M & E HANDBOOKS

M & E Handbooks are recommended reading for examination syllabuses all over the world. Because each Handbook covers its subject clearly and concisely books in the series form a vital part of many college, university, school and home study courses.

Handbooks contain detailed information stripped of unnecessary padding, making each title a comprehensive self-tuition course. They are amplified with numerous self-testing questions in the form of Progress Tests at the end of each chapter, each text-referenced for easy checking. Every Handbook closes with an appendix which advises on examination technique. For all these reasons, Handbooks are ideal for pre-examination revision.

The handy pocket-book size and competitive price make Handbooks the perfect choice for anyone who wants to grasp the essentials of a subject quickly and easily.

THE M & E HANDBOOK SERIES

MANAGERIAL ECONOMICS

J R Davies
BA, MA, ACMA

AND

S Hughes
BA, MA

Pitman Publishing Ltd
128 Long Acre, London WC2E 9AN

A Longman Group Company

© Pitman Publishing Ltd 1977
First published 1977
Reprinted 1978, 1986

ISBN 0 7121 1390 8

Typeset, printed and bound in Great Britain

PREFACE

THE last 10 years have seen a rapid growth in management education in the U.K., and economics has always had an important role to play in the education of future managers. Experience, particularly in the U.S.A., indicated that future managers had a need for something other than a traditional economics course. As managers they are decision-takers and therefore it is essential that the economics they are taught is relevant and gives them practical guidance in arriving at decisions.

Every manager has a limited quantity of factors of production at his disposal—labour, land, machinery, cash, time, etc.—and his greatest problem is in the allocation of these resources to obtain the maximum benefit for the firm. Managers, in other words, are handling scarce resources and it is this problem of scarcity where exchange is involved which gave rise to the study of economics. Should a machine be bought or hired? Should more labour be employed? Should an order be accepted or rejected? These are some of the problems managers have to face every day. How do they evaluate the alternatives to arrive at an optimum solution?

The greatest contribution a study of economics can make to decision-making is in its training in logical and methodical thinking, and managerial economics can be defined as the use of economic logic and principles to aid management decision-making. A course in managerial economics is therefore not a comprehensive economics course. It concentrates mainly upon micro-economics and particularly upon those aspects of micro-economics that aid decision-making. While recognising the importance of macro-economics and the fact that correct internal decisions can only be made if the external forces acting upon the firm are fully understood, we feel that macro-economics should be treated as a study in its own right. The M. & E. HANDBOOK *Applied Economics*, E. Seddon and J. D. S. Appleton, Macdonald and Evans, is recommended to students as a valuable supplement on this topic.

Decisions in practice are complicated because the number of variables is so large that it becomes impossible to solve problems without the aid of mathematical and statistical tools. We have kept the use of mathematics to a minimum in this book on the assumption that a basic course in mathematics and statistics would already be part of a management studies course. We have instead concentrated on getting across the basic ideas and logic of economics that the manager must know. It must be understood, however, that in practice there is no such thing as an economic problem or a finance problem, just problems, and taking effective action to solve them involves drawing together all the knowledge one has. The knowledge of sophisticated mathematics and statistics is, on its own, of very little use in business, but a knowledge of economic relationships and ideas is essential if data is to be assessed, manipulated and analysed accurately. A useful book for business men in the field of mathematics is the M. & E. HANDBOOK *Business Mathematics*, L. W. T. Stafford, Macdonald and Evans.

Managerial decision-making is primarily concerned with optimising, under conditions of uncertainty and subject to various constraints. What is the firm trying to optimise, subject to the constraints of shareholders, general public, government, etc.? In Chapter I we discuss the possibility that the maximisation of profits is merely one objective that the firm can pursue; many more exist. It is not the job of the managerial economist to tell the firm what the objectives should be, but given the objectives he should be able to advise on how best to achieve them.

It is essential when analysing the performance of a firm first to establish what its objectives were. If it aimed for growth or maximum market penetration then it is no use criticising its performance on the basis of profit-maximisation. It will be seen in Chapter I that although there are other objectives in addition to profit-maximisation, a certain minimum profit is always essential and therefore profits always have a part to play. Given the fact that no firm is in existence to make the biggest loss possible, profit-maximisation, while keeping the constraints in mind, is still a good guideline to base decisions upon. We can in fact go further and say that *the firm should take its decisions so as to maximise the discounted value of its future profits subject to the existing constraints*.

We have tried in this book to cover the major decision-areas faced by managers—from the initial step of choosing the form of economic organisation, to demand analysis, cost analysis, pricing policy, investment appraisal and corporate strategy. We thought also that it was essential to include the public sector, since this is becoming so large that virtually every firm comes into contact with it on a day-to-day basis, and it is therefore essential for a manager in the private sector to understand how decisions within the public sector are made.

At the end of each Chapter is a Progress Test which every student is strongly recommended to work through, and there is also Further Reading for those who want to read more about the subject-matter of each Chapter.

The book has been written primarily for students of the Diploma in Management Studies but it would also be extremely useful for those on courses such as Higher National Certificate, Higher National Diploma and the first year of a B.A. in Business Studies. We assume no previous knowledge of economics, yet we move quickly into relevant practical topics. Because of the layout, teachers using this book should find that they can treat subjects at various levels, either by selecting only particular topics or by reference to more advanced work cited in the Further Reading at the end of each Chapter.

April, 1977
J. R. D.
S. H.

ACKNOWLEDGMENTS

WE wish to acknowledge and thank the following institutions and professional bodies for granting their permission to use questions from their past examination papers:

North Staffordshire Polytechnic
Lanchester Polytechnic
Polytechnic of Wales
Institute of Cost and Management Accountants
Institute of Chartered Secretaries and Administrators

Our thanks to Mrs. Ruby Davies for the fine job she has done in typing the manuscript and a particularly big thanks to Lynne who not only typed a large percentage of the manuscript but who also spent many an hour checking completed work and giving valuable encouragement. Our thanks also to Merle and Justin whose encouragement was invaluable in supplying the stimulus needed to ensure completion of the project.

CONTENTS

LIST OF ILLUSTRATIONS

LIST OF TABLES

CHAPTER I

BUSINESS OBJECTIVES

PROFIT AS AN OBJECTIVE AND MEASURE OF BUSINESS EFFICIENCY

THE kind of objectives that a company should set itself to pursue is an issue that has aroused considerable interest and controversy among academics, practical business men and government officials in recent years. Traditionally, the firm has always been regarded as an economic institution and consequently its objectives have generally been thought of as being economic. Indeed, it was the business firm, and the joint-stock company in particular, which was regarded as the main source of economic growth responsible for the relatively high living standards now enjoyed by many parts of Western society. In view of its importance, it was understandable that society should require that the business firm be efficiently run. In a competitive world, the main measure of business efficiency was the profit made by the firm. In a highly dynamic society profitability was essential for the survival of the business, and the inability of some firms to make sufficient profits led to their gradual elimination. It was against this background that both academics and business men came to regard profits as the main objective of business enterprise.

However, society's attitude today towards profits is considerably less indulgent. Indeed, in many circles profit is regarded as socially unacceptable and even immoral. This gradual disenchantment of Western society with the profit motive is in marked contrast to the changing attitude of the Communist world, which is slowly realising that the incentives provided by the profit motive have some role to play in the allocation of resources.

1. Attack on profit-maximisation. This supremacy of the profit motive as the objective of business firms has come under attack for a variety of reasons:

(*a*) Divorce of ownership from control.
(*b*) Difficulties of pursuing profit-maximisation.
(*c*) Problems concerning the measurement of profit.
(*d*) Problems of the corporation and social responsibility.

2. Divorce of ownership from control. The recognition that firms are owned by shareholders and controlled and operated by professional managers has cast doubt upon the entrepreneurial theory that firms always operate in the interests of their owners. Once the owners (shareholders) are separated from the controllers (managers), this relationship is no longer certain. Moreover, it has never been empirically proved that shareholders are more concerned with profitability than anything else. In **7–10** below we shall examine both the extent and the implications of the divorce of ownership from control, and the degree to which managers are aware of, and consequently capable of, advancing shareholder goals. The limited evidence we have demonstrates not only the considerable extent of separation between ownership and control, but also the limited awareness managers possess of shareholder goals. It is clear that profitability is not the sole criterion by which shareholders appraise the performance of a company.

3. Difficulties of pursuing profit-maximisation. The business environment is considerably more complex than when the neoclassical economists first propounded the profit-maximising theory of the firm. The uncertainties which the firm faces often dictate that short-run profit-maximising behaviour be subordinated to the more important objective of long-run survival of the company. The structure of competition is often such that concern with market share and diversification of the enterprise is more important than short-run profit-maximising. For example, the pursuit of "goodwill" is a long-run objective which may adversely affect short-run profit figures. The important point here is that even if profitability is the ultimate objective, the uncertainty and complexity of the business environment and the needs of long-run survival often require that profit-maximisation be pursued by a roundabout route at the expense of short-run profits.

4. Problems concerning the measurement of profit. Traditionally in Western society, profitability has been regarded as the main measure of business efficiency. Economists have, however, never been slow to point out that profitability is not necessarily a good measure of business efficiency, since profits may be the result of imperfections in the market which have resulted in monopolistic exploitation. While this has unquestionably been the case in many industries, more recently an even more damaging attack on this sacred role of profits has emerged by way of criticism of the profit-measurement process itself.

Shareholders rely on accountants to make sure that company accounts really tell them what is going on. However, a series of cases in the 1970s ranging from those of Klinger and A.E.I. to Associated Fire Alarms and Pergamon Press has demonstrated the startling range of financial results that can be produced from the same basic figures. In a report on the Pergamon affair published by the Department of Trade and Industry, the conclusion reached was that "the history of Pergamon Subscription Books Division is a history of the overstatement of its normal trading profits and . . . must have played a significant part in bringing the shareholders of Pergamon to their present unenviable plight".

How is it possible for the same set of basic data to produce staggeringly different sets of profit figures? If a company's annual profit was simply the difference between the cost of what it bought and the income from what it sold, with the company starting in business on 1st January and being wound up on 31st December, there would be few problems in measuring profit. The problem in profit-measurement arises because the company goes on continuously, whereas profits must be recorded at a particular moment of time. On the day of profit-measurement the company possesses a whole host of assets and obligations whose value depends on what is going to happen years ahead. It is the problem of valuing these items that causes the difficulty, since different firms have different systems of valuation. The problem is made worse by the fact that the value of the assets may be so large in comparison with trading profits that relatively small variations in valuation can make a massive difference to the size of the profit reported.

5. Crucial effect of valuation. There are three major areas where valuation is likely to have a crucial effect upon the size of reported profits:

(a) *Valuation of stocks and work-in-progress.* There is a considerable diversity in methods of inventory (stocks and work-in-progress) valuation, even among companies in the same industry. The problem is that price levels and the cost of materials are continually changing.

Two of the best-known methods of valuation are FIFO and LIFO. In valuation by FIFO (first-in-first-out), materials are assumed to be taken from stock in the order in which they are acquired, so that current costs are based on costs of the oldest materials in stock. With LIFO (last-in-first-out), the most recently-purchased materials are assumed to be used up first, so that current costs are based on costs of the most recent acquisitions.

During a period of rising prices FIFO will show unrealistically high profits, since manufacturing costs will be based on the historic cost of materials while inventory valuation will be based on the most recent cost of materials. LIFO will show more accurate costs and hence profits but it, too, may be misleading, since inventory valuation is based on earlier prices and thus remaining stock is undervalued.

Whichever method of valuation is used it is unlikely that the level of profits recorded will be completely accurate. It has been found that inventories were on average worth two and a half times a company's pre-tax profit, which means that a 5 per cent difference in valuation would change profits by 12½ per cent. Correct inventory valuation is therefore a major problem to be solved before accurate profit measurement can take place.

(b) *Depreciation.* The valuation of fixed assets poses as many problems as the valuation of inventory. The value of fixed assets is found by taking them at cost and deducting annually a rather arbitrary sum to allow for the year's loss in expectation of life and efficiency. The larger the sum set aside for depreciation, the smaller will be the reported profits of the firm. The problem is that different companies use different methods of depreciation and this will affect their level of profits.

There are a number of widely-accepted methods of depreciation:

(i) *Straight-line depreciation* is the simplest, with a fixed percentage of the original value of the asset being deducted

annually. By this method, an asset costing £10,000 with a
working life of 10 years would be depreciated at £1,000 per
year.

(*ii*) The *reducing balance depreciation method*, on the other
hand, provides for higher depreciation in the early years,
since the annual depreciation charge is a constant percentage
of an annually diminishing written-down asset value. In
other words, if the depreciation rate was 10 per cent per year a
£10,000 machine would be written down by £1,000 in its first
year, £900 in the second, £810 in the third, etc.

(*iii*) With the *sinking fund method of depreciation*, the
annual depreciation provisions are less than the total capital
cost, the difference being made up from the interest accumu-
lating on the depreciation fund. The amount to be set aside
for depreciation can be calculated from amount of one pound
per annum tables which show the amount £1 a year set aside
at the end of each year that will accumulate at different
interest rates. At 6 per cent, £1 set aside each year for 10
years accumulates to £13·181. Therefore, the annual sum
that will grow to £10,000 over 10 years at 6 per cent is
£10,000/13·181 which equals £759 approximately.

Even a quick glance at these three ways of assessing
depreciation demonstrates the effect that choice of depreciation method can have upon company profits. Moreover, for
companies hiring out commodities such as television sets,
annual depreciation may be more than profits, so that profits
here become exceptionally sensitive to the method of
depreciation.

(*c*) *Capitalisation of costs*. The major problem involved is
when profits should be taken on work done.

EXAMPLE 1: Assume a company bought an asset for £1 m
which is leased out on a 14-year contract at an annual rent of
£200,000, the asset lasting seven years and the company
breaking even after five years. On the one hand, the company
could depreciate the asset at cost over five years, giving a
balance-sheet valuation of £800,000 at the end of the first
year, but in this case no profits would be earned until the
sixth year. Alternatively, the company could take the profits
in the year in which the deal was made, in which case it could
capitalise the asset at seven times its annual rent and depreciate it over 14 years, giving a balance-sheet valuation of
£1,300,000 (i.e. 7 × £200,000 = 1,400,000 which, depreciated
over 14 years, leaves £1,300,000 at the end of the first year).

These are just three of the ways in which profits may be overstated or understated; it is little wonder that profit has become increasingly maligned as a measure of business efficiency.

6. The responsible corporation. The idea of the company being a responsible corporation catering for the needs of all elements in society is not new. Unquestionably, companies have come to realise that the provision of good, well-paid jobs for employees, of cheap efficient services for customers, and a general concern for the economic and social development of the local community can no longer be completely subordinated to the wishes of shareholders.

INTERNAL INFLUENCES ON BUSINESS OBJECTIVES

In a free-enterprise society, it is inevitable that the major determinants of company objectives reside within the firm itself. We will concentrate upon the decision-making process within the firm before going on to consider external influences upon its choice of objectives. Most modern firms consist of three essential elements—shareholders, management and workers—although in smaller business organisations a single person could be responsible for all these functions. The question is which of these three groups plays the major role in determining the objectives of the enterprise.

7. Shareholders. Shareholder demands or goals have traditionally been regarded as the driving force behind business enterprise and have historically been associated with the objective of profit-maximisation. However, the growth of the joint-stock company with the associated divorce of ownership from control has cast considerable doubt upon this hypothesis, the argument being that the managerial team which controls the day-to-day running of the enterprise can have little in common with the owners of the firm, i.e. the shareholders.

This criticism leads us on to two other crucial questions: what powers do the shareholders possess, and are these powers sufficient to ensure that shareholder goals are fulfilled?

(*a*) *Ownership of shares and character of shareholders.* In order to assess the powers possessed by shareholders we first need to know about ownership of shares and their distribution. The main work in this field consists of surveys made by the Department of Applied Economics of the University of Cambridge in 1957 and 1969.[1]

(*i*) Institutions (insurance companies, pension funds, investment trusts and unit trusts) have considerably increased the proportion of shares they hold. In 1957 the personal sector held about 66 per cent by value of the ordinary shares quoted on the Stock Exchange while the institutions held just over 17 per cent. By 1969 the holdings of the private sector had decreased to 47 per cent while that of the institutions had risen to 32 per cent. This has considerable implications for company performance, as we shall see in (*d*) below, since the institutions are in a better position effectively to intervene in company affairs than are private individuals.

(*ii*) The character of private shareholders is likely to limit seriously the effect they can have upon company management. Private shareholders tend to be elderly members of the professional classes and only slightly more are likely to be male than female. Many are disinterested in the affairs of the company so long as their investment is earning them a reasonable income. Moreover, their crucial characteristic, so far as ability to intervene in company affairs, is their desire to limit the risk they undertake by diversifying their holdings. Shareholders tend on average to hold shares in over twenty companies, so that even the most fervent is unlikely to be able to interfere greatly in the affairs of each company in which shares are held. It is for reasons such as these that shareholders have so little control over the destiny of the enterprise.

Thus, so far as the structure of share-ownership is concerned, we can discern two trends likely to have an opposite effect on the shareholders' influence upon business objectives. On the one hand the trend towards an increasing percentage of institutional share-ownership is likely to increase the effect shareholders have upon business objectives, whereas on the other the continuous movement towards diversification of ownership is likely to decrease such influence the shareholders may possess.

(*b*) *Legislative machinery available to shareholders.* In legal terms, the shareholders are the owners of the company and have the power to elect the Board of Directors and to participate in the Annual General Meeting to discuss company policy. However, in both these cases the role of the shareholder is in practice considerably limited, the Board of Directors usually nominating itself and the Annual General Meeting being extremely badly attended and consequently management-controlled. Both of these facts arise from the fragmentation of share-ownership caused by the diversification policy of most shareholders.

Company law has not done much to ease the shareholders' position. It is true that the Companies Act 1967 considerably increased the amount of financial information accessible to them, since all limited companies now have to file their accounts with the Registrar of Companies. However, most shareholders are not in a position to analyse such accounts and would not want to do so anyway. Moreover, to make a resolution under the Companies Act, support has to be obtained from 100 shareholders and holders of at least £10,000 nominal value of shares. With absentee rates of over 99 per cent at Annual General Meetings, and most of the proxy votes going in favour of existing company policy, it is little wonder that individual shareholders have preferred to express their discontent through the sale of stock rather than gather up the requisite amount of support.

Thus current company law gives individual shareholders very little scope to influence business objectives.

(c) *Influence of shareholders.* The individual shareholder has therefore in general preferred to sell his stock rather than engage in the time-consuming exercise of seeking the support of his fellow shareholders. However, even here there is considerably less scope for him than existing literature admits. The detailed studies that have been made of the attitudes of shareholders in specific companies have revealed that shareholders, both private and institutional, tend to hold a company's shares for 10–15 years and that transactions take place (for individuals) either when they have additional funds or when they are short of cash, and (for institutions) when they wish to adjust their portfolios.

And there is good reason for their relative inactivity. As Vernon, Middleton and Harper point out: "On the whole, market prices probably reflect the true value of most companies on the basis of known information, and transaction costs are relatively high, so a 'buy and hold' policy is likely to be best. Without private information or superior insight, consistently above average performance cannot be achieved. Therefore, contrary to first expectations, there are good reasons to justify the private sector's apparent inactivity." [2] Transaction costs and the lack of information available tends, therefore, also to reduce the shareholder's ability to sell out when dissatisfied with company policy.

(d) *Institutional shareholders.* Are the big institutional investors likely to be similarly inhibited? In so far as the ability to sell out is concerned, institutions are likely to be more inhibited: since institutions tend to hold large blocks of shares, any mass selling on their part is likely to drive prices against them. In fact, stability of share-owning is likely to be of enhanced importance to them, since even if share prices are falling, retention of them will restrain the downward trend of the market.

Nevertheless, although the institutional investors are limited in their ability to get rid of the shares of any one company, it is precisely this fact plus the growing trend towards greater institutional share-ownership that is likely to lead to greater interference by the institutions in the affairs of badly-managed companies. The Fisons shareholder survey (1969) concluded that in the 1970s there would be "pressure from and on . . . institutions to take a more active part in company affairs and, if necessary, to intervene in order to safeguard the interests of their own prime investors". [3]

In 1973, Sir Leslie O'Brien, then Governor of the Bank of England, set up the Institutional Shareholders Committee in an attempt to encourage greater involvement by the financial institutions in the affairs of companies in which they held investments. The response of the institutions at the time was cool to say the least, but as companies such as B.S.A., British Leyland, Burmah and Fodens became part of a catalogue of corporate woe that already included Rolls-Royce, Upper Clyde, Alfred Herbert and Vehicle and General Insurance, attitudes began to change. While it is true that the financial institutions still regard themselves primarily as investment managers, there are indications that the Bank of England would like them to play a more active role where it is clear that large companies are falling into financial difficulties.

(e) *Shareholder goals and profit-maximisation.* Much of traditional economic theory has assumed that profit-maximisation and shareholder goals are synonymous, in the absence of any empirical evidence to the contrary. However, until recently, companies made very little attempt to find out what the shareholders really wanted. If companies carried out work surveys among their shareholders they would have a better idea of how to satisfy them, and this could be important in setting business objectives.

In this respect, the Fisons shareholder survey was of very great importance. Shareholders were presented with a list from which they were to choose the best criteria for judging the company. In order of priority, the private shareholder listed management capability, increasing sales, safe investment and widening international interests. Increasing dividends and substantial share-price increases were also well down the list with the institutional investors.

The implication is that private shareholders were mainly concerned with the image and industrial potential of the company, while the institutional investors were more concerned with financial performance, although management image was also important to them. Is profit-maximisation likely to accord with these desires? Further research would undoubtedly go a long way towards providing management with a clearer idea of how shareholder goals may be met.

8. Management. It is unquestionable that the chief executive and top management are responsible for determining the long-term objectives of the company. We must now consider both the extent to which they themselves participate in share-ownership and their ability to maintain control independently of shareholder wishes.

(a) *Executive participation in share-ownership.* Florence [4] has shown that the median percentage of directors' holdings of ordinary shares in very large companies in the U.K. fell from 2·8 per cent in 1936 to 1·5 per cent in 1951. Wildsmith [5] compared data for 1971 on the six companies in Table I with that provided by Nichols [6] for the same companies in 1951. Table I clearly indicates that top management own only a very small percentage of the ordinary shares of these companies, substantially less than 1 per cent in 1971.

(*b*) *The return from share-ownership.* The important thing from the point of view of business objectives is the return

TABLE I: EXECUTIVE SHARE-OWNERSHIP

	Ordinary shares held by the Board (1951) (%)	Ordinary shares held by the Board (1971) (%)
Unilever (Lever Bros.)	23·20	0·01
Imperial Tobacco	4·20	0·04
Courtaulds	1·20	0·16
British American Tobacco	0·20	0·01
Imperial Chemical Industries	0·10	0·02
Dunlop Holdings	0·03	0·04

management receives from its shares, and thus the absolute size of managers' shareholdings is of more importance than the percentage of shares they hold. Florence[7] concluded that the nominal value of the average director's ordinary share-ownership in companies with assets of £3m or over was around £525,000 in 1936 and £21,000 in 1951. The survey carried out by the Oxford Institute of Statistics[8] found that in 1955 the average value of directors' shareholdings was £28,000. On a less general level, Wildsmith[9] presented evidence for six companies in 1971 as shown in Table II.

TABLE II: VALUE OF EXECUTIVE SHAREHOLDINGS

	Nominal value of average director's holding (£)	Market value of average director's holding (£)
Unilever (Lever Bros.)	216	1,565
Imperial Tobacco	3,400	14,864
Courtaulds	8,508	53,308
British American Tobacco	461	5,996
Imperial Chemical Industries	4,500	11,665
Dunlop Holdings	1,074	5,981

It would appear from these figures that income from stockholding within the company is likely to be small in relation to managerial salaries. Indeed, Marris[10] has argued that the proportion of shares held by management would have to increase from 1 to $3\frac{1}{2}$ per cent in order to persuade managers to pursue profits rather than growth.

Thus, despite the growth of stock-option schemes it does not appear that management participation in share ownership is sufficient to ensure strict adherence to profit-maximisation.

(c) *Scope for managerial discretion.* To what extent are managers free to pursue their own objectives? In this respect, management is likely to possess considerable latitude, for three main reasons:

(i) First, as pointed out in **7** (b) above, the Annual General Meeting is very badly attended, and the proxy machinery tends to work in favour of existing management.

(ii) Secondly, management represents a team which cannot easily be replaced and there is no evidence that new managements increase the profitability of the company after a take-over.

(iii) Finally, empirical evidence suggests that unprofitable firms are not in substantially greater danger of take-over than are companies in general. It is for these reasons then that management is likely to play the major role in formulating objectives within the company.

9. Workers' control. Workers can influence the objectives of a company in three main ways.

(a) *Employee shareholding schemes* may present workers with an opportunity to share in the ownership of the company and participate in formulation of objectives by way of the avenues of influence open to other shareholders. However, employee shareholding schemes appear to have been of limited effectiveness in this respect, in that many workers sell their shares shortly after receiving them.

(b) The second way in which workers can influence company objectives is by getting *workers' representatives elected to the Board* and by participation in discussion with management.

While the idea of workers' participation in management has not as yet proceeded very far, workers in some companies are beginning to achieve considerable improvement in their degree of representation at Board level. During the 1970s, a number of firms professed interest in worker participation schemes. Workers at Bristol Channel Ship Repairers, for example, elected four employee-directors to augment the ten-man B.C.S.R. Board. A more revolutionary scheme was that of the government-supported workers' co-operative to run the Triumph motor-cycle works at Meriden, an action prompted by a managerial decision to shut down the Meriden plant and concentrate production at Small Heath and Wolverhampton. In cases such as these, workers clearly possess the ability to influence company decision-making.

(c) The powerful *influence of the trade unions*. In some industries, unions have been extremely successful in raising wages, improving conditions of work, etc. by skilful negotiation and/or the ability to reduce labour supply to zero by the complete withdrawal of the labour force.

It can be seen, then, that employee shareholding schemes and worker participation in management have not as yet proceeded far enough significantly to influence company objectives. Of more importance are the workers' co-operatives, but even here perhaps their real significance is that they show how far workers are prepared to go to protect their jobs. Moreover, the workers' co-operatives have yet to prove themselves and it remains to be seen whether they can survive in a highly competitive environment. Even in the workers' third and most powerful role as trade unionists it is probably true to say that trade-union activity acts as a constraint upon managerial discretion rather than as a direct influence on the formation of company objectives. Nevertheless, in January 1977 the Bullock report with its controversial proposals for worker participation was published. The Committee on Industrial Democracy under Lord Bullock, in its majority report, recommended that employees should have an equal number of Board seats with shareholder representatives, and that these two groups should co-opt a third group of independents which would always have an odd number of members and would be smaller than the first two groups. It would be up to the unions themselves to decide which workers should get the Board seats. The responsiblities of the new Boards would include winding up the company, changes in The Articles of Association, recommendations to shareholders on dividends, changes in capital structure, disposals, the allocation of resources, and the appointment of management.

Since these proposals would apply to all companies with more than 2,000 employees, it is quite clear that their application would affect a large section of British industry (estimated to represent 1,800 companies employing around 6 to 7m people). Moreover, on many of the issues raised above, the shareholders' power would be considerably reduced as would that of management.

In the event, the recommendations of the Bullock report were not implemented, but it did stimulate a national debate on the meaning and application of industrial democracy. The C.B.I. (Confederation of British Industry) made it clear that they were opposed to legislation in this area, but they were prepared to discuss ways of extending employee participation on a voluntary basis. It was not then surprising when the Government in May 1978 published a White Paper on Industrial Democracy which emphasised its preference for voluntary agreements rather than uniform procedures laid down by law. It remains to be seen how much enthusiasm will be generated for the pursuit of industrial democracy via voluntary means.

10. Management power. So it would appear that, at the time of writing, it is the management which is mainly responsible for the formation of company objectives. While no one would seriously dispute that both shareholders and employees exert considerable influence upon management from time to time, it is nevertheless true to say that such pressures constrain managerial behaviour in the event of neglect of shareholder and/or employee desires, rather than that they involve workers and shareholders directly in goal formation.

EXTERNAL INFLUENCES ON BUSINESS OBJECTIVES

While one would expect business objectives to be determined primarily by the internal influence of key personnel within the organisation, it would nevertheless be foolish for the firm to ignore the important external pressures which are brought to bear from time to time. These external pressures come from two major sources:

(a) The first is the influence of the capital market, which imposes major constraints upon the avenues of expansion open to the firm if such expansion requires the use of external finance.

(b) The second pressure has only recently begun to emerge, the corporate social audit, designed to measure the impact of the company on the society in which it operates.

11. Influence of the capital market.

(a) *Capital market constraints.* The capital market has a limited influence on the choice of business objectives in that it is not concerned whether the company is producing jelly babies or washing machines so long as financial and profitability prospects look promising. While the capital market has therefore little influence on specific objectives, it does act as a constraint upon the behaviour of those firms which stray too far from the profit objective, whatever their actual line of business may be.

This constraint operates in the following manner. Most business firms have hopes for growth and expansion. However, expansion requires finance from the capital market, unless the firm is in a position to generate its own funds and so by-pass the capital market, a point we shall return to in (b) below. In order to obtain finance for expansion the firm must be able either to issue new shares or raise further long-term loans. Whichever of these courses of action is adopted, the standing of the existing equity will be of crucial importance since a depressed share price will make it extremely difficult both to issue new shares and raise new long-term debt finance, since both will be unattractive to investors.

Further access to the capital market thus requires a healthy share price, which will only exist if the profit

potential of the enterprise appears good. Consequently, in
so far as firms need to go to the capital market for funds, the
capital market will put such requests to the test of the
market and make it extremely difficult to raise finance for
unprofitable ventures.

(b) *By-passing the capital market.* The key issue relating
to the efficiency of the capital market in creating such
restraint rests with the extent to which firms can by-pass it
by using their own internal sources of finance. For quoted
companies in the U.K., internal sources of finance have
represented about 66 per cent of the total finance raised in
recent years. The introduction of corporation tax in 1965
did not help matters in this respect, since retentions of
profits were taxed only at the corporation tax rate, whereas
distributions of dividend were taxed in addition at the
standard and surtax rates of the individual shareholders.
There is still considerable controversy concerning whether or
not the introduction of corporation tax has therefore led to
an increase in company retentions.

If we are thinking in short-run terms, firms probably
can in practice by-pass the capital market. However, if we
are thinking in long-run terms, the answer is likely to be
very different, for two reasons:

(i) In the first place, most investors like to be assured of a
steady dividend and are unlikely to favour a retentions policy
which does not give a substantial boost to share prices (in
which case, the firm would have been using resources profit-
ably anyway).

(ii) Secondly, most firms are reluctant to limit the pace of
expansion to that permitted by internal finance only.
Consequently, they are forced to go to the capital market in
order to boost the funds available from internal finance.
Despite the fact that the capital-market funds may be the
marginal funds required by the firm, the whole operation of the
firm will nevertheless then become subject to the market test.

In conclusion, therefore, although the capital market does
not impose profit-maximising behaviour upon the firms forced
to use it, it still places a severe profit constraint upon their
behaviour.

12. Corporate social audit. The corporate social audit
attempts to measure the impact the company has on the

society in which it works; in other words, it is a kind of a community balance sheet for industry. It is now by no means certain that what is in the interests of the company is necessarily in the interests of the community. Problems such as industrial pollution, regional unemployment and monopoly exploitation cannot be left to the free play of market forces and the time is coming when companies generally will have to be far more keenly aware of their obligations to society.

(*a*) *Widening management responsibility*. It has been argued that management tends to regard itself as a trustee of corporate property, exercising its powers for the benefit of all those who come into contact with the company, and adjudicating the conflicting claims of shareholders, employees, customers and the general public. Indeed, it has been argued that a company should have a positive strategy for social responsibility and that it should incorporate this in normal corporate planning processes (*see* Chapter XIV).

While many managers would support this thesis in principle, companies have not exactly been falling over themselves to head the social responsibility league table.

This raises the fundamental question of what pressures can be put on managers to make them operate their companies in a more socially acceptable way. There is, of course, government exhortation on issues such as industrial pollution and voluntary price restraint, and it is hoped that the National Enterprise Board will supervise investment plans in order to maintain employment in important industries. However, pressure has also come from sources other than government.

(*b*) *Social Audit*. One of the new corporate pressure groups, the Social Audit (1973), tested the extent to which shareholders would be interested in checking management on social issues. A social audit of Tube Investments was attempted, along with a proposal to get two resolutions (concerned with more disclosure of the company's performance on social issues, and higher pay for its South African workers) put down at the Annual General Meeting. Unfortunately, the social audit failed, partly because Tube Investments refused to co-operate fully and partly because they were unable to get the support of the 100 shareholders required for the resolutions.

Thus, Social Audit and other similar pressure groups have not been particularly successful so far in pressurising companies to act in a more social manner, partly because they have not received the support of the big institutional investors. Nevertheless the Thalidomide issue, when Legal and General and other institutions put public pressure on Distillers, shows that in extreme instances this need not always be so.

13. Economic theory and business objectives. The traditional approach to the theory of the firm has been the neo-classical profit-maximising approach. However, recognition of the divorce of ownership from control subsequently led to two separate new approaches being put forward.

(a) *Maximising a function of the firm.* In the first of these, the profit-maximising objective was replaced by such aims as maximising sales revenue, maximising the growth of the firm, pursuing long-run survival, etc. The distinctive feature of all these theories was that they were concerned with maximising a particular function and were mainly involved with the pursuit of a particular objective. A second feature of these theories was that they usually contained profits or liquidity or some other financial variable as a constraint, so that the objective function was maximised subject to the constraint being met.

(b) *Behaviouralist approach.* This second approach was based upon the behavioural inter-relationships and motivations of the various groups involved in the running of the company. The distinctive feature of these theories was that there was considerably more than one objective, with the result that maximising in a single-utility dimension (profits, sales revenue, etc.) was replaced by satisfying in a number of utility dimensions.

It is quite obvious, then, that there is no universally acceptable objective from which we can begin to study business firms. This conflict about objectives makes economic analysis of business behaviour even more difficult, for without a single objective such as profitability we have no universal yardstick by which we can measure efficiency.

14. Conclusions and implications. Analysis of the operation of the business firm suggests that it is the few top executives in the organisation who are mainly responsible for the formation of company objectives. This is not to deny that pressures exist from other sources, both inside and outside the company, but the fact remains that it is this top level of management who

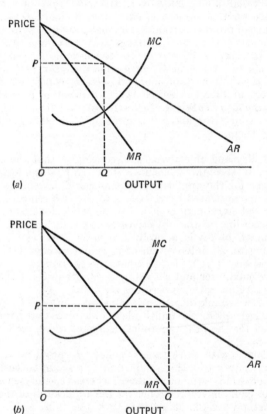

FIG. 1—*The firm as a profit- or sales revenue-maximiser.* (a) Price and output policy of the profit-maximising firm, determined at the height of the demand curve (*AR*) above the intersection of *MR* and *MC*. (b) Price and output of the sales revenue-maximising firm determined at the height of the demand curve (*AR*) above the point where *MR* becomes *O*.

control the destiny of the company and decide upon its level of response to such pressures.

Even if we can decide where decision-making is carried out in the firm, the determination of objectives is a much more controversial issue. Moreover, the collection of empirical evidence on this subject is extremely difficult, because the existence of profit constraints may make the firm's response to a particular environmental change differ according to whether the constraint is effective. In conclusion, one could say that while profit is not the only goal of the business it is nevertheless a very important one, and one that is pertinent to the achievement of all other goals, since profit is necessary to ensure the firm's survival. Nevertheless, each firm must define its own objectives and seek a measure of efficiency which satisfies them.

15. Policy and objectives. The conclusion that there is no universally acceptable business objective has significant implications for the application of managerial economics. This can be demonstrated by reference to the two crucial areas—pricing and investment policy. Pricing policy, for example, will vary according to the objectives of the firm. In Fig. 1, the firm shown in (a) is a profit-maximiser and sets its price according to the intersection of marginal revenue (*MR*) and marginal cost (*MC*). In contrast, the firm in (b) is a sales revenue-maximiser and accordingly sets its price at the level where marginal revenue becomes zero.

These two simple diagrams demonstrate the scope for pricing alternatives among the multitude of objectives that have been proposed for the firm (for fuller details of these, *see* Chapter VII, 4–5).

Similarly, with investment policy, a profit-maximising manager may prefer the application of discounted cash flow techniques of investment appraisal, whereas a safety-conscious manager could have preference for the application of the payback method (*see* Chapter XI).

Despite the meagre findings of this Chapter, it serves to show that managerial economics is simply the application of business techniques, and that the choice of these techniques will depend ultimately on the objective that the business chooses to pursue.

PROGRESS TEST 1

1. Is profit a good measure of business efficiency? (1–4)

2. Is profit-maximisation a realistic objective for the firm? (1–15)

3. Who determines business objectives? Assess the influence of (a) shareholders, (b) management, (c) employees and (d) society. (7–12)

4. Do shareholders want profit-maximisation? (7 (a)–(e))

5. Do institutional shareholders possess more power than individual shareholders? (7 (d)–(e))

6. Why should managers pursue objectives other than profit? (8 (a)–(c))

7. Can companies ignore the influence of the capital market? (11 (a)–(b))

8. What is a "corporate social audit"? Is it likely to have much influence on a firm's behaviour? (12 (a)–(b))

FURTHER READING

1. *The Owners of Quoted Ordinary Shares*, Department of Applied Economics, Cambridge University, in *A Programme for Growth*, Chapman and Hall, 1966.

Moyle, J., "The Pattern of Ordinary Share Ownership 1957–70", *Department of Applied Economics Occasional Paper 31*, Cambridge University Press, 1971.

2. Vernon, R. A., Middleton, M. and Harper, D. G., *Who Owns the Blue Chips?*, Gower Press, 1973, p. 162.

3. Redwood, H., "The Fisons Shareholder Survey", *Long-Range Planning*, April, 1971.

4. Florence, P. S., *Ownership, Control and Success of Large Companies*, Sweet and Maxwell, 1961.

5. Wildsmith, J. R., *Managerial Theories of the Firm*, Martin Robertson, 1973, p. 4.

6. Nichols, T., *Ownership Control and Ideology*, George Allen and Unwin, 1969, p. 76.

7. Florence, P. S., *op. cit.*

8. Klein, L. R. *et al.*, "Savings and Finances of the Upper Income Classes", *Bulletin of the Oxford Institute of Statistics*, November 1956.

9. Wildsmith, J. R., *op. cit.*, p. 4.

10. Marris, R. L., *The Economic Theory of Managerial Capitalism*, Macmillan, 1964, p. 77.

CHAPTER II

THE CHOICE OF CORPORATE FORM

INTRODUCTION

THE choice of an organisational form that every business enterprise has to make is not merely an academic exercise, as much literature would have us believe. For extremely large firms, the attractions of the public company are undoubtedly overwhelming, but for the vast majority of small business enterprises in Britain the choice is by no means as clear-cut.

In its report on small firms,[1] the 1971 Bolton Committee defined small firms in manufacturing industry as those with 200 employees or less, in retailing as those with annual turnovers of £50,000 or less, and in construction as those with 25 employees or less. With this information, the Committee estimated that in 1963 (when the data was obtained), the small-firm sector represented 93 per cent of all firms in the economy, employed 31 per cent of all employees and generated 21 per cent of the net output of the economy.

Despite the rapid turnover of small firms, it is probable that the small-firm sector is still of considerable importance today, representing a sizeable proportion of business enterprise in terms of employment and net output.

It is unquestionable that small firms possess considerably greater latitude in their choice of organisational form than do very large firms, for reasons discussed in 1-6 below. The important point here is that a sizeable proportion of British business, i.e. much of the small-firm sector as defined above, is in a position in which choice of organisational form is not an irrelevant decision. It is a crucial decision, which will be determined largely by the objectives of the owners of the business, in the light of the attractions and disadvantages of the various types of possible organisational form. Before examining these various advantages and shortcomings in detail we shall first enumerate the major types of organisational form available to business enterprise in the U.K.

TYPES OF ORGANISATIONAL FORM

1. The sole proprietor. The simplest kind of business enterprise is the "sole proprietor," called alternatively the "one-man business". These are very small business organisations and, as the name suggests, are under the ownership and control of one person. The sole proprietor may have any number of people working for him, but the essential element of ownership is in the hands of one person. In terms of numbers, this is the most common form of business organisation and is found mainly in the retail trade, service industries and the professions.

2. The partnership. Next in complexity is the partnership form of organisation. This is only one step removed from the sole proprietor, and like the latter it is common in the professions, e.g. doctors and lawyers, and is of comparatively little importance in the manufacturing sector, at least in so far as contribution to net output is concerned. It is possible for the partnership to extend the size of its business by taking on "sleeping" partners, who do not participate at all in the running of the business. Such a move has implications for limited liability which we will consider in **3** below. At this point it is sufficient to say that the limited partnership has not become a popular form of business enterprise in the U.K.

3. The joint-stock company. The most important form of organisation in the U.K. is that of the joint-stock company. This form of organisation was a direct result of the nineteenth-century Limited Liability Acts which were designed to mobilise the savings of the community into company finance.

There are two basic kinds of joint-stock company, the private company and the public company. The legal recognition of the private company came about with the Companies Act 1907. The private company must have not less than two, and not more than fifty, members. This form of organisation is very popular in the retail and wholesale trade and in those sections of manufacturing industry in which only moderate amounts of capital are required.

The procedure for the formation of a public joint-stock company is more elaborate than for that of a private company, and we will examine the legal requirements in **5** below. In contrast to the private company, the public company has no upper limit on the number of members, the only constraint being that there must be a minimum of seven. Unquestionably, it is the public joint-stock company that has been mainly responsible for the growth of large-scale business organisation in the U.K. It has been one of the major instruments responsible for the high rate of economic growth enjoyed by most modern industrial communities in the twentieth century.

Nevertheless, despite the contribution the public joint-stock company has made to modern economic development, such success has not been achieved without reservations—monopoly, exploitation, bureaucracy, etc. Moreover, despite the advantages ascribed to public companies, great private empires have continued not only to survive but to grow successfully. The continued formation of new business enterprises every year and the environmental limitations on growth of many of the existing ones, have continued to provide an outlet for the simpler forms of business organisation.

Against this background of various organisational forms we will turn now to consider the essential factors governing the choice of corporate structure.

CHOICE OF ORGANISATIONAL FORM

4. Why should choice be a problem? The problem arises because the legal, financial and economic environment both affords opportunities and imposes constraints. It is important therefore that the enterprise analyses the implications of these opportunities and constraints so that it can choose the type of organisational form which will enable it to manipulate them in an optimum manner for its particular objectives.

5. Legal requirements and constraints. Legal requirements and constraints differ greatly according to the type of organisational form. The sole proprietor is subject to virtually no regulations, other than the formality of taking out a licence to carry on business. The next best is partnership, which is also subject to few legal requirements other than the contract between the partners. Under the *Limited Partnership Act* 1907, a business may constitute itself a limited partnership by registering with the Registrar of Companies. This involves somewhat more detailed regulation than the unlimited partnership, particularly with regard to the sums contributed by each limited partner. Nevertheless, despite these extra commitments, the legal constraint is not much greater than that of the sole proprietor.

However, when we move on to consider the joint-stock company form of organisation, the legal requirements become much more onerous, with those for the public company being even greater than the private company. The formation of a joint-stock company involves the production of three documents:

(a) *Memorandum of Association.* This includes the name of the company, its objectives, details of the authorised share capital and an indication that the liability of the shareholders is limited (which it nearly always is in practice). In addition, it must be signed by at least two persons in the case of a private, and at least seven persons in the case of a public company.

(b) *Articles of Association.* Standard Articles of Association are laid out in Table A of the Companies Act 1948 and these will be adopted unless the company has articles of its own. This document contains information on the issue and transfer of shares, alteration of capital, dividend policy, borrowing power of the company, regulations governing shareholders' meetings and the power of the directors.

Legally, a private company is distinct from a public company in that it has certain constraints in its Articles of Association. These constraints include restrictions on the right to transfer shares, prohibition of public subscription for the capital of the company and an imposition of an upper limit of fifty on the number of shareholders.

(c) *Statutory Declaration.* This is a declaration by a director or the acting solicitor for the company that the conditions laid down in the Companies Act for the formation of companies have been complied with.

Besides the costs involved in the production of the above documents there is also a registration stamp and fees and a tax of 50p per £100 of authorised capital. In addition to this the public company is also required to file a *prospectus and list of directors* with the Registrar of Companies. The directors must also indicate that the required amount of capital has been subscribed. If the public are not invited to subscribe, then the company may issue a statement in lieu of the prospectus.

6. Operational constraints. In addition to these legal requirements, limited companies also face various constraints upon the operation of their business.

(*a*) The most important of these is the obligation to file their annual accounts with the Registrar of Companies. Prior to 1967 there existed a category of private companies called exempt private companies, which were not required to file their accounts in this manner. However, since the Companies Act 1967, all limited companies are required to conform to this procedure. This legislation removed the outstanding advantage which these exempt private companies possessed—their ability to conceal their accounts from the public.

(*b*) There are also additional requirements for the public company if it wishes to have its shares quoted on the Stock Exchange.

(*c*) Finally, and perhaps most importantly so far as economic analysis of business decisions is concerned, the legal framework of joint-stock companies requires that Annual General Meetings of shareholders be held. Chapter I showed that in certain circumstances it is possible for such meetings to impose serious constraints on company policy, although as was shown in Chapter I, **7** (*b*), the majority of these meetings usually impose a passive rather than an active constraint.

Thus, one of the great attractions of the one-man business, and indeed the partnership form of organisation, lies in the fact that they are easily and inexpensively formed and are subject to few government regulations. This is in marked contrast to the company type of organisation, where the legal requirements are much greater. Perhaps the one weakness of the one-man business and the partnership lies in their impermanence. The sole proprietor form of organisation is bound up with the life of the owner, and the partnership may also involve re-drafting of partnership contracts on the death of one of the partners. In this sense, of course, the joint-stock company has virtual immortality, except in the event of bankruptcy or a decision to wind up the company.

7. Risk for the owners. The biggest single risk which faces anyone starting a business is that which arises from unlimited liability. If a business organisation does not possess limited liability it means that the owners are jointly liable for the debts of the firm. Thus the entire private fortune of a shareholder may be put at risk merely by the purchase of one share in an unlimited company.

In practice, of course, most companies are limited. However, the status of limited liability is not available to the sole proprietor and partnership forms of organisation. It is possible for a partnership to consist of some limited partners, but AT LEAST ONE of the partners must be unlimited. However, the limited partner is not permitted to participate in the running of the business (sleeping partner).

The principle of limited liability is an extremely important one. It means that the shareholder is liable only up to the amount stated on the par value of the share. Once the share is fully paid up, the shareholder has no other liability to the company. In the case of the limited partnership, the amount contributed by each limited partner must be clearly designated.

8. Risk in the joint-stock company. It is quite clear that from the point of view of risking everything in the fortunes of the business, the sole proprietor and the partnership are at a serious disadvantage *vis-à-vis* the limited company. If the business should founder on the uncharted seas of the business environment, the sole proprietor and the unlimited partners risk losing all they possess. Many a small business has gone to the wall, its creditors hovering around like vultures hoping to cut their losses with small pickings from the debris left behind by bankruptcy.

In contrast, the shareholder of a limited company can stand aloof if similar ill-fortune were to fall on one of his companies, knowing that if he has widely diversified his shareholdings among a number of companies, the success of some is likely to cancel out the losses he may incur from one bankruptcy. Yet if he had bought just a single share in any unlimited company, virtually everything he possessed could be seized by its creditors.

It is little wonder, then, that the introduction of limited liability played such a great part in the rapid growth of the

British economy in the latter part of the nineteenth and early twentieth centuries. It was the advent of the joint-stock company and the development of limited liability that led to the channelling of small savings into the investment so necessary for the rapid rate of economic growth which Britain enjoyed during this period.

9. The private investor's risk. Although it is true that shareholders in limited companies do not risk the loss of everything they possess, unlike the sole proprietor or unlimited partners, the value of the shareholdings themselves are nevertheless subject to the whims of the market. Since the Stock Exchange represents the major form of investment in the U.K. (other than house purchase), some investors may find that a sizeable proportion of their assets is continuously at risk. Moreover, it is not merely the prospect of bankruptcy of particular companies that is the risk element here, but also the fluctuating value of the shareholdings themselves. This aspect of risk is of particular significance to those investors to whom liquidity is important, since the value of their shareholdings may not be standing at a desirable level at the time they wish to realise their assets. Indeed over the three years 1973–75 the Stock Exchange Index varied from a low of under 150 to a high of over 450, so that anyone who bought their shares in a boom market was reluctant to realise them at depressed values.

Thus, while it is true to say that the sole proprietor and the partnership form of organisation are exposed to a much greater risk than are the shareholders of a limited company, in that their total realisable assets are at stake, shareholders of limited companies are themselves open to considerable losses, particularly where the extent of their shareholdings is large.

10. Ownership and control. We will now attempt to answer the fundamental question—Do the people who own the business enterprise also control its operations? This question was dealt with extensively in Chapter I, but it must now be related more closely to the choice of organisational form.

If one desires to remain in 100 per cent control of the enterprise, the only form of business organisation to satisfy this is the sole proprietor. The one-man business, as the name implies, means that only one man has the authority to make all the crucial decisions. In the partnership form of organisation, control is shared among the partners to the extent specified in the partnership contract.

Once one moves into the company form of organisation, control by the owners becomes considerably diluted. The private company has a legal maximum of fifty shareholders, thereby placing some constraint on the dilution of control. Similarly, the close company is legally defined as being either directly controlled (i.e. one person possessing 50 per cent or more of the equity) or under the control of five or less participators, so that there is still a large element of control for the owners. The real divorce of ownership from control lies in the large public company, where there may be hundreds of thousands of shareholders. However, as was pointed out in Chapter I, the structure of shareholdings is usually such that control can be maintained with considerably less than 51 per cent of the equity. Where one actually draws the line varies from company to company. Whatever the figure is, the fact remains that for most shareholders in the large public company the divorce of ownership from control is more or less complete in that they have no effective control over operational policy.

So far, therefore, as the maintenance of control by the owners is concerned, the simpler forms of industrial organisation such as the sole proprietor and the partnership are far superior to the company form.

11. Control over the earnings stream. This concept of control has been challenged by Clarkson and Elliott,[2] who argue that it is control over the earnings stream that is important. Referring to the greater degree of control exercised by shareholders of the close company when compared with the large public company, they argue that in many instances the taxation system is so unfavourable to the close company (*see* **15** below) that the after-tax earnings stream they control is smaller than the earnings stream over which they would have had control if the company had gone public.

This concept of control as representing control over earnings seems very pertinent. It is unquestionable that many small businesses have been reluctant to expand because of the fear of losing control of the enterprise. This, of course, raises the fundamental question of whether the largest possible earnings stream was the objective in the first place. We considered this question previously in Chapter I, concerned with the effect of business objectives on the choice of organisational form.

12. Availability of finance. More than any other factor, it is the serious limitation on the ability of the simpler organisational forms to raise adequate finance that has led to the development of the public limited company.

To engage in almost any kind of business activity, the owner must be prepared to provide some of the capital from his own private sources. The one-man business is obviously seriously restricted in the amount of capital it can provide and frequently the owner has to resort to borrowing from close friends and relatives. The partnership form of organisation can provide more capital than the sole proprietor, but it, too, is restricted to the private resources of the partners.

Limitations upon the amount of ownership capital are extremely important, since they severely constrain the borrowing capacity of the business. As a broad generalisation, it can be said that small businesses have adequate access to short-term finance. The major source of such finance is trade credit which generates itself in the course of the business, bank loans which for small businesses are largely determined by the personal contact between the lender and the borrower, accruals in the form of tax owed to the Inland Revenue but not yet paid, and invoice discounting, whereby certain specialised finance companies will convert a certain proportion of the debts of the company into cash. In terms of short-term financing for small businesses, the banks are of crucial importance, for the business can use its own resources to the limit knowing that it can fall back on the bank in times of emergency.

13. The Macmillan gap. While small businesses have not been short of short-term finance, there is no question that in the post-war years they have suffered from a lack of long-term finance. Private companies have been worse off than sole proprietors and partnerships, in that the capital resources required by the private companies were much greater than those required by the smaller business organisations. This problem of financing the long-run capital of private companies became so acute that the Macmillan Committee (1931) was able to talk of a positive "gap" in the financing of these private concerns, a gap which henceforth became known as the "Macmillan Gap".

The findings of the Macmillan Committee led to strenuous efforts to improve the position. These improvements took a number of forms, not the least of which was the setting up of various financial institutions such as the Industrial and Commercial Finance Corporation (in 1945), whose aim was to assist the small firm requiring long-term capital in the range £5,000–£200,000+. Besides the creation of financial institutions such as the Estate Duties Investment Trust Limited (1953), an effort was made to reduce the costs of making small issues on the new issue market which significantly reduced the minimum size of issues handled. The role of the banks in medium- and long-term lending also greatly increased, particularly since the Radcliffe Committee recognised in 1959 that "the banks should be ready to offer loan facilities within reasonable limits, having due regard to their liquidity requirements, as an alternative to a running overdraft for creditworthy industrial and commercial customers".[3]

It appears that private companies now have much greater access to long-term finance than they had at the time of the Macmillan Committee report. Indeed, the Bolton Committee report of 1971 concluded that it did not discover a Bolton Gap and that the gaps identified by the Macmillan Committee and the Radcliffe Committee had been, or were in the process of being, filled satisfactorily.

Nevertheless, there has been growing criticism of the role played by the banking system in recent years, which is of particular importance to small firms since the banks provide at least two-thirds of their funds from institutional sources. The banks have been accused of lack of flexibility and reluctance to take risks, particularly in relation to their demands for excessive security, their tendency to assess firms for their break-up value rather than as going concerns, and their insistence upon relatively low gearing ratios. The Committee of Inquiry set up under Sir Harold Wilson in the late 1970s accepted much of this criticism, and although it recognised the increased competition between the banks, it nevertheless concluded that "We are not as confident as they themselves appear to be that the number of viable enterprises denied access to sufficient funds is insignificant, particularly where new businesses or significant new initiatives are concerned."[4]

14. Advantages of the public company. If we now consider the question of the effect which the availability of
finance has on choice of organisational form, the advantages of
the public company become overwhelming. The sole proprietor
and the partnership have no access at all to the facilities of the
new issue market, and the activities of the private company are
severely limited. The public company can raise long-term
finance merely by the issue of debentures, preference shares or
equities. A debenture-holder is simply a person who has made
a long-term loan to the company at an agreed rate of interest.
The debenture-holder is a creditor of the company, not a
shareholder, and is entitled to a fixed rate of interest every
year and can force the company into liquidation if he is not
paid. Individuals and institutions are prepared to buy debentures from the company because they know that this is the
safest form of investment; they have the first claim on the
assets of the company in the event of liquidation. Note here
that the debenture issues made by a public company are
usually made on a floating charge, whereas the long-term debt
finance available to the partnership and the sole proprietor
usually take the form of a mortgage secured on a specific asset
of the enterprise. Thus, the public company usually has much
more flexibility and autonomy in its use of long-term debt
finance.

In so far as equity financing is concerned, it is the principle
of limited liability which represents the major advantage of the
public company. The public limited company can issue equity
shares which the public will buy because they can then participate in the profits of the company with only the limited risk of
fluctuation in the value of the shares.

Normally the company has some kind of gearing ratio which
will determine the percentage of fixed charge (debentures and
preference shares) to equity capital. The preference share is a
kind of hybrid security: it carries a fixed rate of interest
similar to debentures, but holders are not able to force the
company into liquidation if they are not paid. The larger the
equity base that the firm possesses, the greater will be the
amount of long-term debt it can raise, since the large equity
base will provide some security for debenture-holders, who
are paid first after creditors in the event of liquidation.

Thus if finance, or perhaps lack of finance, is the main
criterion of choice, the advantages of the public company are

outstanding. Not only are they in a better position to attract debt finance but also the advantages of limited liability facilitate the diversification of shareholdings so necessary to the small shareholder.

15. Tax burden. For taxation purposes, business organisations can be divided into three categories: sole proprietors and partnerships; close companies; and finally ordinary companies.

(a) *Sole proprietors and partnerships* are taxed as individuals, and consequently are taxed according to the income of the partners involved. The amount of tax paid depends upon each partner's share of the profits and his individual tax rate. An important point to note here is that the greater the number of partners, the smaller is each individual's share of the profits and consequently the lower is his marginal tax rate. This is one of the main reasons for the conversion of many sole proprietorships into partnerships and family businesses. The tax burden of these simple forms of business organisation varies from the standard income-tax rate of (in 1981/82)30 per cent to the higher-rate tax which increases to 60 per cent. Thus, the sole proprietor and the partnership are faced with a highly progressive system of taxation.

(b) *Close companies* have quite a complex legal definition but are, broadly speaking, small companies under the control of five or less persons. These companies have special tax provisions which represent an attempt to bridge the gap between taxation of individuals and taxation of companies. If these special tax provisions did not exist it would be advantageous for most partnerships to convert themselves into close companies so that they could avoid the higher-rate tax of the partnership system.

Prior to 1973 the close company paid corporation tax on its trading profit at the then prevailing rate of 40 per cent. However, in addition to this the close company also had to pay a shortfall tax. This shortfall tax was a tax on a minimum required dividend distribution, whether or not these distributions actually took place. This shortfall tax was levied upon 50 per cent of the trading profit after corporation tax had been paid and on the whole of the franked investment income. The rate at which this shortfall tax was levied was related to the percentage of ownership held by each director, and the higher-rate tax of each director applied to his own percentage. However, the adoption of the imputation system of taxation in 1973 (*see* (*c*) below) necessitated a complete recasting of the position of the close company. The term shortfall tax has disappeared but the basic concept of the tax remains. What happens now is that the income of the close company is apportioned among the participants if the relevant income of the company exceeds distributions by more than £1,000. The apportioned sum is deemed to be the highest part of the participator's total income. Although no assessment is to be made at the basic rate of income tax, nevertheless, for the purposes of assessment at the additional rates of income tax, there is to be added to the apportioned sums a tax credit at the appropriate rate of advanced corporation tax (*see* (*c*) below). Any individual participator whose apportioned sum is less than £200 or 5 per cent of the total amount apportioned will not be liable to this tax. From the point of view of our analysis of close companies, although the 1973 tax changes have brought about some relaxation of the tax burden on close companies, the complicated provisions accompanying apportionment ensure that close companies cannot secure a tax advantage by withholding distributions.

(*c*) The third taxation category is represented by ordinary companies who pay corporation tax on their trading profit at the prevailing rate and no tax at all on their investment income. Until April 1973 the taxation system favoured profit retention, since while retained profits acquired no further tax liability once corporation tax had been paid, profits distributed as dividends were taxed at the income tax rate and possibly investment income surcharge rate applicable to the individual shareholder. However, since April 1973 with the introduction of the imputation system of corporation tax, both distributed and undistributed profits bear a uniform corporation tax rate.

Under the imputation system a company must still make a payment to the Inland Revenue when it pays a dividend, but the shareholders get an "imputed" credit for having borne income tax at the basic rate. This tax payment on dividends is called the advance corporation tax and it can be set-off against the company's eventual corporation tax liability on that year's profit, thus ensuring that there is no discrimination between distributed and undistributed profits. To make up for the reduction of revenue that this entailed, the government was forced to raise corporation tax from 40 to 50 per cent and eventually to 52 per cent. Companies who consistently distributed one third of their profits were faced with approximately the same tax burden as before, while those who consistently distributed more than one third of their profits paid less than before, and those who distributed less than one third paid more tax than before.

Thus despite the high rate of corporation tax, this category of companies is by far the most favourable treated by the Inland Revenue since if they plough back profits then they incur only corporation tax, while if they distribute profits advance corporation tax is payable but can be set-off against the company's eventual corporation tax liability. The shareholder will, of course, become subject to a capital gains tax when realising the value of his share but this is currently levied at the relatively low rate of half the income tax rate, subject to a maximum of 30 per cent.

In most cases, the choice of corporate structure is determined by factors other than tax. However, circumstances may exist in which a change of corporate structure may reduce the tax burden. This becomes immediately evident when the partnership is compared with the close company. If trading profits are large, the close company may be more advantageous than the partnership, because the heavy higher-rate tax payments of the partnership may more than outweigh the disadvantages that the 1965 Act placed upon close companies. However, if profits are small, it is likely that the disadvantages of the special provisions placed upon close companies will outweigh the higher-rate tax of the partnership, and consequently the partnership may be preferred.

So far as taxation is concerned, the tax advantages to ordinary companies are overwhelming, and the real choice lies between sole proprietor, partnership and close company. In this respect, it is worth noting the recommendations of the Bolton Committee, which suggest that "what is required above all for the health of the small firm sector is an economic and taxation system which will enable individuals to acquire or establish new businesses out of personal resources, and to develop these on the base of retained profits".[5]

16. Conclusion. There is no one single criterion a business man can use to select the correct form of organisation for his enterprise. The whole question of choice is closely related to the objectives of the owners. Generally, most businesses start up with the simpler forms of organisation such as sole proprietor and partnership, where ease of formation and maintenance of control are important. They work their way to the private company and eventually the public company, as the expansion drive of the enterprise becomes stifled by lack of capital and exorbitant taxation.

However, there is no clearly defined point at which one moves from one organisational form to another. There are many sole proprietors who are content to be their own boss and do their own thing rather than expand the enterprise, with the inevitable dilution of control that this entails. Similarly, there are many extremely large private companies that are struggling against lack of capital to maintain their own private empires. One of the classic examples of a large private company being forced to go public by lack of capital was Lord Cowdray's company, S. Pearson. The company had been private for over 130 years, but the need to guard against the inevitability of death duties forced the company to go public. When the company offered ten million of its ordinary shares to the public in August 1969 it was one of the biggest issues the stock market had ever seen, and put a price tag of £71.6m on Cowdray's business interests. If a wealth tax is introduced, it will make it even more difficult for the large private empires to avoid going public. Nevertheless, the example of S. Pearson provides evidence of the ability of businesses to survive in the organisational form of their choice, even when the sheer size of operations suggests that a more appropriate organisational form is required. Other large private empires which have turned public in the 1970s include Pilkington Brothers and J. Sainsbury.

Thus in the last analysis, choice of organisational form is very much a personal issue, although the time must come when every family business must begin to feel the pressure of the factors outlined in 15 above.

PROGRESS TEST 2

1. What are the major types of organisational form which exist in the U.K.? (1–3)

2. In what way would the legal environment influence your choice of organisational form when starting up a business?   (5)

3. Why is limited liability so important to a business? If is it so important why are there so many sole propretors and unlimited partnerships?   (7–11)

4. Why do public companies have greater access to long-term finance than other organisational form?   (12–14)

5. What is a close company? From the tax point of view is it better to be a member of a close company or a partnership?   (15 (b))

6. Should size of operations be the major criterion for choice of organisational form?   (16)

FURTHER READING

1. Cmnd. 4811, "*Small Firms:* Report of the Committee of Inquiry on Small Firms" H.M.S.O., 1971.

2. Clarkson, G. P. E. and Elliott, B. J., *Managing Money and Finance,* Gower Press, 1969.

3. Cmnd. 827, "Report on the Working of the Monetary System", para. 2 H.M.S.O., 1959.

4. "*The Financing of Small Firms*". Interim Report of the Committee to Review the Functioning of the Financial Institutions, H.M.S.O., March 1979.

5. Cmnd. 4811, *op. cit.*, para. 10.40.

CHAPTER III

DEMAND ANALYSIS

INTRODUCTION

UNDERSTANDING the basic concepts of demand is essential for accurate demand forecasting. All the mathematical and statistical tools in the world are useless unless results can be interpreted and analysed. In this Chapter we shall look at the basic demand concepts which explain demand relationships and in Chapter IV we shall look at the methods used to forecast demand, together with the results of empirical research which will help us apply the concepts of this Chapter in practice.

1. Importance of demand analysis. Demand analysis which results in a demand forecast for the firm's product is one of the most, if not the most, important functions within the firm. From the sales forecast the sales budget is established and from the sales budget the firm decides such important questions as:

(a) how much and what type of labour is required to meet future demand?

(b) are existing production facilities adequate?

(c) are existing supplies of raw material sufficient to meet future demand?

(d) will existing warehouse space and general factory area prove adequate in the future?

Regardless of the size of the firm, technology used and over-all efficiency all will be lost unless the product can be sold. It must be determined whether a market exists for the product and what can be done to influence the size of that market.

The demand for a firm's product is influenced by a large number of factors (*see* **2** below) and the value of demand forecasting and the individual factors that are important in each case will vary from firm to firm and from product to product. There are no hard and fast rules that can always be followed. The analysis in this Chapter and Chapter IV must be adapted to suit each individual case.

Demand analysis should be a basic activity of the firm because so many of the firm's other activities depend upon the outcome of the demand forecast. Demand analysis:

(a) provides the basis for analysing market influences on the firm's products and thus helps in the adaptation to those influences;

(b) highlights the factors which influence the demand for one's product and so provides guidelines to help manipulate demand.

FACTORS THAT INFLUENCE DEMAND

2. The demand function. The demand for a product or service is determined by a large number of factors, some within and others outside the influence of a particular firm. In economics we say that the demand for a particular product is a function of, say, price, income, price of substitutes, price of complementary goods, taste, level of advertising, population, government policy, etc.

Stated in mathematical terms,

$$Qx = F(P + Y + Ps + Pc + T + A + \text{populn.} + \text{govt. policy, etc.})$$

Where Qx = total quantity of good X that is demanded.

F = function.

P = price of good X.

Y = income of population.

Ps = price of substitute products.

Pc = price of complementary products.

T = tastes.

A = advertising expenditure.

The demand for X is called the dependent variable, while the other factors are called the independent variables. In practice, however, just how independent the other variables are is open to question. It is the very complicated interaction of these variables that gives rise to the tremendous practical problems of demand analysis and forecasting. The relationship between these variables is never constant, and a product influenced by a given set of variables at one time will be influenced by another set in a later period, or at the very least, if influenced by the same variables, their importance will have changed with time.

In the equation above most of the main independent variables have been included, although for some products other factors not yet mentioned might be of prime importance.

The demand for a product can be defined as the number of units of a good or service that consumers will purchase given a set of circumstances (price, income, advertising, etc.) during a specified period of time (six months, one year or five years).

3. Industry demand and company demand.

In most cases the general factors mentioned in 2 above will affect both company and industry demand, although the value and size of the parameters will vary. Let us take as an example the size of the population. As the population increases demand for the industry's product increases, but unless a firm has 100 per cent of a market, the demand for its own product will increase by a smaller amount than total industry demand.

It is important to know how fast industry demand is expanding because on this depends the future of most firms within the industry. If industry demand is expanding rapidly, then most firms within that industry should also be expanding and it is possible that harmful competition between them will be kept to a minimum. If demand is constant or falling then expansion by an individual firm within that industry can only be at the expense of its rivals—customers can be won through a quality improvement or extra advertising and sales promotion, but both increase the total costs to the firm. A fall in industry demand should be taken as a danger signal by each firm and steps should be taken to seek new markets (diversification) or else preparation made for some very fierce competition.

Many trade associations provide regular forecasts and information on trends within the industry; this is a valuable source of statistics because the individual firm is normally unable to collect such data on its own. The forecasts that are produced must, however, be looked at extremely closely and the basis on which they were drawn up carefully studied before taking action based upon them. What is meant by an industry? What firms do you include or exclude? Is the National Coal Board in the coal industry or just a part of the energy industry? How do we possibly classify I.C.I., whose product range is unending? Such questions still plague industrial economists and any definition adopted is a compromise; therefore one should proceed cautiously.

From this point, our analysis will be concerned primarily with the firm, and therefore company demand, and we shall now look in detail at some of the main factors that influence the demand for a firm's product or service.

PRICE

4. Relationship between price and quantity bought. The relationship between price and quantity bought (*see* Fig. 2) is represented by a demand curve (*D*). The demand curve is downward-sloping, generalising the usual relationship that exists between quantity bought and price, i.e. the lower the price the higher the quantity demanded, and vice versa. There are circumstances in practice where this relationship is seen

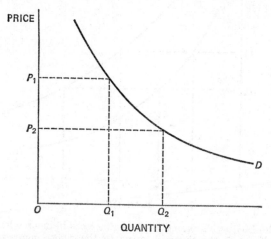

FIG. 2—*The relationship between price and quantity* (assuming that all other independent variables are constant).

not to hold, i.e. price is raised and more is demanded and vice versa. These are cases which involve what are known as inferior goods, the demand curve having shifted due to changes in real income, or where the demand curve is shifted to the right or left due to changes in tastes or expectations.

The demand curve is that part of the demand function which

shows the relationship between price and quantity demanded. To obtain this relationship, however, it must be assumed that all other independent variables are constant. If this assumption was not made, the increased quantity demanded could also have been due to an increased level of income, greater advertising expenditure, rise in the price of substitutes or a change in tastes, etc.

If any of the independent variables change, then a new demand curve will have to be drawn, indicating that the new price/quantity relationship is now based upon different values of the variables. In Fig. 3 an increase in the level of income means that the demand curve shifts to the right—D_1 to D_2—indicating that more is demanded than previously at existing

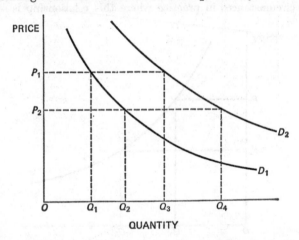

FIG. 3—*Increase in income level.* An increase in income level will normally shift the demand curve to the right, increasing the quantity demanded at all previous prices.

prices because the body of consumers as a whole are better off. At price P_1 quantity demanded increases from Q_1 to Q_3 and at price P_2 quantity demanded increases from Q_2 to Q_4. Even if price is increased from P_2 to P_1, so long as an increase in income shifts the demand curve from D_1 to D_2, quantity demanded will increase from Q_2 to Q_3 instead of falling from Q_2 to Q_1.

5. The firm's demand. The firm's demand curve is constructed by adding together the individual demand curves of all consumers of its product.

EXAMPLE 2: Let us assume that a firm XYZ Ltd has three customers, A, B and C, whose demand curves are as in Fig. 4.

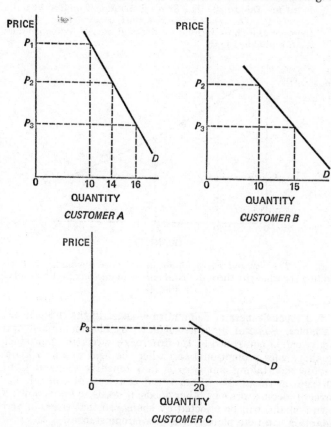

FIG. 4—*Customer demand curves.* As price falls from P_1 to P_3, total quantity demanded increases because: (*i*) existing customers increase their purchases; (*ii*) new customers purchase for the first time.

At price P_1 consumer A will purchase 10 units and consumers B and C will not enter the market. When price is lowered to P_2 consumer A will increase his purchase to 14 and B now enters the market taking 10; C, however, still remains outside the market. When price is further lowered to P_3, A increases his purchase to 16, B to 15, and C enters the market for the first time, taking 20. The firm's demand is therefore 51 units at price P_3. The firm's demand curve is constructed by adding together the three individual demand curves for consumers A, B and C in Fig. 5.

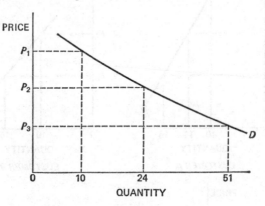

FIG. 5—*The demand curve of the firm.* This is constructed by adding together the three demand curves of customers A, B and C in Fig. 4.

6. Responsiveness of demand to changes in the independent variables. Some of the independent variables mentioned in 2 above can be controlled by the firm (price, advertising, product quality, sales promotions) and what the firm wants to know for decision-taking purposes is how sensitive demand is to changes in them. For those variables it cannot control, e.g. level of income, price of other goods, it needs to know how its own demand will be affected by change so that reaction and adaption can take place to the new circumstances.

In economics the measure of responsiveness is known as elasticity, and this is defined as the percentage change in quantity demanded attributable to a percentage change in an independent variable.

$$\text{Elasticity} = \frac{\% \text{ change in quantity } (Q)}{\% \text{ change in independent variable } (X)}$$

$$\frac{\Delta Q}{\Delta X} \times \frac{X}{Q}$$

Where $\Delta Q =$ change in quantity.

$\Delta X =$ change in value of independent variable.

$Q =$ original quantity of product demanded.

$X =$ original value of the independent variable.

There is thus an elasticity for each independent variable. We shall first look at price elasticity, and introduce the other measures of elasticity as we discuss each independent variable in turn. Once price elasticity has been mastered the elasticities concerned with the other variables will prove easy, as they are merely variations on a theme.

7. Price elasticity. Our main interest in price elasticity arises from the fact that it provides information about the effect of price changes on revenue. The demand curve which was introduced in 4 can also be called an average revenue curve (AR) because each point on that curve represents the average revenue (price) obtained by that firm for selling the number of units indicated, and price multiplied by the quantity sold gives us total revenue. The average revenue curve is extremely important and will form the basis of much economic analysis later.

In Fig. 6 (a), when price is P_1, quantity Q_1 is sold, and total revenue is represented by area P_1XQ_1O. If price is lowered to P_2, total quantity purchased increases to Q_2 and total revenue is now represented by area P_2YQ_2O. The firm's total revenue has increased, because although it has sacrificed revenue P_1XAP_2 by selling at a lower price, it has gained the larger area AYQ_2Q_1. Its total revenue has, therefore, been increased by the difference between areas AYQ_2Q_1 and P_1XAP_2. If the firm had increased price from P_2 to P_1, the opposite would have occurred and total revenue would have decreased, although price per unit had increased.

In Fig. 6 (b), a fall in price has led to a greater quantity being sold, but total revenue has fallen, area P_1RBP_2 has been sacrificed and only the smaller area BSQ_2Q_1 has been gained. An increase in price would of course have led to an increase in

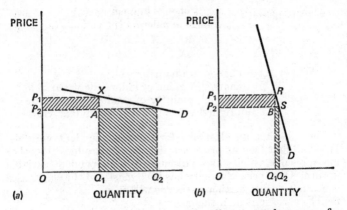

FIG. 6—*Elasticity and total revenue.* The effect on total revenue of a fall in price from P_1 to P_2 depends upon the elasticity of demand. Where demand is elastic (*a*), total revenue will increase, but if demand is inelastic (*b*), total revenue will decrease.

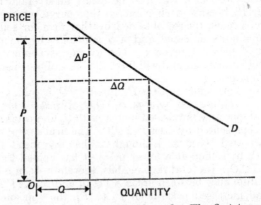

FIG. 7—*Derivation of the elasticity formula.* The first term in the formula $\frac{\Delta Q}{\Delta P}$ is the reciprocal of the slope of the straight line joining the two price/quantity positions under consideration. The second term $\frac{P}{Q}$ relates to a point on the demand curve at which measurement is made.

revenue, although less was being demanded. It is to measure these responses more accurately that the concept of elasticity has been developed.

8. Elasticity formulae. The formula for price elasticity given below is preceded by a minus sign. This is because under normal circumstances (price/quantity relationships) one of the changes will be a minus, i.e. price is reduced from 10p to 8p (-2) while quantity demanded is increased from 100 to 150 $(+50)$. By preceding the formula with a minus sign the answer will always be positive. It is there really for convenience sake, some authorities ignore the signs altogether and merely use the figures as being all positive.

$$\text{Price elasticity} = -\frac{\Delta Q}{\Delta P} \times \frac{P}{Q}$$

The first term in our elasticity formula is the reciprocal of the slope of the straight line joining the two price/quantity positions under consideration (Fig. 7).

The elasticity will vary over a straight-line demand curve not because we are measuring not the slope of the line, but the ratio

$$\frac{\Delta Q}{\Delta P}$$

The second term

$$\frac{P}{Q}$$

relates to a point on the demand curve at which measurement is made. Consequently this formula for price elasticity is used only when the change in price is relatively small (i.e. below 2 per cent) and is referred to as point elasticity of demand.

EXAMPLE 3: When price is £1·50, quantity demanded is 200 units. When price is lowered to £1·48, quantity demanded increases to 300 units.

$$\text{Point elasticity of demand} = -\frac{100}{-2} \times \frac{150}{200} = \underline{\underline{37·5.}}$$

if the change in price exceeds 2 per cent then the formula must be modified, $\frac{P}{Q}$ being replaced by

$$\frac{P_1 + P_2}{Q_1 + Q_2}$$

where P_1 and Q_1 are the original price and quantity and P_2 and Q_2 the new price and quantity. This is the arc elasticity of demand and can be written thus:

$$\text{Arc elasticity of demand} = \frac{\Delta Q}{\Delta P} \times \frac{P_1 + P_2}{Q_1 + Q_2}.$$

EXAMPLE 4: When price is 15p, quantity demanded is 2,000 units, and when price falls to 10p quantity demanded increases to 4,000 units.

$$\text{Arc elasticity of demand} = \frac{2000}{5} \times \frac{15 + 10}{2000 + 4000} = \underline{\underline{1 \cdot 67}}$$

9. Interpreting results. The answer to these calculations is of great importance to the firm because they indicate the effect on revenue that is brought about by a change in price. The results are summarised in Table III.

TABLE III: RELATIONSHIP BETWEEN REVENUE
AND CHANGE IN PRICE

Elasticity of demand	Price rise	Price fall
Greater than 1 ($>$1)	Revenue falls	Revenue rises
Less than 1 ($<$1)	Revenue rises	Revenue falls
Equal to 1 ($=$1)	No change	No change

If the price elasticity of demand as calculated exceeds 1, then demand is said to be elastic (quantity demanded has responded in a greater proportion than price change). This means that if the firm lowers its price it will increase total revenue but if it raises price total revenue will fall.

If price elasticity as calculated is less than 1, the demand is said to be inelastic, a lowering of price leading to less revenue being earned regardless of the fact that more are being sold. However, in this last instance, if price is increased total revenue will rise despite the fact that quantity demanded has fallen.

Finally if price elasticity as calculated is equal to 1, elasticity of demand is said to be equal to unity and total revenue remains unchanged as a result of price moves.

10. Qualifying results. There are two important points to remember when considering the price elasticity of demand:

(a) The measure of elasticity obtained is *only valid for that point in time*. Changes in income or tastes or any other underlying factors will affect the elasticity of demand and, therefore, elasticities calculated last year cannot be relied upon this year. Also, due to the fact that consumer reaction to price changes is not instantaneous, the short-run and long-run price elasticities will differ, e.g. a fall in the price of Ford cars relative to those of British Leyland will result in the demand for Ford cars increasing. In the short-run, those people purchasing for the first time and those replacing older cars will be attracted by Ford's prices. There are many British Leyland car owners who will change to Ford when replacement of their existing car is necessary but if they have just recently bought a new car this decision will not be taken for a number of years.

(b) The elasticity *varies over the length of the demand curve*, it can be elastic at one part and inelastic at another. This is even the case when the demand curve is linear, because as we mentioned in **8** above, although the slope of the curve is the same

$$\frac{dP}{dQ}$$

the ratio

$$\frac{Q}{P}$$

varies along its length. In Fig. 8, D_1 is linear yet the ratio when price falls from 30p to 28p is vastly different to when the price falls from 10p to 8p, $\frac{100}{7}$ as opposed to $\frac{14}{20}$, i.e. increase in quantity demand from 5 units to 10 units = 100 per cent increase in response to a fall in price from 30p to 28p per unit, 7 per cent approximately (*see* **6** above).

Table IV shows how the demand for a firm's product is made up of the demand of three consumers and also how the elasticity of demand varies along the length of the curve. The formula for arc elasticity is used, as the price changes

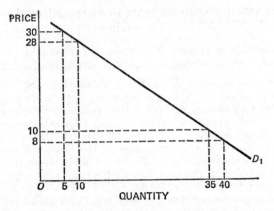

FIG. 8—*Variations in elasticity.* On a straight line demand curve (D_1), the elasticity will vary along its length. Although the absolute changes in both price and quantity are the same, the percentage changes are clearly not.

exceed 2 per cent. It can be seen that price elasticity of demand varies along the length of the demand curve. The student is left to complete the Table, and also graph and calculate the price elasticity of demand for each of the consumers.

TABLE IV: DEMAND FOR A FIRM'S PRODUCT

Price	A	B	C	Total demand	Elasticity of demand
50	100	0	0	100	
45	115	50	0	165	4·7
40	120	60	40	220	2·4
35	125	70	45	240	0·64
30	130	85	50	265	
25	145	100	55	300	
20	150	120	60	330	

11. Marginal revenue (MR). In **7** above we said that the demand schedule facing a firm could also be called an average revenue curve. Associated with this curve and derived directly from it is another curve which will be used frequently in later Chapters, the marginal revenue curve.

Marginal revenue is the revenue obtained by a firm in selling one more unit, and so long as the firm has a downward-sloping demand curve marginal revenue will always be less than price and therefore the MR curve lies below the AR curve. Initially, students are always puzzled how MR as defined above can be less than the price for which the product has been sold. A moment's reflection, however, reveals that to sell an extra unit the firm must sell at a price lower than previously. Units that could previously be sold at a higher price must now be sold at a lower price to ensure that total sales are increased by one. In other words, to gain £X by selling one more unit the firm has had to sell the previous quantity at Yp less each. The net gain, therefore, to the firm (MR) is equal to £$X - (Y$p $\times$ quantity previously sold).

Figure 9 and Table V illustrate this important economic concept.

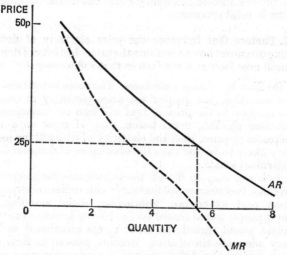

FIG. 9—*The concept of marginal revenue.* Elasticity of demand and marginal revenue are positive and greater than 1 as price falls from 50p to 25p. As price falls below 25p elasticity is less than 1 and marginal revenue becomes negative.

TABLE V: THE CONCEPT OF MARGINAL REVENUE

Number of units sold	Price (AR)	Total Revenue (TR)	Marginal Revenue (MR)
1	50	50	50
2	45	90	40
3	40	120	30
4	35	140	20
5	30	150	10
6	25	150	0
7	20	140	−10
8	15	120	−20
9	10	90	−30
10	5	50	−40

The elasticity of demand between units 5 and 6, when price is lowered from 30p to 25p, is equal to unity. From that point, however, price elasticity is less than 1 (inelastic) and lowering price further succeeds in selling more but at the expense of a decline in total revenue.

12. Factors that influence the price elasticity of demand. Having discussed how to measure the price elasticity of demand, we shall now look at some factors that influence it.

(a) *Number of close substitutes.* The more substitutes that are available, the greater the price elasticity of demand. An increase in the price of beef will lead to consumers substituting chicken, pork, bacon, etc. If meat as a whole increases in price, then the elasticity of demand for meat is very likely to be less than the elasticities of demand for the individual meats.

It is not easy to list all the substitutes for a particular product, because one's definition is wide or narrow depending upon past experience, upbringing, social standing, etc. Some people would regard beef as having no substitute while others would regard the other meats mentioned as being very adequate substitutes. Another person, in fact, could even widen the definition and include eggs as a direct substitute for meat. Clearly personal choice has a large part to play.

(b) *Luxury or necessity.* In (a) above we said that the

definition of a substitute could be a very personal decision; in defining what is a luxury and what is a necessity, personal considerations also apply. You might consider beef steak four times a week to be a luxury while a wealthy person brought up on that diet would consider it a necessity.

However, we can make some general statements regarding luxuries and necessities, and it is the responsibility of the particular firm to use the definition according to its own personal circumstances and from the knowledge it has of its own market. Necessities generally will tend to have an inelastic demand, e.g. foods (*see* Stone's results in **13** below) while luxuries will tend to have an elastic demand.

(*c*) *Number of uses which the product has.* The more uses a product has, the more elastic the demand. A relatively small fall in price will result perhaps not in a very large increase in demand from any one particular market, but when increases are totalled in all the markets, the final increase in demand can be significant. Electricity is a case in point. It can be used for heating, lighting, cooking power and entertainment. An increase in the price of electricity would not lead to a drastic reduction in any one of the above uses, but if economies are made in each a significant reduction in total demand could result. Given a longer period to view the consumer's adaptation to the increase in price, the elasticity in all probability will increase as gas or oil is substituted for electricity in heating or cooking.

(*d*) *Durable or non-durable goods.* By durable goods we normally mean goods which have a long life and wear out slowly over a number of years. A particular feature of these goods is that replacement takes place before the commodity has actually reached the end of its life. People exchange their cars because a new model is preferred; televisions, refrigerators, deep freezes, washing machines, caravans, boats and furniture are all exchanged when they can still provide the service for which they were originally bought. As a result of this, consumers can actually decide just when they want to enter the replacement market. If price rises, they can postpone purchase, or if price falls they might exchange earlier than intended. The impending imposition of Value Added Tax in April 1973 led to a rush to exchange and purchase caravans, boats, etc. in anticipation of the increase in price that would occur.

(e) *Percentage of consumer's budget.* The more expensive a commodity and the bigger the part it plays in the total consumer budget, the more strongly price changes are going to be felt by the consumer and therefore price elasticity will be high. A low-priced product will not necessarily be inelastic, the frequency of purchase also having to be considered to determine the overall part played by that commodity in the total budget. An increase in the price of theatre tickets by 50 per cent is unlikely to affect a person who goes to the theatre only twice annually, but for a person who goes twice weekly the increase in price will have a significant effect. Also, for average households an increase in the price of matches is unlikely to lead to great economies and reduction in demand, but to a pipe smoker using five boxes a week an increase in price could be the last straw that decides him to purchase a gas lighter.

13. Empirical evidence of elasticity. Research in both the U.K. and the U.S.A. has revealed that foodstuffs generally have a low price elasticity of demand. Table VI summarises the results of research by R. Stone.[1]

TABLE VI: CONSUMER EXPENDITURE AND BEHAVIOUR

Commodity	Price elasticity	Income elasticity
Flour	0·79	0·15
Bread	0·08	0·05
Pork	0·67	0·58
Poultry	0·27	1·17
Cream	0·69	1·71
Eggs	0·43	0·54
Sugar	0·44	0·09
Beer	0·87	0·05
Coal	0·50	0·26
Electricity	0·60	0·15

The column relating to income elasticity of demand will be discussed in **19** below.

14. Decisions on elasticity. Each firm, knowing its own market and its own product by applying the above analysis, should be able to decide approximately, as a first step, whether demand is likely to be elastic or inelastic.

Because of the difficulties of the independent variables and in obtaining sufficient information, the accurate calculation of price elasticity of demand is almost impossible in practice: even if sufficient resources within the firm were devoted to its calculation, the results would rapidly become out of date. Nevertheless, although calculation is extremely difficult, if not impossible, the concept of elasticity is extremely important and should be given constant thought and attention by the firm. The factors explained in 12 above are continuously taken into account by firms in determining policy and market price.

15. Importance to the firm of price elasticity. Very simply, profits are the difference between total revenue (TR) and total cost (TC).

$$\text{Profits} = TR - TC.$$

If price elasticity of demand is less than 1 (inelastic), and price is lowered, more will be sold (increasing TC) but as we have shown in 9 above TR will fall. Profits will therefore be reduced.

If price elasticity of demand is greater than 1 (elastic) a fall in price will lead to a greater quantity being sold (increase in TC), but TR will also increase. A decision here to go ahead and lower price can only be made after a cost analysis has been made. No decision can be made by taking the demand conditions solely into consideration. If the increase in revenue (MR) exceeded the increase in costs (MC) necessary to produce the extra output, then the decision to lower price would be favourable.

16. Increase in costs. The elasticity of demand will also determine how much, if any, of the increased costs incurred by a firm can be passed on to the consumer. Given the elasticity of supply, an increase in cost represented by a shift of the supply curve from S_1 to S_2 will lead to a larger fall in quantity demanded and a smaller rise in price, the more elastic the demand curve.

Compare Figs. 10 (a) and (b), where the increase in cost (shift in the supply curve) is the same in both cases yet the effect on price and quantity is very different. Figure 10 (a) shows a smaller rise in price than (b) and also a larger fall in quantity demanded.

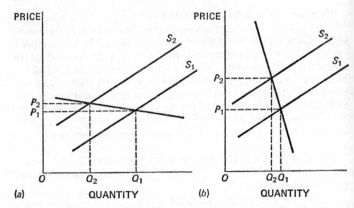

FIG. 10—*Increase in cost.* The more inelastic the demand for a product, the higher the percentage of any cost increase the producer incurs can he pass on to the customer as price increases. In (*a*), where the demand curve is elastic, the producer is unable to pass on as high a percentage of a comparable cost increase as in (*b*), where the demand curve is inelastic.

17. Practical complications. So far we have been discussing a situation in which a firm sells its product in one clearly identified market. In practice, however, this is far from the case, and with products that have many uses (e.g. sulphuric acid) in different countries and different industries, price elasticity of demand is likely to vary from market to market. In some markets elasticity of demand may be high because the elasticity of demand for the final product is high or because substitutes exist, while in other markets elasticity of demand is low and other factors within the demand function are more important than price, i.e. income or advertising expenditure.

INCOME

18. Income. This is the second independent variable shown in the demand function in **2** above. This independent variable is regarded as being outside the control of the firm, although an understanding of how the demand for its product is influenced by variations in the level of income is extremely important, so that adaptation to new circumstances can be judged correctly.

Although an individual firm can do very little to influence the general level of income, firms as a whole through advertising and sales promotion have created an atmosphere favourable to consumption. Consumption creates income, which in turn creates new demand, in turn creating new jobs.

For many goods, income is a major determinant of demand and it is frequently as important, if not more so, than price or advertising. This is particularly true of what we call luxury items, e.g. jewellery, motor cars, holidays abroad, etc. Alternatively, purchases of basic commodities such as salt, bread and matches are not very responsive to income changes, these goods being bought in fairly constant amounts.

In Fig. 11 it can be seen that as income increases the demand curve shifts to the right from D_1 to D_2 and D_3, the result being that more of the good is demanded although price has remained constant at P_1. In fact, if price had increased to P_2 and P_3, it

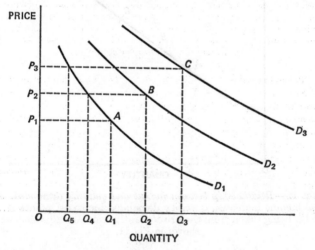

Fig. 11—*Income as a determinant of demand*. As income increases, the demand curve shifts to the right from D_1 to D_3. This increases quantity demanded at the same price, Q_5 to Q_3, when price is P_3, and can also increase quantity demanded when price is increased. When price is increased from P_1 to P_2, quantity demanded would normally fall from Q_1 to Q_4, but because the demand curve shifts from D_1 to D_2, quantity actually increases from Q_1 to Q_2.

would still be possible for more to be demanded if the increase in income more than outweighed the increase in prices. If income had not increased however, quantity demanded would have fallen from OQ_1 to OQ_4 and then OQ_5.

That motor cars are much more expensive today than when first introduced and that the demand for cars is large and ever-growing does not mean there is a positive relationship between price and quantity demanded. What has happened is that the general level of income has increased over the years to such an extent that the increase in the price of motor cars has been outweighed by income rises and increase in the standard of living of the population.

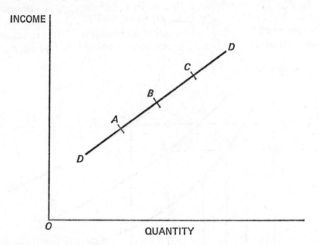

FIG. 12—*Relationship between income and quantity demanded.* As real income increases, quantity demanded increases, points *A*, *B* and *C* being taken from the price/quantity relationships that were shown in Fig 11.

Figure 12 shows the positive relationship that exists between income and quantity demanded, and curve *DD* is taken from Fig. 11, using points *A*, *B* and *C*.

19. Income elasticity of demand. From this second schedule (Fig. 12) we can derive the income elasticity of demand, which is conceptually similar to price elasticity of demand already covered in **8** above.

$$\text{Income elasticity of demand} = \frac{\% \text{ change in quantity } D}{\% \text{ change in income}}$$

In one of the most comprehensive studies undertaken in the U.K. (R. Stone [2]) most foodstuffs were found to have an income elasticity of demand that was positive but less than 1 (*see* Table VI). In other words, as income increased consumption increased, but by a smaller proportion. Consumer durables are more likely to be affected by income changes than any other category, and J. S. Cramer [3] calculated the long term income elasticities of the products shown in Table VII.

TABLE VII: THE INCOME ELASTICITY OF
CONSUMER DURABLES

Refrigerators	1·89
Washing machines	1·28
Motor cars	1·55
Television sets (black and white)	0·83

In interpreting these figures one would say that if income rose by 10 per cent, demand for refrigerators would increase by 18·9 per cent, washing machines by 12·8 per cent, motor cars by 15·5 per cent and black and white television sets by 8·3 per cent.

20. Threshold effects. Just as price elasticity varies over the demand curve, so income elasticity varies over the income demand schedule. One of the reasons for this is that for many goods there tends to be a critical threshold effect: a certain level of income is required to obtain a product. Once you have reached that level of income and once you have bought that product, further rises in income are unlikely to lead to continued purchases. This hypothesis could explain why black and white television sets have an income elasticity of demand of less than 1, when all the evidence points to colour televisions having a relatively high income elasticity of demand.

The importance, therefore, that needs to be placed on income in the demand function depends on the category into which a product is placed, i.e. luxury or necessity, consumer durable or non-durable, and also on the existing level of income, e.g. black and white television sets are consumer durables and were once regarded as luxuries, yet income has reached such a level that the income elasticity of demand has been calculated to be less than 1.

21. Income definitions. Up to now, by "income" we have meant the general level of income in the economy, and the assumption has been that expenditure is based entirely upon the existing level of this income. However, in practice, purchasing power and purchasing ability must be taken into account. The following categories of "income" have been established to assist the practical calculation of income elasticity:

(*a*) *Discretionary income :* disposable personal income less necessary living costs. There is evidence that the sale of consumer durables relates more closely to income after the deduction of certain regular expenses than it does to total income.

(*b*) *Discretionary buying power :* discretionary income plus cash balances plus near-liquid assets plus new consumer credit.

Category (*b*) can be further developed by examining the existing level of consumer credit outstanding, because a high ratio of outstanding consumer debt to current income may suggest a slowing down of purchases based on new debt.

22. Significance of income elasticity of demand to the firm. Firms whose demand functions have high income elasticities will have good growth opportunities in an expanding economy, so forecasts of aggregate economic activity will figure greatly in their plans. Companies faced with low income elasticities, on the other hand, are not so sensitive to the level of business activity. This may be good in that such a business is to a large extent "recession-proof", but since the company cannot expect to share fully in a growing economy it may seek entry into industries that provide better growth opportunities, i.e. diversification.

INTER-RELATIONSHIP OF DEMAND

23. Prices of substitutes and other goods. The third independent variable contained in the demand function is the price of other goods, and as industry becomes more concentrated and the industrial structure becomes oligopolistic (*see* Chapter VII) this independent variable plays a larger and larger role in demand analysis and forecasting. What is important to a firm is not just the price of substitute products or complementary products, but also the price of products that utilise their own output.

(*a*) *Substitute relationship.* Examples of this would be gas cookers and electric cookers, and electric lawn mowers and petrol lawn mowers. An increase in the price of gas would in the long-run lead to an increase in the demand for electric cookers as electric cookers become relatively cheaper to use. A fall in the price of gas would have the opposite effect, an increase in demand for gas cookers and a fall in the demand for electric cookers.

(*b*) *Complementary relationship.* Examples of this would be electricity and electric cookers, pipes and pipe tobacco, caravans and calor gas. If the price of pipe tobacco rose, a large number of people might decide to give up smoking altogether or change to cigarette smoking, resulting in a fall in the demand for pipes. If the price of touring caravans fell, more would be purchased and the demand for calor gas would increase.

(*c*) *Derived demand.* Some commodities are demanded not for their own sake but for their contribution to the manufacture of another product. Bricks, for example, are required for building, the total demand for bricks being dependent on the total demand for buildings of all types.

24. The interaction of demand. The complicated nature of these inter-relationships can be appreciated when we realise that in practice any one product can be affected by all three types of demand simultaneously. For example, steel has numerous uses, each market for its product being affected by different considerations. A fall in the price of electricity will lead to more electricity being used than gas (substitute). The result of cheaper electricity will lead to the demand for electric cookers increasing (complementary) at the expense of gas cookers (substitute). It is possible that the makers of electric cookers who are now faced with a larger demand might be able to lower the price of electric cookers (*see* Chapter V, **12**, on economies of large-scale production). This leads to earlier replacement and also to first-time purchases by people who used gas cookers previously and by those who had no cooker of any sort. Demand for steel increases (derived demand). This is obviously not the end of the chain and further repercussions will occur, but it serves as an example to show how complicated these inter-relationships are, particularly when one attempts to quantify them.

25. Cross elasticity of demand. We can use the concept of elasticity to measure the strength of these relationships, the measure being called cross elasticity of demand.

$$\text{Cross elasticity of demand} = \frac{\% \text{ change in quantity demanded of good } X}{\% \text{ change in price of good } Y}.$$

A negative cross elasticity means that the goods are complementary, while a positive cross elasticity indicates that the goods in question are substitutes. The higher the value, the stronger the relationship and if cross elasticity is 0 or nearly 0 then the goods in question are unrelated. The idea of cross elasticity is of course inseparable from ordinary price elasticity, its importance depending upon the market structure under which it operates and the degree of product differentiation that exists in that market (*see* Chapter IV).

26. Price elasticity of a derived demand. The elasticity of demand of a product that has a derived demand is less than the price elasticity of demand of the final product. The lower its price in relation to the total cost of the final product, the more price inelastic it will become. To clarify this point, consider the following example.

EXAMPLE 5: Firm X produces valves which it sells for £1 to firm Y which produces televisions. These televisions are sold for £100. A 25 per cent increase in the price of the valves from £1 to £1·25 will only cause the final product to increase in price by 0·25 per cent. Unless the final product is exceptionally highly elastic, demand for the valve is unlikely to be curtailed.

In this simple example, we have ignored the possible existence of valves produced by another firm in competition with firm X. If such substitutes exist then firm X would have to consider very seriously the effect on its demand of raising price from £1 to £1·25. If price was the only consideration of firm Y they would cease to deal with firm X, although in practice other factors such as quality, reliability, service, etc. enter into these decisions.

ADDITIONAL FACTORS

27. Sales promotional activity. This is an independent variable that is very much under the control of the individual firm. By sales promotion is meant a host of activities such as advertising, giving trading stamps, prizes, competitions, show-rooms, door-to-door salesmen, etc. We shall concentrate on advertising because this is one aspect of sales promotion with which most of us are familiar, and the general points made apply equally to the other aspects.

In industries where there are a number of competing firms producing very similar products, advertising is used to make the firm's product as differentiated as possible and thus reduce the cross elasticity of demand. By attempting to make one's product unique, it is possible for different prices to be charged for similar products within the industry. It is also used to create problems for new firms attempting to break into the particular market, i.e. create an additional barrier to entry by raising the cost of entry for a new firm.

Advertising can be called a "factor of revenue" because through advertising it might be possible to sell more at the same price, a move from Q_1 to Q_2 in Fig. 13, or sell the same quantity at a higher price, P_2. This is possible because through advertising the demand curve has been shifted to the right and therefore total revenue of the firm will increase. The firm that is advertising hopes that in addition to shifting the demand curve from D_1 to D_2, it will also succeed in changing its shape, i.e. make it less elastic. By building up consumer loyalty the new demand curve becomes inelastic and therefore the cross elasticity of demand is considerably reduced.

28. Cost of advertising. Advertising, in addition to shifting the demand curve to the right, also raises the total cost curve because it is an additional expense. The firm must ensure that the additional revenue (MR) exceeds the additional cost (MC) incurred. As long as the extra revenue being generated (MR) exceeds the additional cost (MC) it will be profitable to con-

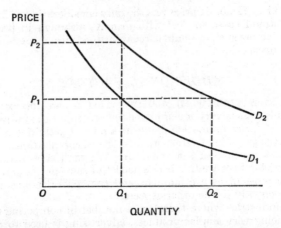

FIG. 13—*Advertising as a factor of revenue.* As the demand curve shifts to the right as a result of advertising expenditure, the firm can increase its revenue by either: (*i*) selling the same quantity, Q_1, at a higher price, or (*ii*) selling a greater quantity, Q_2, at the same price, P_1.

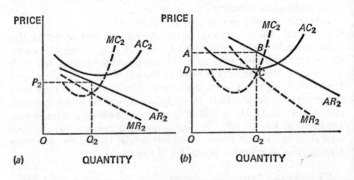

FIG. 14—*Successful and unsuccessful advertising campaign.* (*a*) Advertising expenditure has shifted the cost curves higher than the revenue curves with the result that the firm will make an overall loss. (*b*) The revenue curve has been shifted to a greater degree than the average cost curve with the result that a profit equal to the area $ABCD$ will be earned at output Q_2.

tinue the campaign and to increase the level of advertising expenditure. Indeed, the firm will continue to gain up to the point where MR is equal to MC. Due to the uncertainty of consumer reaction to a particular advertising campaign, advertising is not a guarantee for success and in Fig. 14 (a) the AR and MR curves have been shifted to the right, AR_2 and MR_2, but the average cost curve AC_2 has moved upwards by a relatively larger degree, with the result that total revenue fails to cover total costs. In Fig. 14 (b) the campaign has been successful and a monopoly profit equal to area $ABCD$ is being earned.

29. General environmental influences.

(a) *Population changes* can affect virtually every sector of the economy. An increase in population will mean that more of everything will be required. An increase in the average size of the family could lead to an increase in demand for bigger houses and cars, and furniture, carpets, beds, etc. will wear out more quickly. Even if the population is constant, changes in its composition, such as in sex or age, will lead to changing patterns of demand. As far as the individual firm is concerned, it can only observe population figures as issued by the Central Statistical Office and interpret them in the light of its own product and current demand pattern.

(b) *Size and age distribution of existing stocks.* An analysis of this situation will reveal two important points. First, whether the market has reached saturation point and, secondly, the possible extent of replacement demand and new demand. This distinction is important for consumer durables, because different forces act on each. Some firms in fact divide their demand forecasts between these two categories.

(c) *Government policy* can influence the demand for many goods, particularly consumer durables, through variations in Value Added Tax, deposit and length of repayment of hire purchase debt, level of income tax and general availability of credit. For many people who purchase a consumer durable, the deposit required and the monthly repayment are of greater importance than the total price. A relatively low-priced commodity would be out of their reach if the deposit required was particularly high and the repayment period very short. If the deposit was lower and the repayment period extended, an increase in the price would be secondary. The government's monetary policy can influence the rate of interest and thus the availability of mortgages. This results in a change in the demand for new houses, with a consequent change in demand for all those products and services that are required by house builders.

The scope for government interference in the demand patterns of firms is unlimited, and each individual firm needs to interpret government policy as it will affect the demand for its own particular product.

30. Conclusions. The main influences on demand have been mentioned above. It would be impossible to list all the possibilities. Each firm and each individual product is influenced by factors peculiar to its own market. All factors that influence the demand for the product of your firm must be included in the demand function if an accurate demand forecast is to be established.

It is impossible to quantify all the factors included in the demand function—What is a substitute? How close is a substitute? When does a luxury become a necessity? Until this is the case, forecasting the position and shape of a demand curve will always be extremely difficult.

PROGRESS TEST 3

1. Why is demand analysis essential for successful production planning and capital expansion? (1–3)
2. Is it possible for a demand curve to slope upwards from left to right? (4)
3. What is meant by "price elasticity of demand"? Explain the derivation of the terms in the elasticity formula. (6–8)
4. If your demand curve is a straight line with a constant slope, is the elasticity of demand equal at all points along the demand curve? (8–10)
5. When a firm faces a downward-sloping demand curve, marginal revenue will always be less than price. Why? (11)
6. What is meant by the "threshold effect" in relation to income elasticity? (20)
7. Why is the elasticity of demand of a product that has a derived demand less than the price elasticity of demand of the final product? (26)

8. Advertising is sometimes referred to as being a "factor of revenue". Explain with the aid of diagrams. (27, 28)

FURTHER READING

1. Stone, R., *The Measurement of Consumers' Expenditure and Behaviour in the United Kingdom* 1920–1938, Cambridge University Press, 1951.

2. Stone, R., *op. cit.*

3. Cramer, J. S., *The Ownership of Major Consumer Durables*, Cambridge University Press, 1962.

Authorities in various countries referred to in the theory or policy of ...

CHAPTER IV

EMPIRICAL DEMAND ANALYSIS

INTRODUCTION

In the last Chapter the main theoretical concepts of demand analysis were introduced and we must now study three areas which will help place this knowledge in perspective by using these concepts.

METHODS OF DEMAND FORECASTING

1. Market research. The purpose of market research is to provide a firm with information concerning its current market position, present and possible future trends in the industry, and through the information obtained, help the firm determine product improvement, new product policy, pricing and sales promotion strategy.

The information obtained from market research is merely a first step. It is the analysis and interpretation of information that is important and this is why it is essential to understand fully the concepts introduced in Chapter III.

Any firm embarking upon a programme of demand analysis for the first time should, in the first place, establish a complete market profile for the products it produces at that particular time. Some of the main factors to consider in establishing this are outlined in Table VIII.[1]

Most firms today produce more than one product, and their consumers are obviously not identical; it is therefore essential to look at where the products are sold and to whom and when. Are the product sales concentrated in one area? Are sales concentrated in a particular income group? These questions are of vital importance, as the answers could affect methods of distribution and transportation and even the location of a new plant. The fact that your customers or the customers of a rival firm are concentrated within a certain income group could leave another income group open to attack. Seasonal

TABLE VIII: ELEMENTS OF A MARKET PROFILE

The consumer

Total number of consumers
Regional distribution
Total income
The effect of income and wealth, i.e. measures of elasticity
Income per household
Distribution of income
Consumers' tastes
Behaviour characteristics—where do consumers buy and when do they buy?
Effect of design

The business

Current levels of sales
Current stocks
Trends in sales and stocks
Share of the market
Seasonal fluctuation
Trends in research and development
Company strengths and weaknesses
New product possibilities

The market

The effect of price; measures of price elasticity
Unique characteristics of products
Identification of competitive products
Number and nature of competitors
Institutional arrangements, channels of distribution, etc.
Forms of competition (price, advertising, brand policy, etc.)
Expected technological changes
General price levels
Price of similar commodities

General considerations

Economic climate—level of activity, employment, etc.
Government policy
Taxation

Source: Bates, R. and Parkinson, J. R., Business Economics, Basil Blackwell, 1971.

fluctuations can heavily influence production capacity and size of stocks to be held.

2. Forecasting demand. Once the current position has been established and clearly understood by the firm's management, attempts to forecast and manipulate future demand can be made. Most firms require two forecasts—one covering the short-term, which represents the next three months to one year, and the other covering the long-term, which represents the forecast for any period exceeding one year.

Short-term forecasts are valuable for taking decisions concerning current output, purchases of raw materials and size of stocks to be held, while long-term forecasts are essential in decisions concerning capital investment, factory expansion and recruitment and training of personnel. The actual length of the short- and long-term period will vary from industry to industry, depending upon capital intensity and technical sophistication. The less technical and sophisticated the capital equipment used, the shorter the long-term period.

The forecasts for short- and long-term need not necessarily coincide, and it is possible for apparently conflicting policies to be pursued. Take as an example the market for automatic washing machines—in addition to the price of the product, the general level of income and hire-purchase regulations play a considerable role in determining demand.

A firm might find itself in a situation where, because of inflation and a balance of payments deficit, the government has had to impose credit restrictions which raise the hire-purchase rates of interest and also raise the deposit that must be paid. These actions will affect demand in the short-run and therefore current production will be slowed down; there will be a cutback in the purchase of raw materials and an attempt will be made to keep stocks as low as possible. Despite this, the firm believes that these economic troubles will be solved in the future with the result that the overall prosperity of the nation will increase, as will income per head, and therefore the demand for automatic washing machines will expand. Long-term plans of recruitment and factory expansion will thus continue.

3. Change of priorities. For a firm producing a number of products, the results of demand forecasting could change the whole emphasis of the business by changing product policy. In Fig. 15, product X has for many years been the dominant product of the firm and activities have been geared to its successful production. The demand forecast has revealed that the demand for product Y in five years' time will be greater than that of product X and that the firm should, therefore, cease giving priority to product X and concentrate on building up and supplying the demand for product Y.

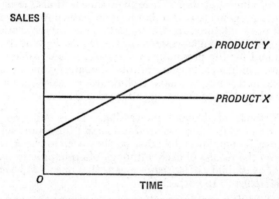

FIG. 15—*Projected demand forecast.* Over a period of time, demand forecasts have predicted that product Y will eventually become more important (in terms of sales) than product X. This will entail a change of management priority within the firm.

A similar graph could be drawn if one product was being sold in two geographical locations; the forecast of demand for each area in the future could affect the plans for expanding the firm at its existing site and involve locating a new plant within a forecasted larger segment of its total market.

4. The three stages of forecasting demand. Once the current market profile has been established the process of forecasting demand can commence. This should proceed through three clearly defined stages:

(*a*) *Stage 1.* An assessment of the general economic and national situation. By this is meant an examination of the implications of existing government policies and proposed policies on general income levels, plus an examination of population trends, technical achievements and discoveries (e.g. North Sea gas and oil).

(b) *Stage 2.* An assessment of the total demand for the product. The rate of increase in total demand is important, because if it is below the aspiration level of the firm, the firm can only expand at the expense of its competitors. Such action is likely to lead to retaliation and thus an expensive price/sales promotion war. The total demand for the product and its increase over time will also issue clear warning signals to a firm that it should seek new markets and new products (product differentiation and diversification).

(c) *Stage 3.* An assessment of the firm's share of the total demand for the product. In this case, it is possible for the firm to influence its share of total demand by manipulating price and using various techniques of sales promotion, i.e. advertising, packaging, after-sales service.

5. Methods of demand forecasting. There are two main methods used for forecasting the demand for a product, and they can be employed together so that a cross-check can be made on the results of each, although often in practice lack of time or availability of statistics means that one must be chosen in preference to the other.

(a) Taking *past information* as a starting point and using various statistical and mathematical techniques to establish relationships that will enable extrapolation and forecasting to take place.

(b) Obtaining information as to the *current intention* of consumers through interviews and surveys, test marketing and opinions of those with knowledge of the trade.

6. Statistical and mathematical techniques. The main techniques employed are those of regression, correlation and time series analysis. Regression and correlation analysis, using past information as a guide, explores the relationship between a dependent variable (sales) and selected independent variables (price, advertising expenditure, income, etc.) and, given a strong relationship, uses the data to forecast the future. There are three stages in the operation:

(a) *Collection of statistics* concerning past values of relevant variables. In most cases insufficient data is available and that which is, is suspect. It must also be ensured that all relevant variables are included in the analysis, otherwise there will be serious distortion of results.

(b) We assume causation between the independent and dependent variables and use correlation analysis to *determine the strength of the relationship*. This relationship will always be subject to some degree of error, i.e. qualified by a significance test.

(c) To *produce our forecast* we now make adjustments to our independent variables used on an assessment of how we think they will vary over the time period considered. Will the general level of income rise and by how much? How much advertising will be employed by our rivals in response to our own advertising budget? What adjustments will be made to their prices when faced with our own price policy?

Although sophisticated mathematical and statistical techniques are being used, the whole process is subject to error and speculation even when the greatest care is taken. The use of such analysis even when past correlation is extremely strong can only provide accurate forecasts if it can be assumed that the same forces that operated in the past will continue to operate in the future, and that the inter-relationship between the variables remains unchanged.

7. Inter-relation of variables. Further problems[2] of a more serious nature arise when there is the possibility that several of the variables themselves may be highly inter-related and, even more serious, where a number of variables interact mutually and are determined simultaneously.

The demand for coal is a good example here. The coal industry demands steel for roof supports, tools and machinery. To produce the extra steel, extra coal is required by the steel industry. To produce extra coal for the steel industry, extra roof supports, tools and machinery are needed, and to provide this equipment extra coal is demanded by the steel industry. Where does one stop? This sort of relationship is not uncommon and the statistician faced with raw data must separate the influence of these simultaneous relationships so that the strength of each independent variable can be assessed. Without such separation the use of regression and correlation analysis on the raw data will provide meaningless results. This is known as the identification problem.

8. The identification problem. Price and quantity in any given situation is the result of demand and supply. It is possible when looking at historical data to plot the line XYZ (Fig. 16). Now this line is downward-sloping, indicating the usual price/quantity relationship (more is bought at a lower

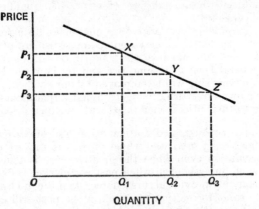

FIG. 16—*An apparent demand curve.* The points X, Y and Z appear to trace out a demand curve. Before accepting it as a demand curve, however, it is important to check that independent variables, other than price, have not moved during the same time period.

price) but it would be extremely naive to assume that points XYZ traced out a demand curve without first investigating whether events had occurred that have shifted the demand or the supply curve.

The demand curve is based on the assumption that "other things remain equal"—in other words all other variables that influence quantity sold are held constant while price is manipulated. Can we be certain that "all other things" have remained constant? In Fig. 17 are the hypothesised and true supply and demand curves for the product in question.

It can be seen that the points X, Y and Z have been produced by the simultaneous solution of supply and demand relationships at three points in time.

The supply and demand curves could have shifted for a variety of reasons—the supply curves because of an increase in technological efficiency, and the demand curves because of an increase in income or an increase in the price of substitute products.

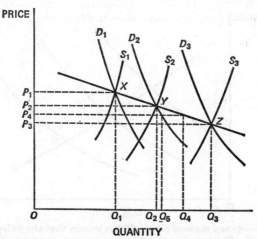

FIG. 17—*Hypothesised and true demand curves*. Misinterpreting the demand to be XYZ instead of D_2 would cause the firm to think it would increase its total revenue by lowering price from P_2 to P_4, with the effect of increasing quantity demanded from OQ_2 to OQ_4. In fact quantity demanded would only increase to OQ_5 and total revenue would fall.

If the firm erroneously interprets XYZ as being its demand curve instead of, say, D_2 at that point in time, it might consider it worthwhile lowering price from P_2 to P_4. It anticipates that quantity bought will increase by $OQ_4 — OQ_2$ and that its total revenue will increase (elastic demand). If the true demand is D_2, quantity bought will only increase to OQ_5, which is less than OQ_4, and the result would be that the firm would sell more (increase in TC) but revenue would be lower than previously (inelastic demand).

9. Overcoming the identification problem. Is it possible to solve this problem in practice? It is, but only if:

(*a*) One curve has remained stable while the other has shifted. For example, assume we know that the general conditions affecting demand over a period have remained stable but due to technological changes the supply curve (Fig. 18) has shifted from S_1 to S_2 and S_3. Each price/

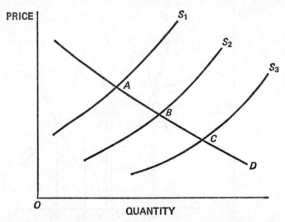

FIG. 18—*Actual demand curve*. If it is known that the independent variables affecting demand have remained constant during a period, but that the supply curve has been shifting, then every price/quantity point must lie on the demand curve.

quantity point (the intersection of demand and supply curves) must be on the demand curve, and the points ABC trace it out;

(*b*) We have enough information to determine just how each curve has shifted between data observations.

Unless such information is available, so that the simultaneous relationships can be identified, the use of regression and correlation analysis is valueless. There are many statistical techniques that have not been mentioned, yet the basic problem is still the same—that of obtaining sufficient information to reflect the true relationship between the variables.

There are two situations where statistical techniques using historical data as a base may not be used:

(*c*) Where the data that is available is inadequate (for reasons stated above) or because no data exists (because the product is new);

(*d*) Where historical data is available, but it is believed that the relationship that once existed between the variables has now changed (change in tastes brought about by a depression, war or government policy, etc.).

In these circumstances, the second method of forecasting demand (**5** (*b*) above) should be used.

10. Intentions of consumers. There are a number of ways to obtain this information, and the method that will be chosen by the firm depends upon how quickly it requires it, what cost it is prepared to incur and the co-operation it can receive from manufacturers and suppliers.

(*a*) The simple method is merely to construct a *questionnaire* and ask consumers in the market what their buying intentions are and what their responses will be to changes in price, advertising, quality, etc. This is obviously the most unreliable method because the answers are likely to be given on the spur of the moment and may be biased to please the interviewer.

(*b*) The firm might construct a *consumer panel* from which to obtain information and sample opinions from time to time. The panel is constructed as a sample of the whole population, and in addition to the human problem of consumers knowing they are taking part in a survey, the greater problem of selecting a sample really representative of the population as a whole arises.

(*c*) The use of the firm's own *field selling organisation*. This method has the advantage of being cheap, in that existing salesmen and retail outlets are used at no extra expense. The results, however, are likely to be biased, normally in an optimistic direction.

(*d*) If the above methods are unsuitable or need supplementing the firm might attempt to *test market* its product. It can do this either by constructing a hypothetical buying situation, and with a random sample of consumers, judge response to changing prices, packaging and advertising, or it can attempt to be more realistic by choosing a geographical area, and with the co-operation of retailers, vary price, advertising, etc. For this test marketing to be successful, however, the following factors must exist:

(*i*) The geographic area chosen is representative of the country as a whole.

(*ii*) The conditions in the market during the experiment are "normal" and similar to conditions that will exist over the country after the experiment. This is a very big assumption, as the firm cannot hope to control all the factors that influence the sale of its product, indeed it is not unknown for a firm, knowing that a rival is conducting market experiments in an area, deliberately to change its marketing and pricing policy so as to sabotage the results of the experiment.

Even if the buying situation is satisfactory the results of the test may be difficult to interpret, particularly if it is impossible to distinguish between initial and repeat purchases.

Due to the high cost of such experiments and the desire to market the product with "other things" remaining as constant as possible, these experiments are normally of short duration. However, it has been shown that time and time again there is a significant difference between impact effect and long-run effect. A fall in price or an intensive advertising campaign might lead to a sharp increase in demand, but for how long will this new higher level be maintained? It is very probable that long-run demand will be higher than formerly but lower than the level indicated by the initial impact of the experiment.

Such experiments can also be very expensive and risky for the firm. Customers lost by an experimental price increase may never be regained from competitive products which they might otherwise never have tried. A 5 or 10 per cent increase in advertising expenditure for any protracted period may be no trivial matter.

11. Forecasting demand for a new product. So far in this discussion we have been considering products which already exist, have been marketed for a number of years and for which some data, no matter how incomplete, therefore exists. If demand forecasting presents such great problems for such products how do we begin to forecast the demand for a new product for which there is no past information and of which the consumer has no experience? Joel Dean [3] has suggested a number of possible approaches.

(a) *Evolutionary*. Project the demand for the new product as an outgrowth and evolution of an existing product.

(b) *Substitute*. Analyse the new product as a substitute for some existing product or service.

(c) *Growth curve*. Estimate the rate of growth and the ultimate level of demand for the new product on the basis of the pattern of growth of established products.

(d) *Opinion polling*. Estimate demand by direct enquiry into the ultimate purchasers, extending the sample to derive the total demand for the product by the population as a whole.

(e) *Sales experience*. Offer the new product for sale in a sample market and from this try to estimate the total demand from all channels and a full-developed market.

(f) *Vicarious*. Survey consumer reaction to a new product indirectly through the eyes of specialised dealers who are supposedly informed about consumer needs and alternative opportunities.

These methods are of course not mutually exclusive, and if possible a combination of several should be used so that cross-checks are available.

DEFICIENCIES OF TRADITIONAL DEMAND THEORY

12. Practical weaknesses. The theory of demand associated with the theory of the firm leaves much to be desired because of the use of static theories of utility and consumer preferences. The practical weakness of the theory stems from two implicit assumptions:

(a) The first is that the consumers have a relatively stable and comprehensive preference system.

(b) The second is the assumption that the consumers' preference systems are independent, i.e. the effect of the decisions of individuals on the decision-taking functions of others are, in this field, sufficiently unimportant to be ignored.

In a "dynamic" theory of demand, instead of adjustments to

price changes among established commodities we emphasise the process of inter-personal stimulation and want creation. This fact was recognized by Duesenberry's [4] "demonstration effect" which portrays the individual coming under the influence of the consumption patterns of those with whom he comes into contact.

13. The process of want creation. "Wants" are largely the product of experience, not only of our own but also of other people's. In addition, most people are constantly searching for new experiences and it is possible to distinguish between "needs" and "wants". A product meets a "need" if it provides the consumer with sensible advantages in the achievement of specific socio-economic aims. But consumers cannot "want" the product until they have experienced it in action, until, in fact, it has been created and is in use. When they do come to "want" it they also "need" it. Before this, the "need" can be described as latent. The commercial process consists of sensing the existence of latent "needs" and exploiting them, i.e. converting them into conscious "wants" by marketing and advertising. It is sometimes argued that "wants" can be created from nothing, without the existence of objective latent needs. If this were generally true, nothing would limit the rate of growth required by the individual firm; the experience of firms in practice, however, proves that unless a product stimulates a latent need no amount of advertising and sales promotion will make it successful. The examples of products in **19** (c) below that have had to be withdrawn from the market lend support to this viewpoint.

14. Group influence. It is in "groups" that opinions attitudes, ethics and ideas are formed: it is a mistake to think of the process of communication as being one purely of transmission and acceptance of messages with nothing in between. There are what are called intervening variables, e.g. exposure, character of media, content, attitude of audience, etc., and a very important intervening variable, in fact the most important, is that of inter-personal relations.

People are influenced by others, and if people did not buy a product until influenced by someone else (want creation) then nothing new would ever be bought. This problem is overcome by the existence of "pioneers".

15. "Pioneers" and "sheep". We can use a simple analogy here. "Pioneers" are active agents for spreading new ideas and "sheep" are those receptive to them. Different people may at different times be "pioneers". Most "pioneers" in their particular field have more knowledge than the "sheep" and to be effective they must be in sufficient contact with their group. One might say that in both pioneers and sheep, "wants" are established by experience as consumers, but with sheep they must first be planted in the mind by another person. Unusual ability to perceive one's own latent "needs", unusual adventurousness or susceptibility to advertisements might all explain pioneering decisions. Products and advertisements must not only reach these pioneers but must also become accepted by them. If the leaders do not pass on information, or if the group refuses to accept it, the flow of influence is blocked. Further, since group leaders or pioneers are better informed, they are harder to influence. They may thus easily reject ideas presented by the mass media.

The total number of pioneers acquired by a product in a given period will be a function of its intrinsic qualities, of the money and skill devoted to advertising and other forms of sales promotion, of its price, and of the social and economic characteristics of the population.

The act of becoming a pioneer is different in kind from that of moving along an established demand curve. Pioneering consists, in fact, of establishing the demand curve itself. Pioneering is thus irreversible: before the act no curve exists, consumption being nil at all prices and incomes, whereas after the act, nil consumption happens only when prices are above a definite positive level.

16. Socio-economic contact. Precisely the same applies to "sheep". When a sheep is stimulated to become a consumer as a result of contact with other existing consumers, a process called activation, he is irreversibly changed. Before, he had no demand curve, now he has. Even sheep can stimulate others and it is possible for a chain reaction to be set up. The number of pioneers must reach some critical figure before the chain reaction will take place. When the number of pioneers reaches this, a condition of criticality is said to have occurred. This is defined as a condition where the probability of a continuing chain reaction tends to unity.

In order to stimulate one another, consumers must be in a state defined as socio-economic contact, able to be influenced by those of similar income and social background. This theory, therefore, by no means eliminates the hard reality of income from consumption decisions. We cannot, however, say for certain that either shared social class or shared income class is an exclusive ingredient.

A socio-economic contact is a person with whom one has a relationship such that his consumption behaviour is capable of influencing one's own. The socio-economic contacts of an individual are therefore limited to those people with whom he is in general contact and, among them, to those with whom he shares enough relevant values for the contact to be economic as well as social.

17. Primary groups and reference groups. This discovery of the pioneer or opinion leader also led to the discovery of the primary group. This was the idea that opinion leaders are not a group set apart, and that opinion leadership is not a trait which some people have and others do not, but rather that opinion leadership is an integral part of the give and take of everyday personal relationships. In other words, all inter-personal relations are potential networks of communication and an opinion leader can best be thought of as a group member playing a key communications role.

Reference groups against which an individual evaluates his own status and behaviour may be of several kinds. First, they may be membership groups to which a person *actually belongs* and may involve either:

(a) small face-to-face groups in which *actual association* is the rule, such as families or organisations whether business, social, religious or political; or

(b) groups in which actual membership is held but in which *personal association is absent*, for example, member-ship of a political party, none of whose meetings are personally attended. These groups may be of the same kind as the former but differing only in the lack of face-to-face association with other members.

Secondly, there may be groups or categories to which a person *automatically belongs* by virtue of age, sex, education, marital status and so on. This sort of reference-group relationship involves the concept of role. For example, before taking a certain action, an individual might consider whether it would be regarded as appropriate to his role as a man or husband or educated person or older person or a combination of all these. What is involved here is an individual's perception of what society—either in general or that part of it with which he has any contact—expects people of his age, sex, education or marital status to do in given circumstances.

Thirdly, there may be *anticipatory* rather than actual membership groups. Thus a person who aspires to membership in a group to which he does not belong may be more likely to refer to it or compare himself with its standards when making a decision than he is to refer to the standards of the group in which he actually belongs but would like to leave. This involves the concept of upward mobility. When such upward mobility is sought in the social or business world, it is usually accompanied by a sensitivity to the attitudes of those in the group to which one aspires.

Fourthly, there may be negative, *dissociative* reference groups. These constitute the opposite side of the coin from the anticipatory membership groups. Thus an individual sometimes avoids a certain action because it is associated with a group (to which the individual may or may not in fact belong) from which he would like to dissociate himself.

18. Influence of reference groups. Reference groups influence behaviour in two main ways. First, they influence aspiration levels, and thus play a part in producing satisfaction or frustration. If the other members of one's reference group (e.g. the neighbours) are wealthier, one may become dissatisfied with one's own achievement and strive to do as well.

Secondly, reference groups influence kinds of behaviour. They establish approved patterns for using one's wealth, etc. They also lay down taboos and may have the power to apply actual sanctions (for example, exclusion from the group). They thus produce conformity as well as contentment (or discontentment).

Although the discussion in **12–18** has taken us into the realms of psychology and sociology these are areas which the managerial economist cannot ignore, particularly as these forces can greatly influence demand for the firm's product.[5]

EMPIRICAL EVIDENCE ON EFFECT OF ADVERTISING AND PRICE IN INFLUENCING QUANTITY DEMANDED

19. Advertising.

(a) *Influence of advertising*. Many claims have been made by the supporters of advertising as to its effectiveness in increasing demand. However, research into the question of whether advertising can increase the propensity to consume indicates that advertising can only cause individuals to change their consumption patterns, without necessarily increasing consumption.

One of the main conclusions of Klapper[6] was that mass communication tends to reinforce rather than to change attitudes and activity. In general, advertising is successful only when it is in agreement with people's basic values, and harnesses existing forces rather than trying to alter them. In other words, it works best when it is reinforcing existing tendencies, or when operating in areas where there already exist no positive or negative trends.

Apart from the psychological and sociological factors which influence the propensity to consume, there is another factor which is extremely important: consumer optimism. Consumer optimism is largely determined by objective factors, i.e. political events, people's personal experiences, and the news they receive through the papers, television and radio.

As long as favourable conditions exist, advertising can, in all probability, have some influence in increasing the propensity to consume. At the same time advertising cannot guarantee this since the basic forces are beyond its control. Unfavourable news may lower consumer optimism and advertising has not and should not have any control over such news. Consumption might lose its glamour or people might become bored with the "new", with the result that the overall trend towards increased consumption might slow down.

It must be kept constantly in mind that while advertising can harness existing forces, it cannot, generally speaking, create them.

(b) *Borden*,[7] who has made the most comprehensive

research into advertising and its economic effects, agrees with these conclusions. In looking at the years 1907, 1914, 1920 and 1929, he concluded that advertising expenditure and economic activity moved together. After the Second World War, a different picture emerged and during four recession periods experienced in Canada and the U.S.A. advertising did not decline, but actually increased.

However, from a long-run point of view, Borden's study concluded that "advertising and aggressive selling have played a large, though not precisely measurable part in the formation of mental attitudes to a high level of consumption especially such attitudes as expectation of change and the nature of progress". In other words, it has helped to develop a mobile as opposed to a static society. The influence of advertising is therefore limited and is dependent on existing attitudes and circumstances. There are many factors that affect consumers' buying habits besides advertising, and this is true for primary and selective demand, just as it is for general demand.

(c) *Product failures.* It is sometimes said that advertising can sell anything. However, the examples below show that even leading firms with lengthy experience of market research techniques and new product launching have had many failures.

(i) From the American car industry came the classic example of the Edsel, manufactured by the Ford Motor Company. This medium-priced car was launched in September 1957 after nine years of planning; yet production was discontinued only two years later in November 1959. This was perhaps not surprising since, despite advertising, consumer resistance whittled sales from 54,500 in the last quarter of 1957 to 26,500 and 29,500 in the years 1958 and 1959 respectively.

(ii) In Germany, quick-frozen foods were introduced in the late 1950s but failed to make headway partly because incomes were low and partly because of strong prejudice against them among people who remembered the low quality of similar products during the Second World War. It took many years to dispel the prejudices which persisted despite improvements.

In the frozen-food market in the U.K., Birds Eye have withdrawn well over one hundred lines which have not been accepted by consumers.

(*iii*) Toiletries and cigarettes are products in which the persuasiveness of advertising and sales promotion techniques are generally considered to be most likely to influence the customer. Yet failures have still occurred. In the early 1960s Strand cigarettes appeared to be a successful new brand supported by a famous advertising campaign and introduced after intensive market research. All this could not prevent the cigarette from becoming a failure.

Some years ago Lever introduced a toilet soap, Lyril, accompanied by an advertising campaign costing some £1 m. During the first few months it gained some 8–9 per cent of the toilet soap market, but thereafter sales began to decline and it was subsequently withdrawn.

At the beginning of the 1960s several large corporations made strenuous efforts to extend the range of sales of men's toiletries. By 1962 at least two of these firms, Beecham and Atkinson, had withdrawn because the market had not expanded rapidly enough to sustain a high volume of sales.

(*d*) *Product life cycle.* In considering the failure of these products one should refer back to **12–18** above concerning the fact that the product must meet a latent need. Advertising is only one of a number of competitive weapons available to a firm (price, packaging, after-sales service, quantity, etc.), and it has conclusively been shown that for most products the influence of these competitive weapons

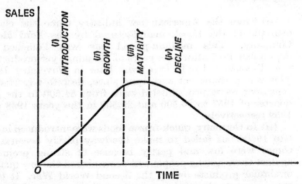

FIG. 19—*Product life cycle.* Every product has a life cycle which passes through the phases shown in this graph. Each firm must vary its marketing mix from cycle to cycle to ensure that consumer response is at its maximum.

varies over the life cycle as shown in Fig. 19. The responsiveness of the consumer to the various marketing weapons employed will vary over this life cycle. It is extremely important, therefore, to ensure that the right weapon is being employed at the right time to ensure maximum consumer response.

For a hypothetical product Dunco, the maximum consumer response may be ensured as follows:

(*i*) Heavy advertising expenditure during introduction to inform as many consumers as possible of the availability of the product.

(*ii*) Once sufficient consumers are aware of the product its reputation will be spread by word of mouth (socio-economic contacts) and therefore will penetrate into the market. Price is lowered and advertising expenditure cut back.

(*iii*) As the product reaches maturity and its reputation is well established, packaging and after-sales service may become prominent.

(*iv*) To delay decline as new- and second-generation products are introduced, emphasis may once again swing back to price and advertising.

(*e*) *Response of competitors.* There is a great attraction for firms to enter a market with an imitative product once the factor of want creation has been overcome. The pioneers' attention must first be captured to prove that the product deserves consideration in comparison with the existing products of similar type. The result of the advertising policy of a firm that enters a market with an imitative product depends upon whether:

(*i*) the market is static or expanding;
(*ii*) existing firms have captured all of the market or only a particular segment.

If the market is expanding the new entrant may be able to capture a large share and produce at a very profitable rate. The advantages are self-evident: the job of starting the chain reaction has already been done, much of the uncertainty has been removed and no act of innovation is required. Providing the existing firm's share of the market has not declined and still continues to grow, retaliation is unlikely. It will take an existing firm some time to calculate how fast the entrant is growing at his expense. Whether the share gained by the new entrant is within the bounds of acceptability for existing firms is a matter of judgment for the new entrant.

If the imitator is faced with a market situation described in (ii) above then he can aim his advertising at that segment of the market so far unexploited and retaliation is again unlikely.

It is where the market entered is static that retaliation is almost certain, with the result that rival advertising expenditures will cancel each other out, thus raising the average total cost curves of the firms without gaining them any particular advantage in demand.

In Fig. 20 this situation is described graphically. We have a firm that is maximising profits (producing where $MR = MC$) and is forced to increase its selling costs to maintain its share of the market, with the result that its profits decline from $(OQ_a)(P_1M)$ to $(OQ_a)(P_1T)$.

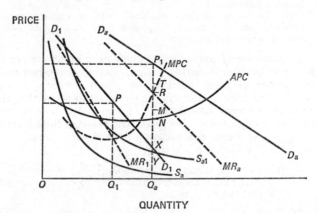

FIG. 20—*Static market situation*. Advertising expenditure reduces profits in a static market. Increased advertising expenditure by rival firms leaves market shares unchanged but increases total costs and reduces profits.

DD is the demand curve for the firm without advertising, MR is the corresponding marginal revenue curve and the firm maximises profits where $MR = MC$. An amount a is spent on advertising represented by rectangular hyperbola

S_a, and this creates a new demand curve, D_aD_a, and the profit-maximising position is at R where $MR_a = MC$ and output is OQ_a and price P_1. Profits are denoted by the rectangle having OQ_a as its base and P_1M as its height, MN of course being equal to Q_aY.

Now if an imitator enters this market, which is static, extra advertising expenditure S_{a1} will be needed to prevent reduction in market share, and even providing that the firm will be fully successful, profits will fall to the area of the rectangle denoted by OQ_a as its base and P_1T as its height.

(f) *Advertising and monopoly power.* From the evidence so far collected it is not at all clear what contribution advertising makes to monopoly power. Some authorities[8] claim that advertising has very little part to play in the creation of monopoly power, and that in fact it is more a weapon of competition. Others, however, see advertising and its attempts to create product differentiation as being a significant barrier to entry into a market. "On the basis of these empirical findings it is evident that for industries where products are differentiable, investment in advertising is a highly profitable activity. Industries with high advertising outlays earn on average a profit rate which exceeds that of other industries. . . . It is likely, moreover, that much of this profit rate differential is accounted for by the entry barriers created by advertising expenditures and by the resulting achievement of market power." [9]

(g) *Distribution of advertising expenditure between product categories.* Advertising will be most effective in situations where:

(i) there is a substantial chance of differentiating the product;

(ii) hidden qualities exist that cannot be judged at the time of purchase;

(iii) strong emotional buying motives exist, such as the protection of health or enhancement of social position; and

(iv) the combination of sales volume and gross margin is high enough to permit the necessary amount of advertising expenditure.

All these tend to make the firm's demand curve more product-inelastic, and the greater the length of the inelastic portion of the demand curve, the more profitable it is to advertise.

How much a product will be advertised depends then on the nature of the product, the nature of the market, the income of the people, their tastes, etc. An analysis of the percentage of advertising to total sales for 125 of the largest advertisers in the U.S.A. in 1965 [10] showed that of thirty-two companies that spent 10 per cent or more of their dollar sales on advertising, seventeen sold medicinal products and cosmetics, four sold soap and cleaners, three sold soft drinks, two sold confectionery and six were in other industries. In other words, the biggest relative users of advertising are concentrated in five industries—drugs, cosmetics, soaps, soft drinks and confectionery. Those companies that spent between 5 and 10 per cent were those selling cigarettes, foods, alcohol and beer.

An analysis of expenditure by product group for the U.K. produced similar results, certain products being heavily advertised to a much greater degree than their importance in the total consumer budget would seem to warrant. For example in 1974, 28 per cent of consumer expenditure was on food and drink, yet the total expenditure on food and drink advertisements on television represented 49·9 per cent of total advertising expenditure. Even more dramatic, chemists' goods represented 1·4 per cent of consumers' expenditure but 14·3 per cent of expenditure on press and television advertising.

(h) *Consumer trust.* The appeal of an advertisement is getting across a message in as brief a time as possible, otherwise the prospective consumer is likely to become bored. The advertising of more technical products on television would not be economical because too much time would have to be purchased in relation to the audience interested. In a newspaper, more information can be displayed, and those interested can study it at their leisure. As products become more expensive and technical, advertising expenditure becomes a smaller portion of total sales expenditure and sales effort becomes concentrated on such things as salesmen and showrooms.

There are thus certain underlying factors which make it profitable to advertise in some situations and not in others. The most important of these is the trust consumers are prepared to place on information provided in advertisements when the commodity is inexpensive. The more expensive the commodity, the less consumers will rely on advertisement information and the more they will plan their purchases. This is not irrational from a maximum utility point of view. Obtaining information frequently costs money and always costs time. This disutility schedule of cost and related time will have a rapidly increasing slope as the number of choices and the number of comparisons expand, and it might therefore not be economical for consumers to spend time seeking small saving opportunities. Studies have in fact shown that an inverse correlation exists between price and the level of advertising.[11]

(*i*) *Allocation of resources to advertising.* Given the scarcity of resources within any firm, what criteria should be used by a firm to determine the size of its advertising budget? Economic theory guides us here. To maximise its profits, a firm should continue to increase its advertising budget until marginal revenue from advertising is equal to marginal cost. This relationship between MR and MC can be interpreted as being either:

(*i*) ($MR - MC$ of advertising) $= MC$ of producing product; or
(*ii*) $MR = MC$ of producing product $+ MC$ of advertising.

So long as the extra revenue being earned exceeds the extra cost, the firm will make a net gain by increasing its advertising expenditure. The moment MC exceeds MR the firm is adding to its costs a greater amount than is being added to its revenue and inroads will be made into profit previously earned (for a fuller explanation of marginal relationships and diagrammatic analysis *see* Chapter VII, **5, 6**). This marginal relationship is unfortunately a short-run concept, i.e. it is concerned with short-run profit-maximisation.

How can we measure MR of advertising expenditure? What time period do we set to measure the MR? These questions have no answer because of three facts:

(*i*) *Delayed response* of public to an advertising campaign. A campaign might have to be in operation for a number of weeks before the public are sufficiently motivated to go and buy the product.
(*ii*) *Lingering response* of an advertising campaign. The purpose of advertising is to establish the product in the minds of the consumers and to persuade them to try it.

People do not cease to buy a product simply because a campaign has ceased. Sales will be made to people motivated by a campaign which finished months ago.

(*iii*) The "*identification problem*" again. Sales might have improved between two dates, but how can we be certain that it was due to an increase in advertising expenditure? Did competitors raise their prices or lower their quality? These influences must be isolated in the statistics before any attempt can be made to measure *MR* and *MC*.

The use of the theoretical concepts of *MR* and *MC* is therefore exceptionally difficult in practice; their importance, however, and their contribution to management decision-making, is that they highlight the relevant (even if unmeasurable) quantities in advertising, as opposed to the irrelevant (but measurable) ones.

(*j*) *Allocation of resources in practice.* Research in the U.S.A. and the U.K. has revealed many methods used by firms for determining advertising expenditure. Five are most popularly used:[12]

(*i*) *Percentage of sales approach.* Determination of the advertising budget as a percentage of past or expected sales. This method cannot be supported by any logic of profit-maximisation, as past sales have no necessary connection with future conditions, and expected sales should be something that the firm intends to influence. There is therefore a confusion as to cause and effect and also—which is extremely important—the expected responsiveness of the public to advertising (promotional elasticity of demand) is ignored. The amount to spend should be determined by the response one expects to receive from the campaign, and not by some arbitrary percentage of past sales, since the relationship between consumer response and advertising has not necessarily anything to do with future response.

(*ii*) *The "all you can afford" approach.* Determination of the advertising budget as an arbitrary percentage share of profits or of liquid resources. Once again the responsiveness of the consumer to advertising expenditure receives secondary consideration, with the result that more money may be spent than necessary, or revenue is sacrificed by less being spent than will be justified by consumer responsiveness.

(*iii*) *Return on investment approach.* This method at least recognises that advertising has a long-term effect, and advertising expenditure is treated as an investment rather than as current expenditure. The practical problems here, however, are immense. To apply investment appraisal techniques an attempt must be made to calculate future cash flows that result from advertising: what proportion of current expenditure will build up goodwill, and by how much, and how much will be necessary to maintain old goodwill at the previous level must all therefore be calculated.

(*iv*) *Objective and task approach.* This approach involves defining objectives, outlining tasks and determining cost of accomplishing them.

Objectives must be set so that they are measurable, but the important problem is to measure the value of the objectives to determine whether they are worth the probable cost of being attained. After the costing process has been completed, objectives can once more be appraised, modified and reformulated in the light of the information produced.

(*v*) *Competitive parity approach.* A firm's advertising budget is based on the output of other members of the industry, e.g. on market shares. It is very difficult to find a rationale for this method although practitioners seem to think that by so setting advertising budgets competitive wars are avoided and market shares preserved. However, future market shares will be directly affected by the policy each firm pursues in the next period, making past market shares irrelevant. In addition, advertising is only one competitive weapon available to a firm, and while a competitor may have a relatively low advertising budget, its effort in other directions, i.e. price, quality, packaging, etc., may be intense. Finally, firms in an industry are unlikely to be pursuing identical objectives and therefore to base advertising on what is spent by another firm is completely irrational. That other firm might be determining its advertising appropriation on your budget.

Using the concept of marginal analysis, none of these methods with the exception of (*iii*) and (*iv*) (properly applied) have economic foundation. Perhaps it is the problem of obtaining sufficient information to apply marginal analysis that has led in practice to the development of these various methods. The identification problem plus the delayed and lingering response of advertising have not helped, with the fact that money value is not a particularly good way of measuring advertising effort and effectiveness because it excludes the important quality aspect. If money outlay represented success, the task of firms would be easier. Practice has shown, however, that this is not the case.

20. Price.

(a) *Influence of price.* Although it is difficult to measure and determine the shape of the demand curve in practice, it is generally agreed that the market demand curve is downward-sloping, indicating that people do respond to lower prices. But price, it must be remembered, is not necessarily the most important influence on consumer demand and to quote from Schumpeter, "as soon as quality competition and sales effort are admitted into the sacred precincts of theory, the price variable is ousted from its dominant position".[13] Some firms are very concerned that sales will fluctuate at any given price and that changes in the conditions underpinning the demand curve, and consequently shifting it, can swamp the most delicate price adjustments.

What empirical evidence exists that can help us apply the concepts of demand theory? It is suggested that because conditions change so quickly, what is required is better research techniques rather than a general hypothesis which cannot be directly applied to individual products. If better research techniques could be developed, definite guidelines could be established for pricing a particular product at a particular time.

(b) *Empirical research.* Research techniques have been developed (notably by P. Granger and A. Gabor in the U.K.[14]) that will help in the determination of consumer attitudes and response to prices. Much work has been carried out in the U.S.A. and the U.K. and in (i)–(iv) below some of the tentative results that have emerged are described.

(i) *Relationship between price and quality.* When faced with a situation in which their information is incomplete, consumers tend to relate price asked with quality. Consumers will therefore purchase more as price falls only up to a certain point. If price continues to fall, quality begins to be questioned and there is the likelihood that continued price reductions will see less being bought.

Figure 21 (a) shows the distribution of consumer response to various prices for a relatively large range of products. Although the curve in Fig. 21 (a) cannot be directly translated into a demand curve unless frequency of purchase by each consumer is known, it is possible that the backward-sloping demand curve in Fig. 21 (*b*) is more common than is thought.

(*ii*) *Price range*. From (*b*) (*i*) above it follows that there is no correct market price but a range of prices which are accepted in the market, and that the differences in price (which can be considerable in some cases) cannot be explained by differences in the quality of the product. The width of

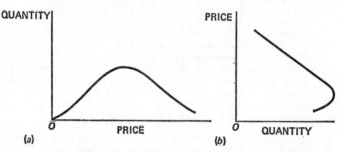

FIG. 21—*Relationship between price and quantity*. As price falls, quantity demanded increases in the normal way. After a point, however, consumers begin to suspect that further price falls can only be achieved by reduced quality of the product. Further price falls are therefore accompanied by reduced demand.

this range varies from product to product—the narrower the range, the less room a firm has to operate. If it wishes to charge a price outside these limits it must work hard to convince the consumer that this is justified. A firm can, however, through advertising and sales promotion, increase this range if it can so convince the consumer. There are two basic reasons why the acceptable range of prices varies from product to product.

(1) *Cost*. The more important the decision for the consumer (i.e. the greater the expenditure) the more information he will automatically seek and therefore superficial qualities will be exposed. This is one reason why marketing effort for consumer durables is channelled into showrooms, and demonstrations, with emphasis on after-sales service, etc. Manufacturers insist, however, that brand names still get prominence because they do widen the range of prices acceptable. *Which* reports on certain consumer durables such as washing machines show that price ranges can vary considerably.

(2) *Experience*. The more difficult it is for consumers to

judge quality through experience, the wider the range of acceptable prices. This explains the heavy concentration of advertising in medicinal and toiletry products where brand image predominates and the learning process through experience of quality is very questionable.

(*iii*) *Impact of price reductions.* It has been suggested that consumers tend to be more responsive to relatively large price cuts, possibly temporary, on a limited range of goods, compared with smaller more permanent cuts over a much larger range. However, further studies have indicated that straight price reductions might not necessarily be the most effective promotional weapon for retailers. Regular customers stock up, so sales fall after the promotion, and customers resent paying higher prices when it ends. Unilever, for example, said (in 1966) that indirect benefits (vouchers reimbursable on next purchase of product) have a larger impact than straightforward price reductions.

A Prices and Incomes Board Report (No. 80, 1968) showed that in the paint market, retailers who reacted to competition by making selective price reductions on some brands found consumer resistance to paying the list prices on other brands.

Granger and Gabor have conducted many experiments with consumers to determine how well they could recall prices last paid, the idea being that this would indicate their awareness of price and its importance in making their purchase. The results showed that price recall varied from product to product, some products registering particularly low recall levels regardless of the fact that they were highly-advertised. This type of result obviously provides important clues as to the marketing strategy to adopt.

(*iv*) *Consumers' attitude to specific prices charged.* A number of experiments by Granger and Gabor showed that before decimalisation in 1971, prices just below a round number, e.g. 5/11 or 4/11, had a definite influence on consumer response (this was not the case for all products). Response fell when prices were increased by one penny to 6/- or 5/-, and in fact tests showed that response increased when price was raised from 5/6 to 5/11, for example. There is no agreed solution to this response except that in certain industries this kind of price structure has come to be regarded by the consumers as being "normal", and as a result, some consumers were unable to regard, say, 4/7 as a price simply because they could not associate it with any specific article.

21. Conclusion. Uncertainty about measuring price effects and about consumer response means that firms prefer to increase the demand for their product by shifting the demand curve to the right rather than by manipulating price. There is also the problem of the reaction of rival firms. If your price reduction is matched by a rival, the end result could be a loss of revenue for both of you unless the total demand curve for the industry is very elastic. A price reduction is easily matched by a competitor, whereas an advertising campaign with an imaginative slogan is much more difficult to compete against. A firm that hits upon a slogan that can capture the imagination of consumers has a clear lead over all rivals because no amount of money spent on sales promotion can guarantee an effective campagin that will counteract it.

PROGRESS TEST 4

1. Is it possible for the short-run and long-run forecasts to conflict? (2)
2. What are the three stages through which a forecast should proceed? (4)
3. Inter-relationship of the variables make the solving of the "identification problem" in practice impossible. Discuss. (6–10)
4. What problems must be solved to ensure that the results obtained from test marketing a product are accurate? (10 (d))
5. Forecasting the demand for a new product poses special problems. How is it possible to overcome them? (11)
6. Why does traditional demand theory need to be supplemented by the process of "want creation" and inter-personal relations? (12–18)
7. Can advertising create demand? (19)
8. What psychological effect does price have in the mind of the consumer in relation to quality? (20 (b))

FURTHER READING

1. Bates, R. and Parkinson, J. R., *Business Economics*, Basil Blackwell, 1971.
2. Baumol, W. J., *Economic Theory and Operational Analysis*, Prentice-Hall, 1972, Chapter 3.
3. Dean, J., *Managerial Economics*, Prentice-Hall, 1961, Chapter 4, p. 172.
4. Duesenberry, J., *Income Saving and the Theory of Consumer Behavior*, Harvard University Press, 1949.
5. Morris, C., *The Economic Theory of Managerial Capitalism*, Macmillan, 1966, Chapter 4.
   Bourne, F. S., "Group Influences in Marketing and Public Relations", *Some Applications of Behavioral Research*, ed.

Leckert, R. and Hayes, S. P., UNESCO, New York, 1957, pp. 205–57.

Katz, S. and Lazartfield, *Personal Influence*, Free Press, New York, 1960.

6. Klapper, C., "What we know about the Effects of Mass Communications", part of "The Brink of Hope", *Public Opinion Quarterly*, 21, 1957.

7. Borden, N., *The Economics of Advertising*, Irwin, Chicago, 1942.

8. Economic Advisory Group, *The Economics of Advertising*, Advertising Association, 1957.

9. Camaron, W. S. and Wilson, T. A., "Advertising Market Structure and Performance", *Review of Economics and Statistics*, November 1957.

10. Backman, J., *Advertising and Competition*, University of London Press, 1967.

11. Doyle, P., "Advertising Expenditure and Consumer Demand", *Oxford Economic Papers*, November 1968.

12. Dean, J., *op. cit.*, Chapter 6.

13. Schumpeter, J., *Capitalism, Socialism and Democracy*, Harper Row, 1966.

14. Granger, P. and Gabor, A., *Nottingham Papers in Pricing*, Nottingham University.

CHAPTER V

COST ANALYSIS IN THEORY

INTRODUCTION

IN Chapters III and IV we studied demand analysis, and saw that its importance to the firm lay in its direct connection with the total revenue (TR) that the firm was capable of earning. We stressed that no decision could be made by taking only TR into consideration and that some attempt would have to be made to forecast the costs that a firm was likely to incur in achieving a specific output level. It is only by comparing the revenue and cost situation that a decision can be made. It is extremely important for the decision-taker to know how costs will behave over various output levels and also what costs to include in making a decision.

COST BEHAVIOUR IN THE SHORT-RUN

1. Trading and Profit and Loss Account. To produce anything a firm must employ various factors of production, and these factors will need to be rewarded for the role they play in the productive process. The Trading and Profit and Loss Account for a firm shows the costs which have been incurred by the firm over the previous year, although the discussion in **16–19** below highlights important costs that should be included in decision-making, but are excluded from the Trading and Profit and Loss Account.

In Fig. 22, sales revenue is derived by multiplying quantity sold by price, and profit is arrived at by deducting all the costs incurred by the firm during that financial year. The figures shown represent the total cost incurred by the firm for its previous year's operations, but for the purpose of cost analysis it is essential to distinguish between those costs that are fixed and those that are variable.

2. Fixed and variable cost. In economics we distinguish between fixed and variable cost, and although in practice it

XYZ COMPANY LTD.

*Trading and Profit and Loss Account for the year ended
31st March 1980*

	£		£
Stock 1st April 1979	5,000	Sales	75,000
Add: Purchases	40,000		
	45,000		
Less: Stock 31st March 1980	8,000		
Cost of goods sold	37,000		
Gross profit	38,000		
	75,000		75,000
Wages and Salaries	12,000	Gross Profit b/d	38,000
Rent and Rates	1,000	Income from quoted	
General Trade Expenses	3,000	investments	1,000
Debenture Interest	200	Income from unquoted	
Auditors' Remuneration	100	investments	500
Directors' Remuneration	3,000		
Provision for depreciation:			
Machinery 2,500			
Motor Vehicles 1,500	4,000		
Net profit c/d	16,200		
	39,500		39,500
Corporation tax based on		Balance b/d from	
profits of the year	8,424	previous year	2,500
Proposed ordinary		Net profit b/d	16,200
dividend 10%	6,000		
Transfer to general reserves	2,000		
Balance carried forward	2,276		
	18,700		18,700

Fig. 22—*An example of a Trading and Profit and Loss Account.*

is no easy task to separate costs into fixed and variable
categories, if correct decisions are to be taken it is crucial that
the effort is made. By fixed cost is meant those costs which are
incurred regardless of the level of output. As long as the firm
remains in business these costs will have to be met. In Fig. 22
examples of fixed cost are rent and rates, debenture interest
and provision for depreciation. Although the output may be
nil and no raw materials or power are used, the rent and rates
must be paid and the debenture holders will demand their
interest. Fixed equipment can also become obsolete and lose
value through lack of use.

By variable cost is meant cost that varies directly with

output, although not necessarily in the same proportion. In Fig. 22 the main item of variable cost would be the stock that was used during the financial period.

The remaining items of expenditure in Fig. 22 cannot be divided on inspection into the fixed and variable categories. Wages and salaries, for example, contain elements of both—the Managing Director's salary and the salaries of the senior managers would tend to be fixed while the salaries of general production employees variable. General trade expenses include heating and lighting, and this obviously has its fixed and variable components.

More information would therefore be required to complete the separation of costs.

3. Short-run and long-run. Which costs are fixed and which are variable depends largely on the period of time being considered. If it is sufficiently long, all costs will be variable, but if it is extremely short almost all costs will be fixed.

By the short-run is meant that period of time during which capacity cannot be adjusted to changing market conditions. This includes, of course, adjustments in response to a contracting as much as to an expanding market.

The long-run is that period of time during which adjustment can be made to meet changing market conditions. No actual period of time can be specified, the length as long or short being influenced by the nature of the industry and the type of adjustment in question. The more technical and sophisticated the factor of production, the longer the length of the short period, e.g. compare the training period of a machine operator with that of a brain surgeon, or the production of cars and lorries with that of aircraft and oil tankers. In most cases contraction takes longer than expansion since if selling one's factors of production is not possible, the only alternative is to let obsolescence and natural wastage reduce capacity.

Most firms are in a constant state of long-run adaptation, the employment of some factors being expanded while others are being contracted, so it is extremely unlikely to find a firm whose total position at any one time can be said to be static. Regardless of this, however, the definition and the concepts of the long- and short-run are extremely important because whether a cost is to be classified as fixed or variable depends entirely on the time period in which the decision is being taken.

4. Fixed cost. When a person is deciding to start in business and has committed himself to no expenditure, his decision and all the costs that will be included in that decision are said to be variable. He has the chance at that point of incurring or not incurring them. For a person already in business, some of his total cost must be fixed, in the sense that it must be incurred regardless of the level of output so long as he decides to remain in business.

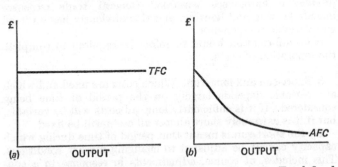

FIG. 23—*Relationship between fixed cost and output.* Total fixed cost (TFC) remains constant over achievable output levels (a). Average fixed cost (AFC) per unit continually falls (b).

In Fig. 23 (a), total fixed cost (TFC) is plotted on a graph against output and it can be seen that cost is constant over the relevant range of output (capacity of the firm). Figure 23 (b) plots the same information on an average fixed cost (AFC) per unit basis, AFC per unit continuously falling as output expands since TFC is divided by a larger number of units.

5. Variable cost. In 2 above it was stated that although variable cost varies with output it *does not necessarily vary in the same proportion* because of the laws of increasing and diminishing returns.

These laws operate because of the fixity of supply of some factors and their utilisation with different combinations of variable factors. Consider the following illustration.

EXAMPLE 6: A firm purchases a machine (fixed factor) that is designed to be operated most efficiently by seven men (variable factors). If initially the firm has a shortage of labour so that only two men can be spared for this machine, some output will be achieved but it will be well below the optimum—the two men have to divide their time between the seven jobs. As further men are allocated to the machine, output not only increases but increases by a greater proportion than the variable factors being employed because each man can now concentrate more time on a single task, and so time delays and material spoilage are reduced (increasing returns). As further men are allocated to the machine, marginal productivity continues to increase until there are seven men fully occupied and specialising on the different operations. Up to this point total variable cost (TVC) has been increasing but output has been increasing at a faster rate. To add further men to the machine now would lead to output being marginally increased but to variable cost (wages) increasing at a faster rate than output (diminishing returns). In Table IX, average output per head increases up to the employment of the seventh man and thereafter it declines, although total output is slowly increasing.

TABLE IX: INCREASING AND DIMINISHING RETURNS

Number of men	Total output (units)	Average output per man
1	2	2
2	5	2·5
3	9	3
4	20	5
5	35	7
6	48	8
7	70	10
8	72	9
9	74	8·2
10	75	7·5

If we calculated the average cost per unit, those costs would vary over the range of output permitted by total capacity as in Figs. 24 (a) and (b), Fig. 24 (a) showing how TVC behaves and Fig. 24 (b) showing how AVC behaves.

Increasing returns are experienced up to output OQ_1, which represents the optimum combination of factors of production, i.e. the lowest AVC per unit. For output levels exceeding OQ_1 diminishing returns set in and AVC per unit increases.

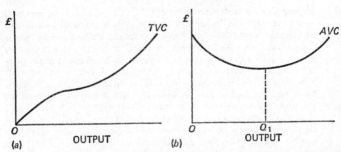

FIG. 24—*Variable cost.* Due to the fixity of factors of supply, total variable cost (*TVC*), although increasing as output increases, increases at a different rate from output (*a*). Average variable cost (*AVC*) per unit at first falls to an optimum, OQ_1, and then increases as diminishing returns set in (*b*).

6. The short-run cost schedule. The total cost incurred by a firm is made up of total fixed and total variable cost, so if we add together the positions in Figs. 23 (*b*) and 24 (*b*) we obtain Fig. 25. Average total cost is obtained by adding *AFC* and

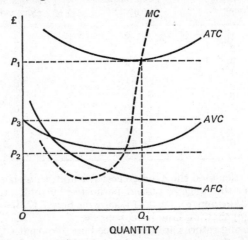

FIG. 25—*The short-run cost schedule. ATC* is obtained by adding together *AVC* and *AFC*. Its shape reflects the increasing and diminishing returns of *AVC*.

AVC together. The optimum point on the *ATC* curve is to the right of the optimum point on the *AVC* curve because initially the increasing *AVC* is offset by the continually falling *AFC* curve. Eventually, however, the increase in *AVC* is large enough to offset the fall in *AFC* and *ATC* starts to increase. Figure 25 shows marginal cost (*MC*), the cost incurred in producing one more unit of output, and as long as increasing and diminishing returns exist *MC* will be different from *AVC*. Table X shows the figures from which Fig. 25 was constructed. As long as a firm varies its output with capacity, the quality of factors of production remaining constant, it will be subject to increasing and diminishing returns. In practice, there is likely to be an optimum area where constant returns are obtained, rather than just the one particular point represented by Q_1.

In that case, the *AVC* and *ATC* curves would have a flat bottom over a certain range of output.

TABLE X: CALCULATING MARGINAL COST

Units of variable factors	Total output	Marginal product	Total fixed cost	Total variable cost	Total cost	AFC	AVC	ATC	Unit MC
1	1	1	10	5	15	10·00	5·00	15	15
2	3	2	10	10	20	3·33	3·33	6·66	2·50
3	6	3	10	15	25	1·67	2·50	4·17	1·67
4	10	4	10	20	30	1·00	2·00	3·00	1·25
5	14	4	10	25	35	0·71	1·79	2·50	1·25
6	17	3	10	30	40	0·59	1·76	2·35	1·67
7	19	2	10	35	45	0·52	1·84	2·36	
8	21	2	10	40	50	0·48	1·90	2·38	
9	22	1	10	45	55	0·45	2·05	2·50	
10	21	−1	10	50	60	0·48	2·38	2·86	

The marginal cost incurred in increasing output from 6 to 10 units is the difference in *TC* (30 − 25 = 5) divided by increase in output, 4, which gives us a unit *MC* of 1·25. The student is left to complete the last column in Table X. Note that when output is increased from 17 to 19 units *AVC* increases by 0·08 and *AFC* declines by 0·07, and thus *ATC* increases by 0·01.

The *MC* curve cuts the *AVC* and *ATC* curves at their lowest point. This must be the case as the *MC* determines the shape of the average curve.

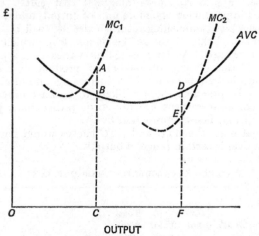

Fig. 26—*Marginal cost.* The relationship between *AVC* and *MC* as shown in this diagram is mathematically inconsistent. *MC* must cut the *AVC* at its lowest point.

In Fig. 26 as long as *MC₁* is below *AVC*, the *AVC* curve continues to fall. As *MC₁* cuts the *AVC* and continues to rise above it, the *AVC* continues to fall which is impossible because you cannot add a higher quantity than the average (*CB*) to the average and expect the average to continue to fall.

Similarly with *MC₂* it is not logical that a lower quantity than the average (*EF*) can be added to *DF* and the average continue to increase. Therefore *MC* must cut *AVC* at the lowest point of the *AVC* curve.

In Fig. 25 a firm would have to cover *ATC* in the long-run to stay in business, i.e. price in the long-run would have to exceed P_1. In the short-run, however, it would be wise to maintain output even if price fell below OP_1, as long as it exceeded OP_2. If price was, for example, OP_3, it would not cover all its costs, but because some of the costs are fixed and will have to be incurred regardless of the level of output, at price OP_3 a net contribution is being made towards these fixed costs because price exceeds AVC (contribution = selling price $(SP) - VC$). The firm pursuing such a policy is minimising its loss. If it ceased production altogether then its loss would be TFC; however, by maintaining production the maximum loss is TFC less net contribution. In the long-run, of course, if price did not increase so that ATC was covered, then the firm would have to reduce its scale of operations, i.e. reduce its fixed cost or go out of business.

7. Break-even point. By putting Figs. 23 (*a*) and 24 (*a*) together, we obtain Fig. 27 which is a break-even chart showing the relationship between revenue, cost and profit at various output levels.

Income and cost are measured on the vertical axis and output, which can be expressed in terms of units, money or percentage capacity, is on the horizontal axis. There are two break-even points X and Y in Fig. 27, because of the economist's

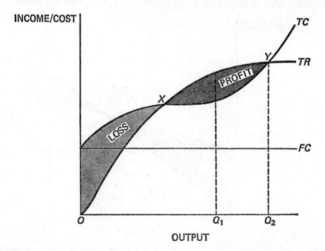

FIG. 27—*Break-even point (economist's assumption).* The firm should produce at output OQ_1 to maximise profits. If output exceeds OQ_1 profits will fall through a combination of diminishing returns and diminishing marginal revenue.

assumption about how revenue and cost will vary over increasing volumes of output. The *TR* curve flattens and could eventually fall because greater quantities can only be sold by lowering price, while the *TC* curve continues to increase since extra output does not have a zero cost. The purpose of break-even analysis should be to indicate that level of output where profits earned are at a maximum, i.e. where the distance between *TC* and *TR* is greatest, Q_1 in Fig. 27.

8. The accountant's assumption about cost behaviour. The accountant differs from the economist in his assumption about how variable cost will behave over different levels of output. While the economist assumes that *VC* varies with output but not in the same proportion, the accountant assumes that *VC* varies in direct proportion to output. The accountant's break-even analysis, therefore, is constructed assuming linear cost and revenue functions, as in Fig. 28.

The problem with this assumption of linearity is that on inspection it seems that the higher the output the higher the profits, and if capacity is represented by output Q_2 then the

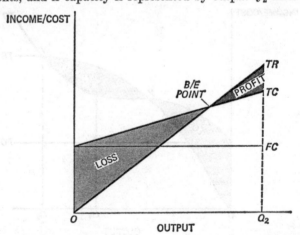

FIG. 28—*Break-even point (accountant's assumption)*. The accountant's assumption of linearity of cost and revenue functions lead one to the misleading conclusion that profit will continue to increase as output increases.

firm will be encouraged to aim for that capacity. Figure 27, which shows the same capacity, Q_2, recognises that the cost and revenue functions are not linear and advises an output level Q_1 at which the difference between TR and TC is at its maximum (i.e. $MR = MC$).

Empirical cost analysis (which we shall study in Chapter VI) has indicated that in fact the true picture might be somewhere in between the views of the economist and the accountant, and as long as cost, revenue and profit analysis is not required at the extreme ends of capacity, the linear assumption might be able to provide reasonable results. The actual shape of the AVC curve appears to be as in Fig. 29, showing a range of constant VC over a significant range of output, OQ_a–OQ_b (for a fuller treatment of break-even analysis, *see* Harper, W. M., *Cost Accountancy*, in the M. & E. Handbook series).

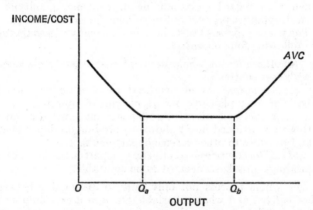

FIG. 29—*Cost behaviour in practice.* In practice it has been found that AVC is constant and at a minimum over a range of output OQ_a to OQ_b.

9. The problem of common cost. So far, we have been looking at cost analysis using examples of firms that produce only one product. As long as that assumption is maintained it is simple to determine the ATC per unit. Once we abandon this assumption, however, and consider the more realistic case of firms which produce more than one product the determination of ATC per unit becomes impossible. It is possible to allocate to any one product certain costs which can be directly associated with it, e.g. raw materials, power, labour, etc., but within any organisation that produces more than one product there will be a residual of cost that cannot be effectively allocated in any logical manner, e.g. salary of Managing Director, canteen and first aid staffs, security forces, depreciation of general buildings and general rates and rent. This is the common cost problem and common costs relate to expenses which cannot be traced directly to any one product.

Accounting practice has developed many ways of allocating and apportioning these common costs—on the basis of machine hours utilised, floor area utilised, direct labour cost or sales value, etc.—yet each method is likely to provide a different answer to what the unit cost of the product is. Therefore, depending upon the method used, different decisions will be taken with regard to expanding or contracting output or even dropping a product entirely from the existing range.

The whole process of cost allotment normally passes through the following four phases:

(a) *Allocation* of whole items of cost directly associated with cost centres.

(b) *Apportionment* of overhead to departments on the basis of some plausible underlying rule of causation.

(c) *Reallotment* of service department costs (including those apportioned in (b) above) to production departments and possibly to other service departments.

(d) *Absorption* from production departments to jobs or products on a basis deemed to be equitable.

This whole process not only fails to distinguish between what is fixed and what is variable but also uses a number of arbitrary allotment procedures to share out the common cost. These common costs are important, and it is vital to the continued operation of the firm in the long-run that all costs should be covered. Yet for the purpose of making decisions in a time period when some of the costs incurred are sunk, misleading results can emerge from attempting to allot every expense on a unit basis.

EXAMPLE 7: A firm produces four products—A, B, C and D. Variable cost is allocated directly to each product and the common cost (fixed cost and variable cost that cannot be

directly allocated) is apportioned on the basis of either sales
revenue or units produced. The important points to note
here are that the *TR* and *TC* facing the firm are the same
regardless of the method of apportionment chosen and the
total profit in each case is £5,800. Every product makes a
positive contribution to the overheads, yet by attempting to
apportion the common cost by *TR*, the value of product *C* is
brought into question and the firm will consider dropping it.
Under the apportionment method of units produced, both
products *C* and *D* appear to be making an overall loss. By
dropping these products the firm would still have the total
common cost to bear, £10,000, yet it would have lost the
contribution being made by *C* and *D* of £5,000 (£2,000 +
3,000) (*see* Tables XI and XII).

TABLE XI: CONTRIBUTION TO OVERHEADS

Product	A	B	C	D	
Price	100	80	50	20	
Units produced	120	150	200	300	
TR	12,000	12,000	10,000	6,000	40,000
VC per unit	60	40	40	10	
TVC	7,200	6,000	8,000	3,000	24,200
Contribution	4,800	6,000	2,000	3,000	15,800

TABLE XII: COMMON COST APPORTIONMENT
(*Total figures rounded to nearest ten*)

Product	A	B	C	D	
Common costs		£10,000			
Apportionment on basis of sales revenue	3,000	3,000	2,500	1,500	
Profit	1,800	3,000	(500)	1,500	5,800
Apportionment on basis of units produced	1,558	1,948	2,597	3,896	
Profit	3,242	4,052	(597)	(896)	5,800

10. Determinants of initial scale. Clearly the scale which the firm chooses as being appropriate will depend on the level of output which it expects to supply. However, many firms choose a scale which is greater than the expected average level of output. There are a number of reasons why firms adopt such a policy, mainly arising from the difficulty of forecasting the precise volume and pattern of demand.

(*a*) The demand from the firm's regular customers may be higher, or their orders more bunched, than expected. If the firm was unable to meet these orders some customers might transfer their trade on a permanent basis to rival suppliers.

(*b*) The converse of (*a*) is where a firm hopes to gain customers by providing quick service when they have failed to gain that service from their regular supplier.

(*c*) It is not normally possible to choose a scale to match precisely current requirements because of the indivisibility of the factors of production. Thus the choice is between a scale smaller or larger than currently needed, and if the firm has growth ambitions it will of course choose a larger scale.

In making decisions concerning what quantities of the various inputs will be required, the greatest attention will usually be given to the amount of plant and equipment to be installed. Although some flexibility in the utilisation of plant may exist by way of overtime or extra shift working, the firm may not be able to rely on this, so that the capacity of the plant and equipment will become the factor which limits the level of output. This may be a very serious limitation, since there is often a considerable time lag between a decision to expand the amount of plant and equipment and the ability to obtain and install it. This lag may be partly due to the inability of the suppliers to meet orders immediately (a delay of several months) and partly to the need to create space for the new equipment. This delay could be very considerable as it may involve purchasing land and building a factory.

COST BEHAVIOUR IN THE LONG-RUN

11. The decision to expand. As the demand for the firm's product grows beyond the optimum output level of the plant, it will find itself capable of meeting that demand only by producing in that section of the ATC curve where diminishing returns exist, and therefore AC per unit is increasing. Extra shifts will be created, workers will be paid bonuses and over-time pay, wear and tear of machinery will increase and bottle-necks and delays become more frequent. The firm will there-fore have to consider expansion. This decision is extremely important because it results in increasing the level of fixed cost. In Fig. 30, when the firm is operating with ATC_1 the

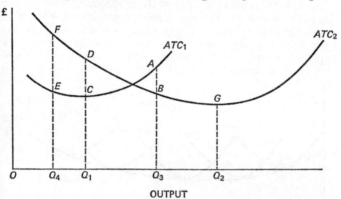

OUTPUT

FIG. 30—*The decision to expand.* Once the decision to expand has been taken, production at old output levels OQ_1 and OQ_4 will result in higher AC per unit, Q_4F and Q_1D as opposed to Q_4E and Q_1C.

optimum output level is at OQ_1, with AC per unit Q_1C. To meet an increase in demand and produce output OQ_3, AC per unit increases to Q_3A because in increasing output from OQ_1 to OQ_3 diminishing returns have set in.

By increasing its scale of operation so that it now operates from ATC_2, it can produce output OQ_3 for AC per unit of Q_3B and it can increase output to OQ_2 and continue to lower its AC per unit. Beyond OQ_2 diminishing returns once again set in. The firm must be certain that the increase in demand is permanent, otherwise it will find itself with excess capacity and a higher level of AC per unit than previously. If in Fig. 30 the level of demand fell so that only OQ_1 was required AC per unit with the new capacity would be Q_1D and if demand fell further so that output was limited to OQ_4, AC per unit would increase to Q_4F.

The firm must therefore be certain that the expansion in demand is permanent before it commits itself to a higher level of fixed cost. The incentives to expand, however, are great because the new optimum AC per unit is lower than the previous optimum, Q_2G as opposed to Q_1C. Why should AC per unit decline as scale increases?

12. The economies of large-scale production. The answer lies in large-scale production. These economies are a function of the size of the plant, and are economies which can be gained by a firm entirely through the size of its operation; they explain how unit cost tends to decrease as output and scale of operation increase. Figure 31 shows the long-run average

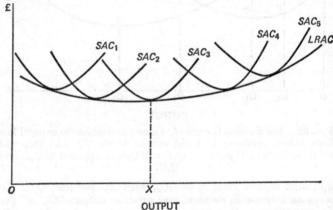

OUTPUT

Fig. 31—*Economies of large-scale production.* In the long-run cost schedule, AC per unit falls up to output OX, due to economies of large-scale production. Any increase in scale beyond plant size SAC_3 results in increasing AC per unit because of the existence of diseconomies of large-scale production.

cost curve ($LRAC$) that exists in a hypothetical industry at one particular time. The industry consists of five firms, each of a different size. It can be seen that AC per unit declines as scale increases up to the size of Firm 3 (SAC_3), yet AC starts to increase once scale exceeds Firm 3. The increase in AC per unit beyond output OX is due to diseconomies of large-scale production, which will be discussed in **15** below.

It is important to realise that *LRAC* does not show what would happen to a firm's *AC* per unit as it increases its scale over time. The *LRAC* curve shows the extent of economies of scale in a given industry at a particular point with a given state of technical knowledge. The curve should really be termed a scale curve rather than a *LRAC* curve because the latter term implies that it shows what would happen to the firm if it grew through time. It certainly provides an incentive for firms to increase their size of operations, but with the continuous advancement of technical knowledge the *AC* per unit over the whole possible range of outputs would be changing.

Although it is assumed that the state of technological knowledge is given, this does not mean that all firms regardless of size use the same technology. They all, regardless of size, have available the current pool of technological knowledge. Yet some of the techniques can only be utilised economically when output is high, with the result that smaller firms, although aware of these technological advantages, cannot incorporate them in their production process. Large firms also may be committed for a number of years to an out-dated technology because of the costs of plant replacement.

Economies of scale are often classified as internal economies and external economies.

13. Internal economies. These economies arise through the growth of a firm and are enjoyed only by that firm, i.e. the economies are internal. Sources of internal economies are normally:

(*a*) *Economies of increased dimensions.* For many types of capital equipment, initial and operating costs increase less rapidly than capacity. An outstanding modern example of this is the super oil tanker. The cost of building a 200,000 ton tanker is not double that of two 100,000 ton tankers; you do not need twice the power to power it or double the crew to run it. Providing no special technical problems have to be overcome because of increase in size, this source of economy is quite common.

(*b*) *Economies of specialisation.* The larger the output of the firm, the more feasible it becomes to organise production on a flow basis and automate each process. Specialised machinery can be introduced and the labour force can concentrate on various tasks, thus increasing efficiency. Increased output will also enable the firm to employ specialist managers. Greater output therefore facilitates specialisation which would not be economical at lower levels of production.

(c) *Economies of marketing*. A larger output means that raw materials will be purchased in larger quantities with the possibility of quantity discounts and favourable treatment from suppliers. The cost of administration of sales does not rise in the same proportion as their total value, and the sales force can be employed more economically. It has already been pointed out in Chapter IV that a "threshold effect" exists with advertising expenditure, i.e. a certain minimum has to be spent to achieve any impact; in addition, the structure of advertising rates in the press and on independent television ensures that the cost per column inch or per second decreases as quantity increases.

(d) *Economies of finance*. The very size of a firm and the value of its assets will enable it to obtain long-term finance at more favourable rates than smaller firms (*see* Chapter II on the Bolton Committee report). In addition, the actual administration cost of raising long-term finance (per unit of money raised) falls, the larger the size of the issue, as Issuing House fees and prospectus costs are spread.

(e) *The "learning effect"*. The longer the production run, the more research and development costs will be spread; knowledge gained through producing the product can lead to slight modifications in the production process that lead to a significant lowering of the *AC* of production.

14. External economies. These are economies which arise through the growth of an industry, and are enjoyed by all firms in that industry, regardless of their size.

(a) *Ancillary trades*. The growth of an industry in an area such as the textile industry in Lancashire or the pottery industry in Staffordshire, draws to it ancillary trades which exist to serve the needs of the main industry. Because of their willingness to specialise in various functions or processes they provide an invaluable service. The large number of relatively small firms in the Midlands which specialise in providing certain components to the main motor manufacturers is a prime example here. If the output of the main industry becomes large enough it will become profitable for firms to exist to handle only their waste products, paying the main industry for these products that previously would have had no value. This therefore helps to reduce AC per unit.

(b) *Pool of skilled labour.* The growth of an industry in an area leads to a pool of skilled labour gradually being created which acts as an attraction to firms entering the industry for the first time. The local labour develops a high degree of skill that would be difficult to find and expensive to train elsewhere. The continued existence of the furniture industry around High Wycombe and the pottery industry in and around Stoke-on-Trent are largely explained in this way.

(c) *Educational, professional and commercial services.* These also gradually become geared to the needs of that industry. The colleges of further education in the area will organise training courses for the industry. Bankers and accountants become familiar with the business problems of the industry and this knowledge improves the services they offer.

All these economies cause the $LRAC$ curve to fall from the left to the right, up to output OX in Fig. 31.

15. Diseconomies of large-scale production. These arise through the decline in the efficiency in use of production factors as scale increases.

(a) *Management efficiency.* As the size of a firm increases the strain placed on management will also increase. Decisions take longer, communications become more difficult and problems of co-ordination tend to increase at a faster rate than growth in actual size. A decline in morale is also possible as managers of all levels see themselves as small cogs in a big machine with very little control over current events.

(b) *Labour relations.* There is evidence that labour relations deteriorate as the size of firm increases. Employees feel that industrial relations are becoming more impersonal as they find themselves (through the management hierarchy) further from the actual decision-takers. The length of production runs and the repetitive nature of the work lead to boredom and dissatisfaction, with a resultant decline in productivity.

(c) *Marketing costs.* If a firm grows at one location its distribution costs will tend to increase rapidly as it attempts to deliver to sections of its market many miles away. The advertising and sales promotion expenditure necessary to boost its sales to a higher proportion of the total market will eventually become prohibitive, e.g. the cost of increasing sales from 20 to 30 per cent of the total market is likely to be much lower than the cost of increasing sales from 70 to 80 per cent of the total market.

(d) *Technical problems.* To increase capacity beyond a certain point, special technical problems will emerge which will result in production costs increasing, e.g. once storage tanks exceed a certain size the walls have to be strengthened, and if the size of machinery within a factory is increased a special building might be required or the existing building modified by strengthening the floors and ceilings to withstand the greater vibrations.

To the right of output *OX* in Fig. 31, the diseconomies of large-scale production cause *AC* per unit to increase. The economies of scale listed in **13–14** do not cease to operate to the right of output *OX*. What has happened is that the diseconomies of scale have begun to outweigh the economies.

COSTS FOR DECISION-MAKING

16. Incremental cost. For decision-making, the costs to be taken into account should only be those costs that are going to be incurred as a direct result of taking that decision. If a particular cost is unchanged by a given decision, the incremental cost for the action undertaken is zero. Although this description of incremental cost may seem straightforward, its application in practice involves great care and the following factors must be taken into consideration:

(a) *Opportunity cost.* Opportunity cost is the cost of using an asset with the most profitable alternative foregone, because the asset is employed in its present use rather than for something else. This cost does not appear in the trading

and profit and loss account and therefore the figures there
may well understate, and in some cases overstate, the actual
costs incurred by a firm.

EXAMPLE 8: A business should charge itself for the use of its
own money. If it had not been utilised in the business, at
the very least it could be earning interest in a bank account.

EXAMPLE 9: A firm has a highly specialised machine that has
no alternative use but a book value of £5,000. The opportunity cost of using that machine is nil, because it has no
alternative use.

(b) *Long-run consequences.* Unless the long-run implications of a decision are considered, there is a danger that the
calculated incremental cost will be too low.

EXAMPLE 10: A firm accepts an order in a period of depressed
business at a price which exceeds the short-run incremental
cost but is not high enough to cover its total cost. Business
soon recovers and customers who have been paying higher
prices return. Very soon the firm finds itself in a situation
where it is working at full capacity and unless it acquires
extra capacity (increases its commitment of fixed cost) it
will have to turn away profitable business. The firm now
realises that it has not taken into account the long-run
effects of accepting the contract in the depressed period. If
the firm is not prepared to invest and increase its capacity,
the long-run opportunity cost in accepting the original
order would be the extra profit which will have to remain
unearned due to the lack of capacity to meet the more
profitable orders.

(c) *Factor prices.* This point is important because firms
do not buy factors of production and use them immediately.
If they did, the cost would be the price paid for the factor.
However, when items are purchased and stored and, even
more complicated, when a fixed asset is used over a period
of years, what then is the cost of using such assets? Historical
costs may in these cases be unimportant and if used misleading; the liquidity crisis faced by British industry in
1974 was aggravated by the use of accounting conventions
that give emphasis to historical costs.

EXAMPLE 11: A furniture factory purchases lengths of timber
at 30p per foot and has stocks to the value of £10,000. The
price of timber increases to 60p per foot and the firm has to

make a quotation for a contract. What cost should it use?
The answer is the current cost per foot (60p), because it
would cost the firm £20,000 to replace its stocks. Addition-
ally it could sell its stocks on the open market for 60p per
foot (opportunity cost).

To apply the concept of incremental cost successfully in
practice, it must be possible to predict how the firm's cost will
behave with variations in activity, and to classify the costs faced
by the firm into fixed and variable categories.

In 1–15 above, considerable time was spent examining how
a firm's costs will behave in the short- and long-run; now we
must concentrate on the problems of classifying costs into the
categories of fixed and variable.

17. Identifying fixed and variable costs.

(a) The *dividing line* between what is a fixed and what is a
variable cost is not the same for all decisions. Let us take,
for example, direct labour cost. It makes a difference
whether a decision to accept a particular order requires the
addition of overtime (variable cost) or can be managed with
the use of available idle time (fixed cost). It is possible in
practice for direct labour to be a fixed or variable cost
depending upon whether output is expanding or contracting.
In Fig. 32, as output falls from OX to OT, management is
reluctant to lay off workers although the direct labour is
employed in quantities that are only justified by output
OX. If output continues to fall, however, say to OS, labour
will be released. A *ratchet effect* therefore exists, with a
factor being treated as both a fixed and a variable cost. The
decision-maker must select the classification suited to his
purpose.

(b) It is wrong to assume that an expense must be *either
fixed or variable*; it can be semi-fixed or semi-variable.
Depreciation, for example, is composed of two parts—wear
and tear (variable) and obsolescence (fixed period cost).
Other examples of semi-fixed and semi-variable costs are
electricity, gas and telephone charges, which contain a fixed
charge and a charge based on consumption.

In practice, various methods exist to determine the fixed
and variable components of a certain expense. These
methods vary from using an accounting classification where
everything is either fixed or variable, to engineering esti-

mates and to the use of statistical methods. There is no one approach which is superior to others; it is a question of deciding which is the most suitable for the costs under consideration. The biggest sin is to become too inflexible, so that an item will receive a once and for all classification into either fixed or variable.

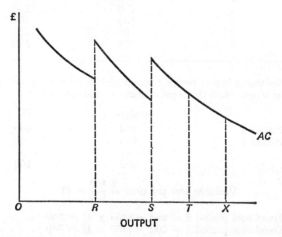

OUTPUT

FIG. 32—*Direct labour as a fixed and variable cost.* As output contracts from OX to OT, direct labour is treated as a fixed cost and AC per unit increases. As output contracts further, however, from OT to OS, labour is treated as a variable cost (the firm releases labour from its employment), and AC falls.

To illustrate the use of one of these methods let us see how fixed and variable cost can be determined by the use of one of the more simple statistical methods that merely compares a period of high with a period of low activity.

EXAMPLE 12: Owain and Justin own a small factory producing kitchen tables. Table XIII compares the cost of maintenance of the machinery in their factory with the output produced over the last six periods.

To separate the fixed and variable components of the total cost we need to compare the highest and lowest levels of activity and assume that the cost difference is purely variable and incurred directly through increased production. Applying

TABLE XIII: MAINTENANCE COST AND OUTPUT

Period	Cost of maintenance (total cost (£))	Output (units)
1	620	270
2	600	250
3	615	260
4	700	350
5	680	320
6	650	300

the variable cost per unit to our high and low outputs enables us to establish the fixed element of the total cost:

	Output	TC
Period 2	250	600
Period 4	350	700
	100	100

$$\text{Variable cost per unit} = \frac{100}{100} = \text{£}1$$

Fixed cost period 2 = 600 − (250 × 1) = 350
Fixed cost period 4 = 700 − (350 × 1) = 350

More sophisticated statistical techniques can be employed, e.g. regression and multiple regression analysis, but the results must be interpreted with caution. There are numerous factors in addition to volume which cause costs to vary. There is also the tendency in practice for the accountant to use unadjusted historical data and assume that all other factors are constant during the period to which this data refers.

(c) Factors which are said to be a fixed cost tend to be fixed to various degrees, and it is important therefore to distinguish between different kinds:

(i) Costs which are fixed as long as operations continue, but which are escapable if operations are shut down, e.g. salaries of supervisory staff.

(ii) Costs which run on even if production is halted but which are escapable if the company is liquidated, e.g. security and heating to prevent damage to machinery and equipment.

(*iii*) Costs which are at the discretion of the management. Examples are advertising, research and development expenditure and consultants' fees. These expenses go under the names of "programmed fixed costs" or "discretionary expenses".

18. Additional problems. In addition to the understanding, classification and analysis of a firm's costs, the accuracy with which future costs can be estimated will depend upon a number of factors.

(*a*) If the product in question has been supplied by the firm for some time, then costs which have been incurred in the past will provide an invaluable guide. On the other hand, if the product is new to the firm *cost estimation* will be far more difficult. If the product is new to the firm but not new to the industry, some guidelines will exist. For a new product concept, there will be no guidelines. Figures will be available from the development project and pilot studies, but practice has shown only too often that the costs incurred in proceeding to full production can be vastly different from those gained by extrapolation of pilot study results. If the product is one that involves new technology the uncertainty will increase.

(*b*) *Uncertainty* may exist regardless of the fact that the product is not new, if the production method is changed utilising a new set of factors of production.

(*c*) Average cost per unit is dependent upon the level of production and the firm has to rely on demand forecasts to *calculate its AC per unit*. We saw in Chapters III and IV, however, how difficult and uncertain demand forecasting can be.

19. Conclusion. To determine the costs for decision-making, it is more important to develop a logic and a system of thinking than a number of mechanical procedures. It was demonstrated in **17** above that the distinction between fixed and variable costs is far from being easy and that the decision being considered at the time will determine how costs are to be regarded. It is essential to consider the implications of making a decision, and the concept of opportunity cost (although never easy to apply) makes one think of the alternatives foregone and the true cost of making a decision. In a firm that produces more than one product, never attempt to allocate the common cost, because even if a technique were devised that would guarantee correct allocation, incorrect costs would be used in making a decision. Only the costs that are to be affected by a decision need to be taken into account.

PROGRESS TEST 5

1. What items of cost are normally regarded in practice as being fixed? (2)

2. Why is it important to distinguish between the short- and the long-run? (3)

3. How does cost vary with output during the short-run? (4–8)

4. "It is extremely dangerous to make decisions by using full absorption costing." Discuss. (9)

5. Why should economies of large-scale production exist? (11–15)

6. "The concept of opportunity cost is central to the logic of good decision-making." Discuss. (16)

7. What are semi-fixed and semi-variable costs? (17)

8. Classify the following items into categories of fixed cost, variable cost, semi-fixed and semi-variable cost:

    (*a*) Salaries
    (*b*) Direct wages
    (*c*) Heating of factory
    (*d*) Power for factory
    (*e*) Salesmen's commission
    (*f*) Telephone bill
    (*g*) Spoilage of materials
    (*h*) Depreciation of machinery
    (*i*) Wages of canteen staff
    (*j*) Electricity bill.   (2, 17)

FURTHER READING

1. Harper, W. M., *Cost Accountancy*, Macdonald and Evans, 1974.

2. Sizer, J., *An Insight into Management Accountancy*, Pelican (Penguin Books), 1972.

3. Hart, H., *Overhead Costs: Analysis and Control*, Heinemann, 1973.

4. Boer, G. B., *Direct Cost and Contribution Accounting*, J. Wiley, 1974.

5. Solomans, D., *Studies in Cost Analysis*, Sweet and Maxwell, 1970.

CHAPTER VI

COST ANALYSIS IN PRACTICE

INTRODUCTION

IN the last Chapter, the short- and long-run average cost curves were described as being U-shaped over different levels and scales of output. How do we attempt to determine their shape in practice?

A knowledge of how costs are going to behave over different levels of output is extremely important, because this will help the firm determine price and output policy. A knowledge of how costs are going to behave at different scales is also important as this will help a firm determine its future capacity requirements and thus its capital expenditure.

In this Chapter we need to answer three major questions:

(*i*) How does one determine the short-run average cost curve?

(*ii*) How does one determine the long-run average cost curve?

(*iii*) What has been the result of empirical research into their general shape?

ESTIMATION OF THE SHORT-RUN AVERAGE COST CURVE

1. Statistical method. If one assumes that the firm in question has been operating efficiently, or if it is possible to isolate and account for inefficiencies that actually occur, then time series regression analysis can be used for estimating the firm's short-run variable cost function. The total variable cost function is regressed rather than the total cost function, because the complicated problem of allocating overheads in a multi-product firm can then be avoided. Also, for short-run decision-making, fixed costs assume a secondary role, and all decisions should be based on the behaviour of variable costs.

2. Problems of using accounting data. The data available for estimating the short-run cost function will be provided by the accounting department. However, such information needs to be used with caution, for the following reasons:

(a) Care must be taken to ensure that *output and costs are correctly matched*. It is possible, due to lags, for costs to be incurred for a particular output, yet not to appear until a following period, e.g. heavy production in Period 1 leads to extra maintenance costs being incurred in Period 2. Unless these maintenance costs are allocated to the output which was responsible for them (Period 1) under-estimation of costs will occur for Period 1 output and over-estimation of costs will occur for Period 2 output.

(b) The data will be historical cost, and due to inflation the *costs of more recent periods will seem high in comparison to periods further in the past*. It is therefore essential that this bias is removed so that cost variations shown reflect the efficiency of the production system.

(c) The length of the observation period must be adequate to ensure that *sufficient information is available at different output levels*, yet it must not be too long or else plant changes will occur which will make earlier and later data observations incompatible.

(d) There are finally the conceptual problems already mentioned in Chapter V, concerning costs for decision-making in the short-run and the fact that accountancy records do not reflect opportunity cost in any way.

3. The form of the cost function. Once the problems of obtaining accurate data have been solved it is then necessary to decide the functional form of the cost curve. The linear form is normally most popular although there may be theoretical reasons why this cannot be used. Thus quadratic or cubic cost functions become necessary. Reliance should not readily be placed on estimates established from data at the extreme ends of the data range, and particularly on extrapolations outside the range of observed data available. In Fig. 33 the dotted line represents the actual form of the cost function and the solid line the estimated cost function. It can be seen that for the range of available data the estimated and actual are very close, yet once one begins to move outside the available range divergence increases.

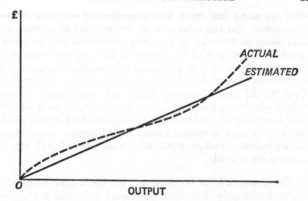

Fig. 33—*The form of the cost function.* For a considerable range of output, actual and estimated total variable cost are close.

ESTIMATION OF THE LONG-RUN AVERAGE COST CURVE

4. Complexities. The estimation of the long-run cost curve tends to be more complex than the estimation of the short-run cost curve, for the following reasons:

(a) *There are many dimensions to economies of scale.*[1] It is not simply a matter of the size of output at a particular time, it also involves rate of output and length of period over which the output is produced. In addition, a simple discussion on economies of scale normally assumes a single product produced in a single-plant firm, whereas in practice firms are multi-plant and multi-product. In this case, economies of scale vary, depending upon whether one is discussing the plant, the firm, a particular product, or a group of products. Choosing to expand to gain a particular economy of scale may involve diseconomies elsewhere in the firm, and therefore the decision to expand must be based upon a compromise and a calculation of the net benefit to be gained by the firm through expansion.

(b) It will be remembered that in Chapter V economies of scale referred to the effect on average cost of producing a given product at different scales, at an existing level of technical knowledge. *A given state of technical knowledge does not mean that every firm regardless of size uses the same techniques.* On the contrary, it means that at a given time and state of knowledge the best technique will be used to produce an output of a given size. Having said this, it will be appreciated that it is almost impossible to measure the economies of scale by studying just one firm. Although the firm would grow through time, the techniques it would adopt would be those of future time periods as it evolved, and any analysis based on such observations would tend to show how cost is reduced over time through improvement in techniques rather than how cost is reduced through economies of scale.

5. Three methods of estimation. We shall now look briefly at three techniques that have been used to estimate the shape of the long-run average cost curve—the survivor technique, the engineering technique and cross-sectional regression analysis.

6. The survivor technique.[2] This technique, which was developed by George Stigler, is based upon the assumption that in competition with each other, firms with the lowest average cost would grow at a faster rate than firms with higher average costs. By examining the size of an industry through time, it should be possible to determine the shape of the long-run average cost curve. The application of the technique would proceed as follows:

(*a*) An industry is chosen for study and the firms in that industry are classified into groups, by size and share of industry output.

(*b*) The share of industry output at a future date for the groups is compared to the shares established in (*a*) above.

(*c*) If the share of industry output has increased, the firm is assumed to have minimum costs and if the share of industry output has increased at a slower rate or has declined, average costs are assumed to be higher.

(*d*) The shape of the curve can now be established.

7. Limitations of survivor technique.

(*a*) For this technique to be useful, the firms in question must be competing against each other in a free market. If this is not so, then the classifying mechanism will be absent.

(b) Geographical separation and local conditions may make the costs of two firms producing the same product entirely different for reasons that have nothing to do with scale economies.

(c) If firms pursue different objectives then their results are again not entirely comparable.

(d) The survivor technique only provides the shape of the long-run cost curve, and not necessarily its actual position. If all the firms in the industry are producing at a level which is not their optimum, then the economies of scale will be under-estimated because the long-run average cost curve will be higher than it actually could be.

8. The engineering technique. This technique makes estimates of the cost of producing different levels of output with the best technology available at that time. It obviously has the great advantages of:

(a) basing estimates at the current level of technical knowledge;

(b) overcoming the problems of comparing different firms who use different accounting procedures with regard to depreciation;

(c) allowing for the fact that firms being observed might not be operating at their optimum point.

This technique was used by Pratten and Dean[3] who have conducted the most comprehensive survey made into economies of scale in the U.K.

Although this technique overcomes many of the problems posed both by the survivor technique and by the statistical technique (9–10 below), special care must be taken in making estimates concerning production levels beyond those currently being produced. Experience has shown that such estimates tend to be optimistic, with disastrous results for the firm that expands on the basis of such figures.

9. The statistical technique. In an attempt to overcome the complexities in **4** above, the statistical technique of cross-sectional regression analysis has been used. For this technique not one, but a number, of firms of a different size are studied, and these are compared at one point in time, regressing total cost against a set of independent variables.

10. Limitations of the statistical technique.

(*a*) Variations in accounting procedures between firms will tend to give variations in the cost of production.

(*b*) Regional variations might distort the cost of factor inputs.

(*c*) All the firms being studied may not be producing at their optimum point, with the result that the long-run average cost curve obtained will be distorted.

11. Availability of data. The choice of technique will be determined by the data available, although in many cases the engineering technique, because it eliminates many of the statistical collection problems, is becoming very popular and in the future is most likely to become the main technique.

RESULTS OF EMPIRICAL RESEARCH

12. The short-run average cost curve. The general picture to emerge from the research which has taken place is that the relationship between cost and output is linear, which means that MC and thus AVC is constant over a significant range of output. The average cost curve, instead of being of the U-shape assumed by economic theory, with one optimum point, tends to have a flat bottom, with average cost per unit being at a minimum for a range of output levels.

13. Managerial implications. Perhaps the greatest managerial implication arising from this research is the extra time that management is given in making a decision on whether to expand capacity. In Chapter V it was emphasised that the decision to expand is very important because once undertaken the situation was virtually impossible to reverse. If a firm was expanding in anticipation or in response to an increase in demand, then that firm had to be certain that the increase in demand for its product was permanent. Faced with the theoretical cost curves where AVC, and then ATC, increased after a certain level of output, the firm was pressurised into taking a decision to expand capacity. In Fig. 34 at output OQ_1 ATC is at a minimum. To produce any output

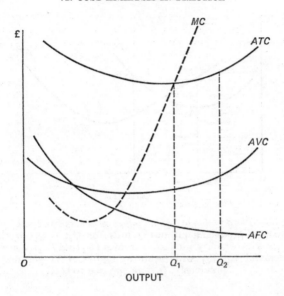

Fig. 34—*The decision to expand (taken under pressure)*. An increase in output from OQ_1 to OQ_2 increases ATC per unit. If price is relatively constant, profit per unit is reduced, and possibly total profit. Such a situation causes management to think immediately of increasing capacity.

in excess of OQ_1, i.e. OQ_2, means facing higher ATC per unit. If the firm expands capacity it moves on to a new AVC curve, ATC_2 in Fig. 35, and for output OQ_2 ATC is lower. If this increase in demand is only temporary, however, and demand contracts to OQ_1, ATC per unit will now be Q_1B, which is AB per unit higher than it was with the old level of capacity.

With a significant range of output being produced under conditions of constant AVC, the firm has more time to assimilate the total situation before arriving at a decision whether to expand capacity. In Fig. 36 the AVC of producing output OQ_1 and OQ_2 are the same. It is only when output exceeds OQ_3 that AVC begins to increase.

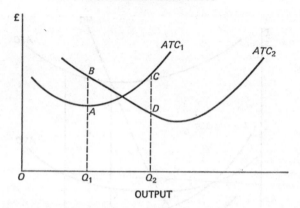

FIG. 35—*The decision to expand (effect on demand and cost per unit).*
The cost of producing output OQ_2 falls from Q_2C to Q_2D as the firm
increases its capacity and moves from ATC_1 to ATC_2. Contraction
of demand to OQ_1 will result in higher ATC per unit than
previously, Q_1B as opposed to Q_1A.

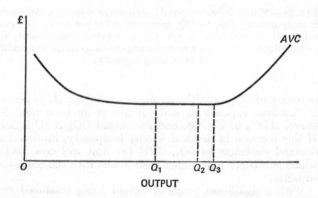

FIG. 36—*The decision to expand (taken under conditions of constant
average variable cost).* The existence of constant AVC over a range
of output reduces the pressure on management to expand capacity.
More time is available to establish whether the increase in demand
is permanent.

14. The long-run average cost curve. Once again in this case, as with the short-run average cost curve, the majority of the empirical evidence [4] indicates quite strongly that the shape of the curve is different in practice from in theory. Whereas the theoretical long-run cost curve was a shallow U, the curve in practice is L-shaped. This L-shape does not mean that diseconomies of scale do not exist, or that economies of scale are constant after a certain scale. There is enough evidence to show that diseconomies are real enough and therefore the L-shaped curve could indicate that after a certain point the effects of cost on economies and diseconomies of scale are equal, resulting in constant costs. In theory, after a certain point, economies of scale are outweighed by the effects of diseconomies. The authorities in this field, although agreeing on the L-shape, are not unanimous in their interpretation of the information available, as to whether costs are constant or gradually declining.

15. The importance of economies of scale. One way of estimating the importance of economies of scale is as follows:

(a) Determine the long-run cost curve for an industry.

(b) Obtain from the curve the point at which average cost becomes constant. This point will then be known as the minimum efficient scale (MES).

(c) Ask what increases in average cost would occur with a plant size some fraction of the size of the MES. If the increase in average cost is significant—say greater than 10 per cent—it can be said that economies of scale are important.

This was the approach adopted by Pratten and Dean and Table XIV is constructed by taking a sample of their results.[5]

These figures relate to technical economies of scale; other economies, such as financial and managerial, have not been measured. In the industries that were chosen it can be said that technical economies would be of greater importance than any other, yet their omission must mean that those shown must to some extent under-estimate the total economies of scale available.

From the sample of industries selected in Table XIV, it can be seen that the importance of economies of scale varies from industry to industry, ranging from the extremes of aircraft production and computers where 100 per cent of the market is required for *MES* to be attained, to footwear, bricks and bicycles where 10 per cent or less of the market is necessary to obtain all the technical economies of large-scale production. To judge fully how important economies of large-scale production are we must look at what happens to average cost at 50 per cent of *MES*. Table XIV shows quite a varied picture.

TABLE XIV: ECONOMIES OF SCALE

Product	MES as % of market	% increase in costs per unit at 50% MES
Bicycles	10·0	Negligible
Bricks—plant	5·0	25
Aircraft	100·0	20
Newspapers	30·0	20
Computers	100·0	8
Steel rolling—plant	80·0	8
Refrigerators, etc.	50·0	8
Footwear—plant	0·2	2
Cement—plant	10·0	9
Cars	50·0	6

Although *MES* as a percentage of the market is the same for bicycles and cement production, the importance in terms of cost of not reaching that size in the case of bicycles is negligible while for cement it has the effect of increasing the average cost of production by 9 per cent. Similarly, compare aircraft production and newspapers, where the share of the market to achieve *MES* is quite different, yet the effect on cost of not reaching that size is the same. These figures really tell us the shape of the long-run average cost curve (*LRACC*), and in Fig. 37 (*a*), where the left-hand side of the curve is steep, we have a *LRACC* similar to that found in the newspaper and brick industry. Having an output OQ_2 which is 50 per cent of *MES* (OQ_1) increases *AC* per unit by *AB*. In Fig. 37 (*b*), the *LRACC* has a shallow shape, and the effect on *AC* of having an output 50 per cent of *MES* is not so great, only *DC* per unit. This situation is similar to what appears to exist in computers, steel rolling and the refrigerator industries.

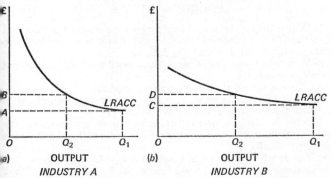

FIG. 37—*Minimum efficient scale.* The cost advantages of being at minimum efficient scale are greater for firms in Industry *A* than firms in Industry *B*.

16. Managerial implications.

(*a*) For the industries studied by Pratten and Dean there were significant economies of scale to exploit, although in many industries firms were at no great disadvantage if they were utilising only 50 per cent of *MES*.

(*b*) The greatest economies available are for the scale of output of individual products. The availability of economies of scale by widening the product range was not so large, although it was possible through general growth in size to obtain economies of scale in relation to finance and management.

(*c*) If the market is not big enough to exploit all the economies of scale available, it is the responsibility of the firm to increase its market to enable exploitation to take place.

(*d*) The existence of *X*-inefficiency (*see* Chapter VII, **19**) means that firms are not minimising average cost per unit to the maximum extent possible.

(*e*) The continuation of technical progress can change the *MES* completely. With a given technique it is possible for a firm, 50 per cent the size of the existing market leaders but with the latest equipment, to have lower *AC* per unit.

(*f*) Economies of scale can provide a strong inducement for firms to expand and grow, both internally and externally.

PROGRESS TEST 6

1. Why is it that the accounting procedures adopted by different firms make the determination of the short-run and long-run average cost curve difficult? (1, 2, 9, 10)

2. Why is it dangerous to extrapolate results outside the area of observed data? (3)

3. "Economies of scale have many dimensions." Discuss. (4)

4. What limitations exist in using the survivor technique to estimate the long-run average cost curve? (7)

5. Why is the engineering technique superior to both the survivor technique and the method of cross-sectional regression analysis? (7–10)

6. The result of a range of constant variable costs means that the manager is not pressurised into expanding capacity. Why? (13)

7. The long-run average cost curve is L-shaped. Does this mean that diseconomies of scale do not exist? (14)

8. What is the significance of the minimum efficient scale (*MES*)? (15, 16)

FURTHER READING

1. Silberston, A., "Economies of Scale in Theory and Practice", *Economic Journal*, 1972, pp. 369–91.

Pratten, C. F. and Dean, R. M., "The Economies of Large Scale Production in British Industry", *Department of Applied Economics Occasional Papers*, No. 3, Cambridge University Press, 1965.

2. Stigler, G. J., "The Economies of Scale", *Journal of Law and Economics*, Vol. 1, No. 1, October 1958, pp. 54–71.

3. Pratten, C. F. and Dean, R. M., *op. cit.*

4. Johnston, J., *Statistical Cost Analysis*, McGraw-Hill, New York, 1960.

Hymer, S. and Rashigion, P., "Firm Size and Rate of Growth", *Journal of Political Economy*, December 1962.

Haldi, J. and Whitcomb, D., "Economies of Scale in Industrial Plants", *Journal of Political Economy*, August 1967.

Pratten, C. F. and Dean, R. M., *op. cit.*

Bain, J. S., "Economies of Scale Concentration, and the Conditions of Entry in Twenty Manufacturing Industries", *American Economic Review*, 1954.

5. Pratten, C. F., "Economies of Scale in Manufacturing Industry", *Department of Applied Economics Occasional Papers*, No. 28, Cambridge University Press, 1971.

CHAPTER VII

MARKET STRUCTURES

INTRODUCTION

1. The neo-classical model. Traditionally, economic theory texts have concerned themselves with the neo-classical model of price and output determination in different market structures. This process was based upon an objective of maximum profit and was undertaken in a general equilibrium framework in which no change in price and output policy would be desired once the optimum profit position had been reached. The various forms of market structure were then appraised according to the proximity of each outcome to the allocative efficiency (*see* **3-8** below) required by the neo-classical model. The optimum outcome was generally regarded as being price equal to marginal cost and average cost at its minimum.

2. Criticism of the neo-classical model. Many criticisms have been levelled at the neo-classical model, not least of which have been those concerned with alternative objectives described in Chapter I. More important from the point of view of this Chapter is the recognition that the subject of market structure embraces many more variables than that of price alone. Indeed, the current vogue is to analyse market structure in terms of the triplicity of structure–conduct–performance, where certain characteristics of market structure are assumed to lead to certain types of behaviour which in turn lead to certain performance features. In this Chapter we propose to examine some of the relationships which exist between market structure and performance. In particular, we will examine the relationship which exists between market structure and pricing behaviour, profits, progressiveness and efficiency. This is not meant to be an exhaustive list but it will nevertheless provide some of the basic elements involved in appraising the performance of a given industrial structure.

MARKET STRUCTURE AND PRICE THEORY

The efficiency of the resource-allocation process has been the central feature of neo-classical price theory.

3. Efficient resource-allocation. In simple terms, price theory divides market structures into the three main types of perfect competition, monopoly and imperfect competition. As we shall see, it is only under the theoretical ideal of perfect competition that efficient allocation is achieved.

The resource-allocation process in economic theory is based upon the assumption of profit-maximisation. As shown in Chapter I, this assumption has received much criticism. However, for the purposes of this Chapter we will accept the assumption and analyse its implications for the efficiency of the resource-allocation process. It is in fact profits which play the central role in the resource-allocation process, industries expanding and contracting in relation to the generation and elimination of short-run abnormal profits.

4. Identification of revenue and cost curves. In order to examine the resource-allocation process in any market structure, we must first identify average revenue, marginal revenue, average cost and marginal cost, and then apply the criteria required to create a comparative static equilibrium. Average revenue is simply the total revenue (price × output) divided by the number of units of output. Marginal revenue is the addition to total revenue received from the sale of the last unit of output.

Normally, the average revenue curve is assumed to be downward-sloping, since the firm will need to reduce its price in order to sell more output. Moreover, with a downward-sloping demand curve, marginal revenue will also be downward-sloping and will be less than average revenue since the firm has to reduce the price of all the other units of output in order to sell the extra marginal unit. On the cost side, average cost is simply the total cost divided by the number of units of output and the curve is generally assumed to be U-shaped in the short-run because as the firm's output expands the spreading of overhead costs and the advantages of the division of labour will tend to reduce costs per unit. Eventually, as output continues to expand, diminishing returns will set in caused by increased variable factors becoming less productive as they are applied to fixed factors (the upturn in the long-run is assumed to be caused by diseconomies of scale). Marginal cost is the addition to total cost of producing the last unit of output and is mathematically linked to the average cost curve, being below the average when the average is falling, above the average when the average is rising, and intersecting the average at its minimum point where average cost is constant.

5. Equilibrium. The criteria required for a position of equilibrium is that the firm should be maximising its profit so that it does not want to change its price and output policy. This will be achieved where $MR = MC$, since as long as the firm is adding more to its revenue than to its cost ($MR > MC$) it will wish to increase its output, while if it is adding more to its cost than to its revenue ($MR < MC$), it will want to reduce its output. The industry will be in equilibrium (i.e. no firms wishing to leave or enter) only when normal profit is being earned, so that no new firms are attracted in and no firms in the industry wish to leave. This will be achieved where $AR = AC$ since the calculation of AC includes a normal profit element. If $AR > AC$ abnormal profits would be earned and new entrants would wish to come in, whereas if $AR < AC$, less than normal profit would be earned and some firms would wish to leave the industry.

We can now use these two criteria to analyse the resource-allocation process.

6. Perfect competition. Perfect competition is a hypothetical ideal which assumes product homogeneity, many buyers and sellers, freedom of entry and perfect information. Given these assumptions, the firm is faced with a horizontal demand curve, since it supplies such a small part of the total market that it can vary its output without affecting price. Equilibrium is therefore achieved at output Q in Fig. 38, since it is only at this level of output that $MR = MC$ and $AR = AC$.

The two important features about perfect competition from a resource-allocation point of view are that price $= MC$, and AC is at its minimum. The former represents an optimum resource-allocation from the consumers' point of view, since their marginal valuation of the product (as measured by the price they are prepared to pay) is equal to the marginal valuation of the resources used up in its production (as measured by the marginal cost). Economists regard price = *MC* as essential for the maximisation of economic welfare, and

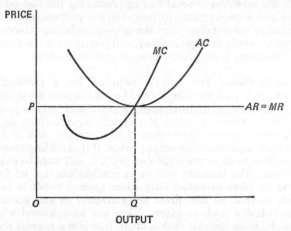

FIG. 38—*Perfect competition*. Price and output policy of a perfectly competitive firm, faced by a perfectly elastic demand curve, determined where simultaneously *MR = MC* and *AR = AC*.

as we shall see perfect competition is the only market structure which achieves this optimum allocation of resources. In addition, *AC* at its minimum ensures that from the production side there is an optimum combination of factors of production in existence.

7. Monopoly. Monopoly represents the opposite extreme to perfect competition. It assumes that there is only one firm in the industry, and that it will be faced with a downward-sloping demand curve since variations in the firm's output will substantially affect the total supply. Obviously, only the single criterion of profit-maximisation is required here, so that equilibrium will be at output *Q* in Fig. 39.

Note that we no longer have the ideal conditions of the perfectly competitive model. Price is now greater than *MC*, implying that optimum resource-allocation requires more resources to be devoted to this industry, since at the margin the consumers' valuation of the product exceeds the cost of the resources involved in its production. Moreover, *AC* is no longer at its minimum and this would occur only by chance alone. Monopoly profits are shown by the area *PABC*.

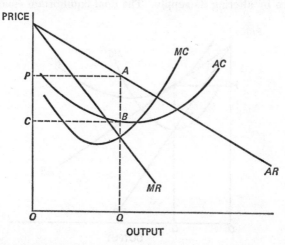

FIG. 39—*Monopoly*. Price and output policy of a monopolist, determined at the height of the *AR* curve above the intersection of *MR* and *MC*.

8. Imperfect competition. This term can be applied to cover all forms of competition which exist between the two extremes of perfect competition and monopoly. The problem is that the degree of market imperfection is so varied that many models of imperfect competition have been devised. Such models range from Chamberlin's monopolistic competition (in which there are many firms selling different products that are close substitutes for one another) to the oligopolistic models, with their complex reaction functions.

The imperfectly competitive models are not easily handled by the tools of traditional price theory. Indeed, it was only by making the now famous assumption concerning uniform demand and cost curves for all firms in the group, and by requiring that any adjustment of price or product by any firm would have a negligible effect upon its competitors, that

Chamberlin was able to achieve his famous tangency solution. The outcome of such assumption is shown in Fig. 40. The revenue curves are once again the normal downward-sloping ones, since each firm is in a position to influence the market price by altering its supply. The dual equilibrium conditions

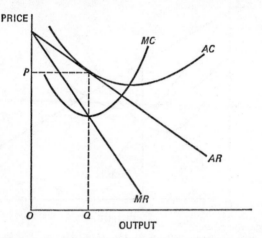

FIG. 40—*Imperfect competition*. Price and output policy of an imperfectly competitive firm determined at the level of output at which $MR = MC$ and $AR = AC$.

are satisfied where AR is tangential to AC. Mathematically, the tangency solution with $AR = AC$ also means that MR must $= MC$ at output OQ and price OP, because of the relative slopes of the average curves, i.e. if the slopes of AR and AC are equal at output OQ, then the addition to revenue must be equal to the addition to cost at that point (i.e. $MR = MC$).

As with monopoly, this model of imperfect competition results in a solution in which price is greater than MC, and AC is not at its minimum at the equilibrium output. These departures from the ideal of perfect competition are a consequence of product differentiation, with too many firms working at excess capacity.

9. Indeterminate solution. Chamberlin's model of imperfect competition could only be analysed by the tools of traditional price theory as a result of the "heroic" (to use his own word) or major assumptions he made. However, once we move to the more concentrated end of imperfect competition (i.e. oligopoly), these assumptions quite clearly become invalid and the price/output solution becomes indeterminate; the tools of traditional price theory, i.e. individual demand and supply curves for each firm, cannot be determined. Nevertheless, in view of the important role oligopoly plays in our economy (70 per cent of industrial output is produced in industries with oligopolistic structures) it is worth considering some of the more important aspects of oligopolistic theory.

10. Oligopoly. Oligopoly is a situation in which output is highly concentrated in the hands of a few firms. Consequently, actions taken by any one of these firms may significantly affect their rivals.

(a) *Absence of price competition*. One of the central features of oligopoly theory is the absence of the continuous price competition which arises in competitive models. This may be the result either of collusion or of price leadership, or because price competition is too costly to the participating firms.

Monopolies and mergers legislation in the U.K. and anti-trust legislation in the U.S.A. have made it less likely that prices will be set by firms operating in a cartel. Nevertheless, price competition is still likely to be absent, either on account of informal collusion or because of the development of price leadership.

Price leadership may be either dominant or barometric. Dominant price leadership occurs when the leading firm is powerful enough to set a price which all other firms will be forced to follow. Barometric price leadership occurs when the leading firm is followed merely because the price it sets reflects market forces and the needs of other firms in the industry.

Price wars between major firms tend to be very rare, one of the most famous being that between Unilever and Procter and Gamble in the detergent industry in 1955. A major price war has recently been raging in the U.K. petrol retailing business where the four major companies, Esso, Shell, B.P. and Texaco, control about 65 per cent of the retail market. It is interesting to note that the increased price competition stemmed from the small operators being able to buy petrol surpluses at keen prices on the Rotterdam market. The major firms reduced their prices in defence of their market share with the result that some independent service stations were driven out of business.

Moreover, once the price war has achieved its purpose of driving out firms or establishing leadership, the industry quickly reverts to other forms of competition.

(b) *Price rigidity.* Another important feature which emerges from the absence of price competition is that of rigid prices. This is a direct result of the kinked demand curve theory. This theory is based on the assumption that the firm believes the demand curve facing it is such that, whichever way it changes price, its total revenue will fall. This situation arises because of assumptions made about the reactions of rivals. In Fig. 41, if the company raises its price above OP it will be faced with an elastic demand curve (because the other firms will not raise their prices) and will consequently lose revenue, while if it lowers its price below

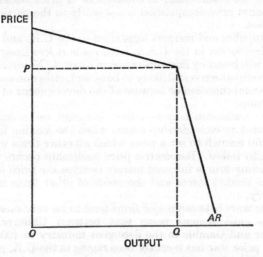

FIG. 41—*The kinked demand curve.* Price and output policy of an oligopolist faced by a kinked demand curve.

OP it will be faced with an inelastic demand curve (because other firms will also lower their prices) and will similarly lose revenue. Thus price rigidities are likely to be a feature of industries in which firms hold these beliefs about elasticities.

(c) *Pricing to discourage competition.* Because of the oligopolistic concern for maintaining market shares oligopoly theory has been particularly concerned with the threat of potential competition. Consequently, one branch of oligopoly theory suggests that oligopolists will set a price low enough to discourage potential competition. At what level this price needs to be will be dependent upon the height of barriers to entry to the industry, such as economies of scale, absolute cost advantages, product differentiation, etc. The higher the barriers to entry the less the industry will be concerned with potential competition. It may be, of course, that the profit-maximising position may be lucrative enough to justify neglecting potential competition altogether.

(d) *Non-price competition.* Another feature of oligopolistic market structures is the prevalence of non-price competition. This takes the form of product development, improvement, changes in marketing expenditure, after-sales service, etc. Non-price competition is generally preferred to price competition by oligopolistic firms partly because it has less disastrous consequences and partly because it cannot be quickly imitated. Moreover, product differentiation reduces the cross-elasticity of demand between products and thereby gives the firm great control over its own market.

There are numerous advantages of non-price competition in British industry. The motor car industry, for example, is concerned with model competition within particular price ranges while the detergent industry was heavily criticised by the Monopolies Commission in 1966 for excessive marketing expenditures.

11. Market structure and price policy: empirical evidence. As we have noted in **6–7** above, price theory in the extreme cases of perfect competition and pure monopoly tends to predict that market structure (number of sellers) influences conduct (selection of price and output) which in turn determines performance (the amount by which price exceeds marginal cost). However, imperfect competition is much more complicated in this respect, in that market structure can give rise to many patterns of conduct and performance, depending upon the assumptions one makes about collusion, interdependence, etc.

The empirical evidence indicates that where a powerful monopoly exists in the absence of public policy, price levels are significantly above costs. Similarly, where there has been significant market power and conducive demand conditions, price discrimination has been prevalent. Such prices may be enormously above costs, as for example with certain products in the drugs industry. The Monopolies Commission found that Kodak's prices of colour films were 35 to 55 per cent above competitive levels, at a time when it held a 77 per cent stake in the British colour films market.[1]

The effects are much more difficult to disentangle in oligopolistic markets. W. G. Shepherd concluded that "price effects are minimal in loose oligopolies. . . . In intermediate and tight oligopolies with entry barriers, the effects tend to range between 10 and 30 per cent, and may go much higher."[2]

MARKET STRUCTURE AND PROFITABILITY

12. Abnormal profits: theory. The traditional price theory set out in **6–10** above, demonstrates that market imperfections enable firms to compete in market situations in which abnormal profits have not been completely eliminated. This divergence of AR and AC at the equilibrium point is a direct result of market imperfections. Hence the effort made by firms to differentiate their products, advertise and use the whole range of variables in the marketing mix to extend their market power. In terms of traditional price theory the objective of manipulating the instruments in the market mix is to push the demand curve facing the firm further to the right and at the same time make it more inelastic. This enables abnormal profits to be earned, as can be seen from Fig. 42. At the initial equilibrium price and output of P_1Q_1 only normal profits are earned since $AR_1 = AC$. Product differentiation or a successful advertising campaign may shift the firm's demand curve to AR_2, so that the new price and output combination would be P_2Q_2. AR_2 now exceeds AC at the equilibrium point, so that abnormal profits of P_2ABC are earned for as long as the new market power exists.

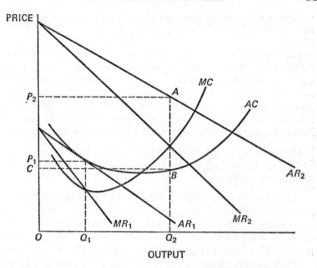

FIG. 42—*Abnormal profits*. The use of advertising to shift the demand curve to the right (AR_2) enables abnormal profits to be earned.

13. Abnormal profits: empirical evidence. The empirical evidence is inconclusive, at least so far as the British economy is concerned. U.S.A. findings suggest that company size itself significantly affects profits. However, British evidence suggests that although small firms received more variable profits, it was in fact the small firms which received the largest.[3] In so far as market structure is concerned, almost all U.S.A. concentration profits studies which have been undertaken (with the exception of Stigler's) have yielded significant positive relationships between concentration and profits. Even in the U.S.A., however, the studies suggest that an increase in concentration would not significantly increase profits. Also, much of the variation in profit rates is unexplained by the evidence. British studies have so far found no evidence that high profits and high concentration are correlated.[4] It is clear, therefore, that much more evidence is needed before a final judgment can be made.

MARKET STRUCTURE AND TECHNICAL PROGRESS

14. Two views. There exist two opposing views on the relationship between market structure and technical progress. On the one hand there is the now famous Schumpeter–Galbraith hypothesis that large firm size and an oligopolistic market structure represent the best means of promoting technical change. On the other hand, there is the hypothesis that competition is an important stimulant to technical change.

15. Advantage of size. The belief that large size and technical progress are positively related is based upon a number of premises:

(a) The costs of the research and development necessary for innovation are so great that only large firms can afford to employ the skilled teams of scientists and engineers, expensive plant and equipment, etc., required for success.

(b) The large firm can afford to diversify its research and development portfolio, thereby reducing the risk involved.

(c) The large multi-product firm will be in a better position to make use of any developments that arise from the research process than single-product firms.

16. Advantage of competition. However, there are equally impressive arguments in favour of the competitive hypothesis. It can be argued that a monopolist may become complacent, whereas competitive firms are stimulated by the fear that other firms may innovate first. Moreover, it is only competitive pressure that forces firms to search for better techniques and ways of doing things.

17. Empirical evidence. The empirical evidence both on the relationship between firm size and technical progress, and market structure and technical progress, is by no means clear. In so far as firm size is concerned, there appears to be a "threshold" effect: a company must be of a certain size before it can meaningfully undertake research and development. However, some studies indicate that beyond a certain size there are substantial diseconomies of scale in research and development. Large firms do not tend to be proportionately more important producers of major innovations. For most industries it is likely that the threshold level of firm size will be below the size of the largest firms in the industry. A similar conclusion appears to emerge from evidence on market structure. Some increase in concentration up to the range of loose oligopoly appears to increase technical progress, but further increases in concentration may hinder progress, e.g. where the combined output of the four leading firms in the industry exceeds 55 per cent of the total output of that industry.

MARKET STRUCTURE AND TECHNICAL EFFICIENCY

There are two aspects of efficiency with which we are concerned here. The first is whether the firm is operating at a sufficiently high level of output to reap the full benefits of economies of scale, and the second is whether the firm is actually operating at minimum cost for each level of output.

18. Market structure and economies of scale. The importance of economies of scale will clearly indicate the number of firms economically viable in an industry if they are to be of optimum size. Bain's studies demonstrated that in the U.S.A., optimum-sized plants required no more than 10 per cent of the total market in eighteen out of the twenty industries he investigated.[5] Pratten and Dean undertook a major investigation of British industry and found that with one or two exceptions, the level of concentration required for minimum efficient scale was quite low, allowing room for several firms in the British market.[6] Moreover, the slope of the long-run average cost curve to the left of its minimum point was found to be quite gentle in most cases, so that even at 50 per cent of optimal capacity not many of the industries in Pratten's study suffered cost disadvantages of more than 10 per cent. Also, it would appear that there is quite a wide range of output over which costs are constant, so that once the minimum efficient scale has been reached, further expansion of output will be unlikely to reduce unit costs.

The empirical evidence has clear implications for the choice of optimum size of firm—the minimum efficient size of firm. On grounds of technical efficiency there is little point in increasing firm size beyond this point, which for most industries in Britain is well short of a monopoly situation. Indeed, it is likely that there is more concentration than is merited purely by the existence of economies of scale, and there may be a case for the breaking up of some firms into several smaller firms. On the other hand, Bain's analysis also revealed that the industries he studied generally had a fringe of inefficient small plants that supplied 10 to 30 per cent of industry output. Once again it is likely that there is a threshold effect, with some form of mild oligopoly being appropriate for many industries.

19. Market structure and internal efficiency. The relationship between market structure and internal efficiency has received little attention until recently. It was Leibenstein who first drew attention to the fact that the existence of market power enabled firms to be less cost-conscious, since in the absence of competition, minimisation of costs was no longer a condition of survival.[7] It is thus argued that monopolistic market structures provide less incentive for cost minimisation, with a resulting loss in efficiency. This concept of internal efficiency was termed X-efficiency by Leibenstein in order to distinguish it from allocative efficiency (inefficiency arising from a divergence of marginal cost and price).

Leibenstein argues that the loss arising from X-inefficiency is considerably greater than that arising from the price distortion effect (allocative efficiency), since X-inefficiency represents a raising of the entire cost curve and therefore affects all units, rather than just marginal units, of output. Unfortunately, the empirical evidence concerning X-inefficiency is so far extremely limited. Nevertheless, what evidence we have seems to suggest that X-inefficiency does exist and that it may be an important cause of the high cost structure of British industry.

APPRAISAL

20. Difficulty of measuring market structure. There is no unambiguous measure of market power. A large number of dimensions of market structure have been suggested, such as the degree of seller concentration, the degree of buyer concentration, the extent of product differentiation, the condition of entry, etc. For public policy purposes, the main index taken has been that of seller concentration. However, there is no single measure of concentration. There are in fact a number of techniques for measuring concentration, such as the absolute concentration ratio, the Lorenz curve, the Herfindahl index, etc., each with its own limitations as a measure of market power. Problems such as local markets, collusion, international competition, product differentiation, etc., all make it difficult to obtain an adequate measure. It is clear, therefore, that inferences concerning market power based on concentration data should be viewed with some suspicion.

21. Difficulty of measuring performance. A major problem here is that there is no exact measure of performance. A large number of indices have been suggested to measure performance, such as profitability, rate of return on capital, technical efficiency, productivity, technical progressiveness, etc.

Even if we were to choose just one of these, say, profitability, we would still be faced with serious problems. High profits cannot be directly compared with low profits because of differences in the degree of risk involved. Similarly, profits may be low simply because the firm is internally inefficient and has allowed its costs to rise. There are also so many different accounting conventions that it is difficult to compare the profits of different companies, and therefore extremely difficult to find out the precise relationship between market structure and profits.

Similar problems arise in analysing any of the other indices of performance, indeed, the measurement problems are even more hazardous in areas such as technical efficiency, productivity and technical progressiveness. Despite the uncertainty surrounding the concept, this is one of the main reasons why profitability has remained the foremost indicator of performance in British industry, even in the public sector.

22. The problem of causation. In examining the relationship between market structure and performance, the implication so far has been that certain kinds of market power such as concentrated market structures bring about certain features of behaviour which affect performance, i.e. they have implications for pricing, profits, research and development, etc. However, the direction of causality is not all one way. In the textile industries, for example, poor performance as measured by low profitability led to rationalisation schemes which brought about more concentrated market structures. The relationship is thus complicated. Pickering is surely correct in asserting that "not only is structure an influence on present conduct and

performance but in a dynamic framework today's market
structure is a result of yesterday's conduct and performance".

In conclusion, it is worth noting that there is still very little
empirical evidence on structure/performance relationships in
the British economy. Moreover, what evidence there is does
not always accord with that on the U.S.A. economy. Extreme
caution should therefore be applied in formulating policy on
the basis of such evidence.

PROGRESS TEST 7

1. Explain what is meant by the term "allocative efficiency".
Which market structures are likely to be most successful in
achieving it? **(1–8)**

2. Account for the relative importance of price competition
and non-price competition in oligopolistic industries. **(10)**

3. Do concentrated market structures lead to higher prices and
profits? **(11–13)**

4. Are large firms better innovators? **(14–17)**

5. Explain the role played by economies of scale in determining
the minimum efficient size of firm. Are there any advantages to be
gained from going beyond this size? **(18)**

6. Explain what is meant by the term "X-inefficiency". Do
you think that it applies to British industry? **(19)**

7. What limitations should be borne in mind when considering
empirical estimates on the relationship between market structure
and performance? **(20–22)**

FURTHER READING

1. Monopolies Commission, *Colour Films*, H.M.S.O., April 1966.

2. Shepherd, W. G., *Market Power and Economic Welfare*,
Random House, 1970.

3. Samuels, J. M. and Smyth, D. J., "Profits, Variability of
Profits and Firm Size", *Economica*, 1968.

4. Hart, P. E., "Competition and Rate of Return on Capital in
United Kingdom industry", *Business Ratios*, No. 2, 1968.

5. Bain, J. S., *Barriers to New Competition*, Harvard University
Press, 1956.

6. Pratten, C. F. and Dean, R. M., *The Economics of Large Scale
Production in British Industry*, Cambridge University Press,
1965.

7. Leibenstein, H., "Allocative Efficiency versus X-Efficiency",
American Economic Review, June 1966.

8. Pickering, J. F., *Industrial Structure and Market Conduct*,
Martin Robertson, 1974.

CHAPTER VIII

PRICING IN PRACTICE—PRIVATE ENTERPRISE

THE COMPLICATIONS OF PRICING

THE pricing decision is one of the most difficult decisions to be made in business, because the information required is never fully available. It is impossible to quantify all the information necessary to make pricing decisions, and therefore qualitative information can prove as valuable as quantitative information. In addition, the price of a commodity can also convey particular messages to the consumer as we saw in Chapter IV where price can be associated with quality, where a "right price" for an article is said to exist in the mind of the consumer, or where odd prices, i.e. £1·99, £695, etc., have an influence on consumers' reactions.

For the firm's long-run survival, the price charged must yield sufficient revenue to cover its total costs. Therefore cost must play an important role in determining price, although the importance of cost in the pricing decision depends upon the product in question, the market structure and the customer.

The price charged is also expected to achieve objectives other than revenue-generation, such as creating a favourable image in the mind of the consuming public or deterring possible new entrants from the industry.

1. The uses of marginalism. In Chapter VII the main market structures of economic theory were examined and the price was determined in each structure by the method of marginalism, i.e. output was determined where marginal revenue was equal to marginal cost and price was obtained from the demand curve directly above the intersection. The empirical work in the U.S.A. and U.K. has revealed, however, that firms do not set prices according to the logic of marginalism.

(*a*) The theory rests on the assumption that profit-maximisation is the prime objective, yet Chapter I showed quite clearly that this is not necessarily the case.

(b) Economic theory deals essentially with the firm maximising its position in the short-run, whereas in fact such short-run maximisation policies may harm the long-run position of the firm.

(c) Economic theory assumes that the firm has more information than is actually available to it. Very few firms (if any) can draw up revenue and cost functions and so most operate and make decisions with incomplete information. Chapter III indicated the difficulties that arise in demand analysis, that the many variables that influence the demand for the firm's product are constantly changing and the "identification problem" is impossible to solve in practice. The firm can attempt to assess the influence of some variables on the demand for its product by test marketing, yet the results here can never be guaranteed because no one can be certain that the area chosen for the test is representative of the market as a whole or that the conditions which existed in the market during the period of the test were what the firm thought they were, i.e. that other manufacturers had maintained their existing prices and advertising budgets.

For these reasons many pricing techniques are adopted, and in 2–8 below we shall describe in detail some of those most commonly used. It is advisable at this stage for the student to reread Chapter V, because when we describe the various pricing techniques used it is essential that the concept of incremental cost is kept constantly in mind. We shall attempt to describe each technique and point out, where necessary, its weaknesses.

PRICING TECHNIQUES IN USE

2. The background to the pricing decision.

(a) The price should be chosen in order to achieve a company objective. That objective could be profit-maximisation (short-run); profit-maximisation (long-run); sales-maximisation; growth-maximisation; establishment of favourable image with public or government; or limitation of competition. An objective must be chosen and the price, when eventually set, should aim to help achieve it.

(b) The pricing decision involves all departments within an organisation and is not the prerogative of accountancy or marketing. Price determines quantity demanded, and therefore it is essential that before price is finally determined the production department is consulted to establish whether there is the capacity to meet this demand created by the price set. To satisfy demand, this production capacity must exist and raw materials must be available in sufficient quantities and at the right price.

(c) The importance of cost depends upon the way in which price is determined and the market conditions under which the firm competes. Some firms have argued that demand is the most important influence, while others have argued that it is cost. The truth lies somewhere in between. Demand and cost are both important, but the product in question and the market environment under which the firm operates will determine which factor is the most important for it.

3. Full-cost pricing.

This is the simplest of the pricing methods and is based on full absorption costing plus a mark-up for profit. The firm must take into account variable and fixed production costs, variable and fixed selling and administration costs, and a mark-up that provides for profit.[1] This technique, although one of the most popular in practice, has come under severe criticism:

(a) It demotes the influence of demand. Cost is regarded as being the prime influence in determining price and the influence of the market tends to be ignored.

(b) Because of (a) it fails adequately to reflect competition.

(c) It overvalues the precision of allocating costs (see Chapter V).

(d) It is based upon circular reasoning, i.e. quantity demanded is determined by the price charged, price charged is dependent upon cost per unit, and cost per unit is in turn dependent upon quantity demanded.

To some extent one can understand the logic of this technique: it is based upon the business man's fear of failing to cover total cost and hence of going out of business. Total cost must be covered by total revenue and this technique is supposed to ensure that this is achieved. However, this method will only guarantee that total cost will be covered if budgeted sales and actual sales coincide. If for some reason actual sales are less than budgeted sales, fixed cost will not be fully recovered. One also has the problem (highlighted in Chapter

V) of distinguishing between fixed and variable cost and allocating the fixed cost between various products in a multi-product firm.

4. Government contracts and cost-plus. For some contracts to supply the government, a cost-plus arrangement is insisted upon. In most cases this is advantageous to the firm because the products being produced or developed are of a highly technical nature and extremely high-risk in terms of fore-casting the cost of production, e.g. aircraft, aero-engines, missiles, etc. Government auditors check costs incurred by the firm to ensure that no excessive wastage and inefficiency has occurred and a mark-up is added, based upon a figure negotiated by the government and the firm in question. Such contracts have been criticised because it is said that there is no incentive for cost-saving; however, it is possible to introduce incentives. For example, a target cost may be agreed at the beginning of a contract, e.g. £50,000 for a jet engine, and the incentive to reduce cost is an additional agreement that the firm will be paid 50 per cent of all cost-saving it makes, e.g. if the cost of the engine is eventually £40,000, a saving of £10,000, the government will pay the firm £45,000 for each engine. In addition to this, it can also be agreed that the government will only pay 50 per cent of the cost in excess of the target figure, e.g. if the cost of production was £60,000, the firm would receive only £55,000.

5. Target rate of return pricing. This is merely a refinement of the full-cost pricing described in 3 above, an attempt being made to relate the mark-up to the rate of return on capital employed. Regardless of this refinement, the criticisms of full cost-plus pricing in 3 apply equally to this technique. A simple formula has been devised which enables one to apply a mark-up on cost that will give the desired rate of return.

$$\text{Percentage mark-up} \atop \text{on cost} = \frac{\text{Capital employed}}{\text{Total annual cost}} \times \frac{\text{Planned}}{\text{rate of return}}$$

Capital employed   £3 m
Total annual cost   £6 m
Planned rate of return   20%

Percentage mark-up = $\frac{3}{6} \times 20 = \underline{\underline{10\%}}$

If total cost per unit	= £50
10% mark-up	= 5
Selling Price	= £55

If a firm is to use this technique and is changing from some other pricing method, it must ensure that:

(a) the price will result in the demand projected;

(b) the price chosen will not be significantly out of line with competitors' prices, unless such differences can be easily justified;

(c) problems are not created by new prices which are significantly different from the old ones.

Although the logic of this technique is extremely suspect, it is true to say that given the right conditions it can be quite successful. The right conditions, however, must exist, otherwise pursuance of this policy could be disastrous.

(a) The firm must be able to set and control its own price.

(b) The firm must be able to estimate sales data successfully.

(c) The firm must be able to take a long-run view of its operations,[2] i.e. it must be aware that excessive profits might lead to new entrants into the industry, which will increase competition and reduce profit in the long-run. It may be more beneficial to earn moderate profits for a long period than high profits for a short period, and then low profits after new entry has taken place.

6. Acceptance pricing. This technique is used in the situation where a price-leader has emerged, i.e. a firm initiates price changes and the other firms in the industry merely follow the pattern set by the leader—they accept his leadership.

Before we describe this technique further it is necessary to explain why price leadership and acceptance exist. The main reason is the desire of firms in the industry to avoid harmful cut-throat competition. As concentration increases, firms', awareness of each other increases, with a resulting desire to limit harmful competition. There is not necessarily any direct communication between firms, but an informal understanding becomes established and a leader emerges. The leader does not have to be the largest firm in the industry.

Another of the leader's roles is to alert the other companies to the need for a product price change.

So far as the price-follower is concerned, this technique involves evaluating whether the new prices set by the leader should be accepted or not.

7. Acceptance pricing: evaluation. To evaluate whether the new price should be accepted, the firm should:

(a) compare the new price with the incremental cost of production;

(b) compare the total cost and revenue situation for various activity projections.

In determining desirability, the price-follower must be thinking in terms of his own long-run profitability. Profitability must be sufficient so that capital is drawn into the firm and capital it already has can be retained.

EXAMPLE 13: Glampol Ltd. is a price follower who has to evaluate whether to accept a new price of £25 set by the price-leader. The old market price was £24. The first step is to compare the new price with the projected average variable cost per unit. From Table XV it can be seen that a contribution of £5 per unit will be made.

TABLE XV: VARIABLE COST PER UNIT FOR GLAMPOL LTD.

	£
Raw Material	8·00
Direct labour	8·00
Variable overheads	2·00
Total variable production cost	18·00
Variable selling distribution cost	2·00
Total variable cost	20·00
Contribution	5·00
Selling price	25·00

Having established that a clear contribution is earned over the variable cost, the next step is to evaluate each possible strategy that the firm could pursue. It could pursue three:

(i) Glampol Ltd. prices at the new price and all other firms change to the new price.

(*ii*) Glampol Ltd. prices at the old price and all firms except Glampol Ltd. go to the new price.

(*iii*) Glampol Ltd. prices at old price and all other firms remain at the old price.

In Table XVI we have the profit projections of these three strategies. Strategy (*i*) is to be preferred to strategy (*iii*), yet strategy (*ii*) results in even greater profits for the firm.

TABLE XVI: PROFIT PROJECTIONS

	(*i*) All at £25		(*ii*) All except Glampol Ltd. at £25		(*iii*) All at the old price	
$TR = 5,000 \times 25$		125,000	$7,000 \times 24$	168,000	$5,500 \times 24$	132,000
Less TVC $5,000 \times 20$		100,000	$7,000 \times 20$	140,000	$5,500 \times 20$	110,000
Contribution		25,000		28,000		22,000
Fixed cost		18,000		18,000		18,000
		7,000		10,000		4,000

£10,000 profit, however, will only arise if other firms in the industry will allow Glampol Ltd. to stay at the old price. If they respond to Glampol Ltd.'s refusal to raise the price and lower their own to the old price, profit will fall to £4,000. This is a situation where *qualitative* information on the behaviour of rivals must supplement quantitative data, and if past experience has shown that rival firms will react in this way, the best strategy to pursue would be that of price acceptance.

8. Acceptance pricing: a variation. In 6 and 7 above, price-leaders and followers emerged through the market conditions that existed in that particular industry. It is also possible for price acceptance to exist through the nature of the product. Conditions then would be similar to theoretical perfect competition, i.e. there would be many producers producing an homogeneous product using equipment that was not partticularly expensive or difficult to obtain. The result would be that barriers to entry would not exist.

A firm must first recognise that it is operating in such an industry; if so, it must then decide what stage the industry has reached. Has the individual firm still some control over price or must it merely accept the market price? If it still has some control over price, then it must decide between maximising short-term or long-term profits. By charging a high price, profits in the short-run would increase but this would attract entrants into the industry. Supply of the product would increase and profits would fall.

EXAMPLE 14: A firm must decide which stategy to pursue. Which one will ensure greatest profits in the long-run? The product has a life of 10 years and if a price of £10 is charged entry will be prevented. If a price of £12 is charged entry will take place although it will take 3 years for new entrants to become effective. Variable cost per unit is £7 and the quantity demanded at various prices is as in Table XVII.

TABLE XVII: QUANTITY/PRICE RELATIONSHIP

	Price	Quantity demanded
	10	10,000
	12	9,000
after entry	8	8,000

Strategy (i): Price to keep out new entrants

Total revenue	$10,000 \times 10 = 100,000$
Total variable cost	$10,000 \times 7 \ \ = 70,000$
Total contribution	30,000
Total contribution over 10 years	300,000

Strategy (ii): Charge high prices in short-run

Total revenue	$9,000 \times 12 = 108,000$
Total variable cost	$9,000 \times 7 \ = 63,000$
Total contribution	45,000
Total contribution over 3 years	135,000

Plus

Total revenue	$8,000 \times 8 \ = 64,000$
Total variable cost	$8,000 \times 7 \ = 56,000$
Total contribution	8,000
Total contribution over 7 years	56,000
Total contribution over 10 years	191,000

If new entrants could not become effective for 6 years, then the firm would benefit by charging £12, although new entry would occur. The student is asked to calculate the total contribution over the 10-year life of the product if entry does not take place until the end of the 6th year.

If the price charged in the past has attracted entrants into the industry the firm finds itself in a situation where it must accept the ruling market price and produce, or reject, the price and seek new markets. If market price is lower than average variable cost it must shut down immediately but if price exceeds average variable cost it will be advantageous for the firm to continue to produce regardless of the fact that price is lower than average total cost. Fixed costs have been incurred and, therefore, any contribution towards them is advantageous, Even this, however, is a short-term policy because total cost must be covered in the long-run. During this short-run period the firm's executives should be seeking alternative uses for the firm's products.

9. Bid pricing. In this situation it is the buyer through direct contact or advertising who initiates the procedure, by requesting firms to bid for the supply of a good or a service. The buyer will specify his requirements and in many cases the product requested will be completely new.

10. Bid pricing: uncertainty with new product. The problem in making a bid for a new product is uncertainty. One might have to work raw materials that one has never worked before, or employ labour and machines of a new type. Data concerning usage, price, wastage, efficiency, etc., do not exist and, therefore, must be estimated. The danger is that once the bid has been accepted and a contractual obligation been undertaken, any adverse divergence from the projected costs will be harmful to the firm.

11. Bid pricing: uncertainty with existing product. Where one makes a bid for a product one already produces, the uncertainty of **10** above no longer exists, but a new set of problems emerges. The major one is of the effect of the bid on the net income of the firm if it is accepted.

(a) If the customer is a current customer the acceptance of the bid could lead to a lowering of income. If, however, the bid is lost income will fall further.

(b) If the bid is for units sold by a competitor, acceptance will increase income, but loss will leave income unchanged.

(c) If the bid is to a previous non-buyer, then what happens to income depends upon what the buyer does with the purchased goods. If he uses them himself, income will increase. If he resells them to your customers your income will still have increased, but by an amount less than the revenue you lost by his resale to your old customers.

12. The minimum bid. The minimum bid price is the incremental cost in each case, but the price chosen is not necessarily close to the minimum bid. The minimum bid as established by incremental cost is the rock-bottom price that could possibly be accepted. The actual price chosen will be set by considering competition for the bid and previous experience of the prices that have been accepted. It is essential, as it is for all these pricing techniques, that the price is evaluated in terms of its effect on the firm's income.

EXAMPLE 15: A small shipyard is making standard sailing boats with a production capacity of 100 per year. At present it is operating at 80 per cent capacity and the incremental cost of producing additional boats is £2,000. A firm of boat distributors would like to purchase twenty boats and is offering a contract in which it is prepared to pay £50,000 for them. Present selling price is £2,750. Comparing the price with the incremental cost indicates to the firm that the contract should be accepted, because a net contribution of £10,000 is earned. However, before acceptance the firm should ask itself a number of questions:

(*a*) What is the possibility that boat sales to normal sources will increase to 100 per cent of existing capacity? If demand from normal sources increased, the firm would not be able to meet the demand and would therefore be sacrificing £250 per boat.

(*b*) Is the availability of raw material sufficient to produce the extra boats without increasing the cost of this raw material?

(*c*) Is sufficient labour available at current wage rates to produce the twenty extra boats?

(*d*) What is the possibility that the buyer may purchase more boats in the future?

(*e*) Will the buyer of the twenty boats resell some of them to your existing customers? If the answer is yes, then revenue gained from the extra sales will fall by the amount of sales made by the buying firm to your old customers.

Evaluation of the minimum bid should therefore always take into account these five contingencies.

THE CORRECT APPROACH TO PRICING

13. Conclusions. Looking at these techniques, what have we learned? What common thread of knowledge exists that can help a firm in the situation where a pricing decision must be taken?

(*a*) Clear objectives must exist and price must be tailored to help meet those objectives.

(*b*) The true cost of the decision must be known (incremental cost).

(*c*) The total demand situation must be analysed.

(*d*) Qualitative and not just quantitative information must be taken into account.

(*e*) Total revenue and total cost must be evaluated at different price levels with varying assumptions.

(*f*) The establishment of a price must involve the participation of the accounting, marketing and production departments.

In the long-run, total revenue must exceed total cost, and this need for long-run survival has made full-cost pricing exceptionally popular. For TR to exceed TC there must be a mark-up added to total cost. All pricing therefore must be a form of full-cost pricing: where criticism is justified is in the determination of the mark-up. The pricing problem is too complicated for some general formula to be applicable in every case. We must understand the logic and develop a general approach to pricing, so that as we systematically ask the right questions and obtain relevant data our final task of applying a mark-up will be made easier. Incremental cost will always be the rock-bottom price but the price eventually charged will be determined by information concerning market structure and competition and government policy. Once a price has been established it is not necessarily kept indefinitely or charged to every customer. Future action with regard to price will depend upon the answers to the following questions.[3]

(*a*) Do we apply the price indefinitely into the future? (Product life cycle)

(*b*) Do we apply this price to everyone? (Individual negotiations)

(c) Do we apply it regardless of the quantity bought? (Discounts)

(d) Do we apply it regardless of the time factor? (Peak load problem)

(e) Do we apply it regardless of geography? (Price discrimination)

(f) Do we have to evaluate its effect on other products? (Inter-relationship of demand)

(g) Do we apply the price within the company? (Transfer pricing)

PROGRESS TEST 8

1. Why is it, in practice, difficult to price through the use of marginalism? (1)

2. "The pricing decision is the prerogative of the accountant because costs are the most important influence in pricing." Discuss. (2)

3. What are the main criticisms of full-cost pricing? (3)

4. Given the figures below, calculate the selling price assuming the firm is aiming for a target rate of return of 30 per cent.

Capital employed	£3 m
Fixed cost	£2 m
Variable cost per unit	£20
Normal production	£3 m (5)

5. What conditions must exist if target rate of return pricing is to be relatively successful? (5)

6. Explain what is meant by the minimum bid price. (12)

7. If no one formula can determine the price to charge, what should be the approach adopted by each firm? (1–12)

FURTHER READING

1. Lanzillotti, R. F., "Pricing Objectives in Large Companies", *American Economic Review*, Vol. 48, No. 5, December 1958, pp. 921–40.

Haynes, W. W., "Pricing Practices—Small Firms", *Southern Economic Journal*, Vol. 30. No. 4, 1964, pp. 315–24.

Hague, D. C., *Pricing in Business*, George Allen and Unwin, 1971.

2. Vere, J. C., *Pricing Techniques for the Financial Executive*, J. Wiley, 1974, pp. 149–50.

3. Davies, J. R. and Hughes, S., *Pricing in Practice*, Heinemann, 1975, Chapters 5 and 6.

CHAPTER IX

PRICING IN PRACTICE—PUBLIC ENTERPRISE

NATIONALISATION

1. Private v. public enterprise. Despite the emotive issues surrounding the concept of nationalisation there is nothing mystical about the purpose of public enterprise. It is simply an alternative way of providing the same basic service as private enterprise, namely, to provide goods or services for which there is a demand.

The government can interfere in industry in two main ways. The first involves regulation of the private sector not only by general fiscal and monetary policy, but also by a number of specific incentives such as investment grants and allowances, encouragement of research and development, regional incentives and other financial aids. Similarly, where discouragement of specific private enterprise behaviour is required, the government can introduce legislation relating to such issues as control of restrictive practices or monopoly legislation, and even prevent firms expanding in congested areas by the refusal to grant industrial development certificates. In this way, the government possesses a variety of instruments by which it can regulate the behaviour of the private sector.

However, where the government regards the performance of private enterprise to be so grossly inadequate that it does not respond to indirect action, then it can invoke the second alternative, that of seeking a solution through public ownership. Of course, in the case of nationalisation the issues are not only economic (*see* **10–12** below).

Public enterprise, then, simply involves a more direct form of government regulation of industry, in that the production process itself is publicly owned. The operation of public enterprise faces the same kind of problems that are met by private enterprise. However, in three respects public enterprise differs from the average private enterprise firm. In the

first place public enterprise is usually much larger than private
enterprise and often possesses a considerable degree of monopoly power. Secondly, because the nationalised industries are
publicly owned, they are accountable to Parliament and are
subject to political influence and control, particularly over the
achievement of commercial objectives. Finally, the nationalised industries have extremely high overhead costs which have
important implications for pricing policy (*see* **6–8** below).

It will not be possible to look in detail at the economic
problems of the nationalised industries. Since they vary so
widely it would demand a separate study of each industry.
The purpose of this Chapter is to examine briefly the general
principles governing the operation of the nationalised industries
in so far as they differ from that of private enterprise.

2. The trend towards nationalisation. It was during the
period 1946–51 that a significant part of British industry was
brought under public ownership. In 1946 the Labour government nationalised the Bank of England, the coal industry and
the air corporations. This was followed by the Transport Act
1947 nationalising the railways and other transport industries;
1947 saw the nationalisation of the rest of the electricity supply
industry. The gas industry was nationalised in 1948 and a
large part of the iron and steel industry in 1949.

On the whole, subsequent Conservative governments
accepted the fact of nationalisation, largely because it had been
concerned with the basic public utilities like gas, electricity,
etc. Indeed, the only service industry denationalised by the
1951 Conservative government was the partial denationalisa-
tion of long-distance road haulage. The most serious party-
political issue on nationalisation during this period involved a
manufacturing industry, steel, and it was no surprise when the
steel industry was denationalised by the Conservative government in 1953 (with the one exception of Richard Thomas and
Baldwin), and subsequently renationalised by the Labour
government in 1967.

During the 1970s the issue of public ownership again became
heated. The Conservative government of 1970–74 favoured a
policy of selling off the profitable sections of the nationalised
industries, although even they were forced to nationalise
Rolls-Royce when the company ran into financial difficulties
in 1971.

The Labour party returned to power in February 1974, and in the following August produced a White Paper on their proposals for nationalisation.

3. The 1974 White Paper. The most significant points to emerge from the White Paper were as follows:

(a) Development land, shipbuilding, aircraft building, ports, and parts of the road haulage and construction industries would be taken into public ownership and control, and the government would also hold a majority stake in North Sea oil.

(b) A National Enterprise Board would be set up whose main functions would be:

(i) to take over and purchase shares in selected manufacturing firms;

(ii) to act as a holding company to control the management of such firms;

(iii) to take over some firms in danger of collapse;

(iv) to provide investment capital and managerial help to firms in need;

(v) to help restructure industries; and

(vi) to start new business ventures.

(c) All firms under private control with sales in excess of £50 m p.a. would be invited to sign planning agreements, for three years ahead, with the government and their own workers. Such agreements would cover investment, prices, productivity, jobs, exports and regional development.

It is clear that this Labour government not only intended to extend considerably the scope of public ownership, but also to tighten significantly the reins of control over the private sector. It is not the intention here to argue the relative merits of these proposals but rather to consider the performance of the existing nationalised sector in the light of these far-reaching proposals.

FINANCIAL BURDEN OF COMPENSATION

4. The nature of compensation. Nationalisation involves the compulsory purchase of property. Naturally, the owners of such property expect to be compensated, and the terms on which such compensation is agreed can sometimes place a heavy financial burden on the operation of the nationalised industry.

The Nationalisation Acts in Britain have not been particularly good in providing general guidelines on the principles of compensation. Sometimes it was based on the market value of the acquired assets, sometimes on the net maintainable revenue that would have accrued to those assets in the absence of nationalisation, and sometimes on the annual debt charge of the undertaking.

(a) In the case of the *railways*, compensation was based upon the market value of the securities, and the owners were given freely-negotiable new government stock in exchange. In the event this turned out to be an over-generous compensation. Railway stock had been relatively overvalued because of the transfer of traffic to the railways during the war years. More importantly, the replacement of equity by fixed-interest stock meant that the annual fixed charges were now considerably higher. As M. Webb points out: "This increased the likelihood of the railways in future making financial losses, and given the need to borrow to meet current interest obligations, future debt charges would be increased and the possibility of profitable financial operations reduced." [1]

(b) In the case of both *electricity and gas*, compensation was far less generous, mainly because it was a transfer of assets within the public sector—from the local authorities to the new boards. The new boards simply took over the annual debt charges, thus undercompensating those local authorities which had ploughed back profits or redeemed their electricity and gas loans.

(c) The *coal industry*, on the other hand, is an example of compensation based upon the principle of net maintainable revenue, i.e. what the assets would be expected to earn if they were not nationalised. A tribunal valued the coal industry at £164·6 m, and government stock to this value was given as compensation.

5. Heavy fixed interest charges. The examples in **4** (a)–(c) above strikingly illustrate the variety of compensation principles which were applied to the nationalised industries. However, the important point is that the compensation payments, which were met by the issue of government-guaranteed stock, formed the initial capital of the various nationalised industries, and the annual interest charge forms part of their cost.

In view of the heavy fixed interest charges on the nationalised industries arising from the nature of compensation, it is not surprising that from time to time debts have been written off. Indeed, during the 1970s the nationalised industries were even compensated by the government for holding their prices down. It was for this reason that they were released from the obligation of paying their way between 1971 and 1974.

FEATURES OF THE NATIONALISED INDUSTRIES

In general, the nationalised industries incorporate a number of distinctive features not possessed by the vast majority of private firms, particularly opportunities and constraints which affect their operation.

6. Monopoly problems. The nationalised industries are monopolies and most are in a position to exploit their monopoly power. It is, of course, true that usually there are close substitutes, in that oil is a close substitute for coal, gas or electricity. Nevertheless, the National Coal Board has a monopoly of coal production and is clearly in a position where it could substantially raise the price of its product without significantly reducing its sales in the short-run. In the long-run, such a policy would undoubtedly lead to a switch to other fuels as consumers switched their appliances from coal-based to alternative energy sources. However, despite the greater degree of price elasticity in the long-run, it is still likely that high initial conversion costs would enable the National Coal Board to maintain a relatively high level of output even in the long-run. Moreover, coal is an important input to other fuels so that this, too, tends to reduce the extent of substitution that takes place.

Whether or not one would have agreed with this analysis prior to the 1974 oil crisis, it is now abundantly clear that the nationalised fuel industries are in a much more powerful position to exploit their monopoly power should they wish to do so. A profit-maximising private enterprise would take advantage of the relatively inelastic demand facing the coal industry. However, the National Coal Board is expected to show restraint in the way it exercises its monopoly power.

7. Cost structure. The cost structure of most nationalised industries is such that fixed costs form a relatively large, and running costs a relatively small, part of operating expenses. The nationalised industries are enormous users of capital equipment, and the need to finance such heavy capital expenditures was one of the major reasons for their nationalisation.

Besides the sheer cost of financing such expenditures, there is also the problem of arriving at efficient pricing criteria, since the cost-allocation problem is likely to be an enormous problem where overheads form such a large part of total costs. Perhaps more important in this respect are the financial problems caused by marginal cost-pricing in decreasing cost industries. Thus, not only do the nationalised industries have the problem of identifying marginal cost (the cost-allocation problem), but also the financial problems of operating a marginal cost-pricing policy in decreasing cost industries. We will return to these problems in **16** below.

8. The public interest. The nationalised industries were regarded as being so important to the economy that they should be officially designed to serve the "public interest". In this respect it is worth noting that the nationalised industries provide important inputs to the rest of the economy, particularly to fuel and transport. It was with the ideal of the "public interest" in mind, and with the desire to maintain parliamentary control over the nationalised industries, that the systems of ministerial control and public accountability through Parliament were established.

However, the concept of the public interest proved to be extremely elusive in practice. This was due partly to inadequate definition of the term and partly to the blurring of responsibility between ministers and nationalised industry boards.

WHAT WAS NATIONALISATION TO ACHIEVE?

9. Objectives. The objectives of nationalisation are economic, political and social in nature, the relative weighting of these components varying with the value judgments of the individual.

It has, however, been a noticeable feature of nationalisation debates in Britain that such issues tend to be dominated by economic considerations. The reason for this is not that economic considerations are regarded as more important than anything else, but simply because they tend to be a more acceptable rationale for nationalisation.

10. Economic issues.

(a) *Scale.* Because of the co-ordination required, for example between different regional transportation networks, it was essential that these should be brought under one control in order to provide an efficient service. It is clear that technical economies of scale can only be achieved by integration and central co-ordination of the public utilities.

(b) *Wasteful competition.* As already pointed out in **7** above, the nationalised industries are enormous users of fixed capital and it would consequently be ridiculous for different companies to provide different sets of railway lines, electricity cables, etc., all of which would be under-utilised. It is essential, therefore, in industries with heavy overhead costs, that capacity should not greatly exceed demand. Such an outcome is only possible by restricting competition.

(c) *Problem of finance.* In any industries that are heavy users of fixed capital, the problems of capital replacement and expansion are severe. In Britain, this problem was worsened by the Second World War which saw the run-down of fixed investment in basic industries such as the railways, electricity and coal. Private enterprise at this time was in no condition to raise the vast amount of capital required, and so it became essential that such finance should come from public sources.

11. Political issues.

(a) *Government planning.* Most of the ideological issues concerning nationalisation were based upon the fundamental belief that control of the so-called "commanding heights" of the economy is essential to any kind of government planning and control. The "commanding heights" were identified as the provision of fuel, power and transport. It is quite clear that these are strategic industries whose control is fundamental to any effective economic planning. It is worth noting the havoc created in Western economies by the upward price adjustment of Arab-produced oil. Although it is true that reduced demand forced the oil-producing countries to moderate their policies, it will take some time to rectify the damage inflicted on the world's economies by the oil pricing policies of 1974/5.

It is little wonder then that control of fuel and transport were regarded as essential for economic planning purposes.

(b) *Redistribution of income.* It was hoped that national-isation would bring about a better distribution of national income. In some quarters this was seen as a gradual move-ment towards public ownership of the means of production and the eventual elimination of private property.

12. Social issues.

(a) *Social services.* It was recognised that the operation of transport services on purely profitable lines would lead to the closing down of many rural transport services, causing great inconvenience to the local communities involved. It was argued that nationalised industries were owned by the public and should provide a good service to all members of the community. Thus social services, such as rural trans-port facilities, are very much part of the operation of nationalised undertakings.

(b) *Regional unemployment.* All post-war British govern-ments have emphasised their commitment to full employ-ment. Moreover, the plight of the depressed areas brought many social issues to the forefront. Government attempts to attract new industry to the depressed regions have met with only limited success. It was against this background that the uneconomic coal pits were closed at a much slower rate than would have been dictated by purely financial considera-tions. The steel industry in 1976 faced extreme difficulties in tackling its over-manning problem not only because of a high level of general unemployment but also because much of the cut-back needed would have taken place in depressed regions such as South Wales.

HOW IMPORTANT ARE PROFITS?

13. Government guidelines on profitability: the 1961 White Paper. In the past, government legislation has not been particu-larly helpful. The major statutory requirement in the 1940s was that the nationalised industries should pay their way taking one year with another, which meant that deficits and surpluses would cancel out over a period of time. These guidelines were extremely inadequate since they gave no indication of the kind of pricing and investment policies which would achieve this objective. The result was that some of the nationalised industries made a loss while others earned a low rate of return compared with the private sector.

The inadequacy of these guidelines led to the 1961 White Paper [2] which decreed that:

(a) surpluses should cover deficits over a 5-year period;

(b) provision should be made for depreciation at replacement cost rather than at historic cost;

(c) an overall rate of return would be negotiated with each industry according to its circumstances, particularly the extent to which the industry would be required to undertake unprofitable ventures; and

(d) investment would be allocated according to a 5-year capital development plan.

Once again, however, there were no basic guidelines as to how these objectives were to be achieved, particularly pricing and investment policies.

14. The 1967 White Paper. The deficiencies in the 1961 White Paper were remedied in the 1967 White Paper [3] which decreed that:

(a) if the average target rates of return set for each industry conflicted with the application of correct pricing and investment rules, then it was more important that the correct pricing and investment rules should be applied;

(b) prices should be based upon long-run marginal cost;

(c) cross-subsidisation may be justified in some cases;

(d) the financial responsibilities for social obligations lay with the government; and

(e) discounted cash flow techniques or social cost/benefit analysis should be used for investment appraisal purposes.

However, despite the impressive array of pricing and investment techniques available since the 1967 White Paper, the nationalised industries were released from the obligation to pay their way during the early 1970s which was notable for being a period of indiscriminate subsidies. However, from 1975 onwards the emphasis was placed upon making the nationalised industries profitable. The major price rises necessary to achieve this were followed by the publication of the 1978 White Paper which reiterated the prominant role that profitability was to play in the new strategy for the industries. The White Paper stated bluntly that "the Government intends that the nationalised industries will not be forced into deficits by restraints on their prices".[10] The main guidelines decreed in the new White Paper were:

(a) financial performance to be evaluated by means of a financial target to be set for each industry on a 3 to 5 year basis;

(b) new investment was to be required to earn a real rate of return of 5 per cent before tax;

(c) there was also to be non-financial performance indicators so that the public could be better informed on the industries' "success" in controlling costs and increasing efficiency.

Thus once again an impressive array of financial criteria was laid down for the nationalised industries. However, in practice, the operation of the guidelines laid down in the 1978 White Paper has become subservient to the desire to meet the cash limits imposed by the Government.

15. Economic efficiency and profits. In terms of the limited economic objectives of removing wasteful competition and stimulating economies of scale, the nationalised industries have achieved some degree of success. However, in terms of the operation of efficient pricing and investment criteria they have met with a large degree of failure. As already pointed out in **14** above, it was not until 1967 that the industries received technically correct guidelines from the government, but even these became quickly inoperative as price restraint and investment regulation became more important foundation stones of the government's macro-economic policy.

Moreover, even without the distortive effects of government interference, the heavy fixed-cost structure of many of the nationalised industries makes it difficult to achieve efficient pricing policies simultaneously with a profitability target.

Economic theorists generally regard marginal cost-pricing as the most efficient pricing technique in terms of achieving the optimum allocation of resources. The problem is that in industries with very heavy overhead costs, marginal cost-pricing will lead to deficits, since the decreasing cost-structure will mean that marginal cost will be less than average cost.

16. Marginal cost-pricing. Figure 43 demonstrates that as long as AC falls with an expansion of output (since overheads will now be spread over more units of output), MC must be below AC, so that a pricing policy based upon MC is bound to lead to deficits. In Fig. 43, OP and OQ are the respective

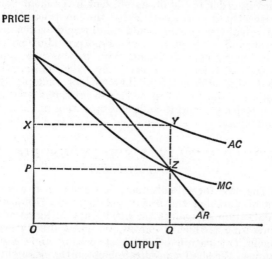

Fig. 43—*Marginal cost pricing*. Deficit caused by marginal cost pricing in an industry where AC is continually falling since price will be equal to MC which is less than AC.

price and output resulting from marginal cost-pricing, but because of the continuously declining AC curve this price and output policy leads to a deficit equal to $PXYZ$. This is the inevitable outcome of a pricing policy based upon marginal cost in a decreasing-cost industry.

Thus decreasing-cost industries are faced by the dilemma of whether to optimise the use of existing resources by applying marginal cost-pricing techniques or whether to disregard this ideal in favour of a policy that will be profitable. The 1967 White Paper sought a way out of this by suggesting that prices should be based upon long-run marginal cost. By making all costs variable in the long-run it was pointed out that all costs would be covered. Moreover, a sensible pricing policy would also enable the nationalised industries to apply efficient investment appraisal techniques in the same manner as private enterprise.

It must be recognised, of course, that long-run marginal cost-pricing does entail some welfare loss in the use of existing facilities, but it is generally accepted that this is a necessary sacrifice in order to obtain an efficient investment policy. In this respect it is worth noting that the low prices that short-run marginal cost-pricing would entail would artificially stimulate demand while at the same time providing no efficient base for investment decisions. Seen in this light, long-run marginal cost-pricing is a necessary compromise, which, if pursued with sufficient flexibility (as, for example, efficient utilisation of short-run capacity), will provide a solid foundation on which to build the efficient operation of the nationalised industries.

SHOULD NATIONALISED INDUSTRIES BE SUBSIDISED?

17. The case for subsidisation. This rests upon the relative merits of pursuing the social and ideological objectives of nationalisation as against the inefficiency in terms of pricing and investment which it entails. We have already examined the inefficient nature of incorrect pricing and investment techniques. We shall concentrate here on the possibilities for, and implications of, subsidisation in a number of specific cases.

18. Subsidisation of public road-passenger transport. The major argument in favour of subsidising public road-passenger transport lies with the assumption that if so subsidised, less people would use their cars, with a consequent saving in congestion costs, i.e. the extra cost each motorist imposes on other road users by congesting the roads. However, a fare reduction on public road-passenger transport would not only divert traffic from private cars to public transport but would also induce some non-motorists to make journeys that have a value to them less than their resource cost. While the traffic diverting effect would reduce congestion, the traffic generating effect would increase congestion. Thus estimates of price elasticity of demand for each of these groups is particularly important here.

The major problem of subsidisation is that motorists tend to belong to high income groups and are relatively unresponsive to price changes in public transport. Baum[4] demonstrates that estimates of demand elasticity by motorists are from 0.1 to 0.4 and concludes that the effect of fare reductions on traffic diversion is small. Similarly, Moses and Williamson[5] have estimated that even completely free public transport in Chicago would cause only 13 percent of motorists to switch for their journeys to work.

In the light of this evidence it would appear that motorists' demand for public transport is likely to be less elastic than that of non-motorists. Moreover, the majority of public transport journeys are already made by non-motorists. The combination of these two factors is likely to mean that the traffic generating effect will be more important than the traffic diverting effect. As E. V. Morgan points out: "Any possible reduction in fares is unlikely to have more than a marginal effect on the volume of private motoring (and hence traffic congestion) and any benefits derived therefrom are quite likely to be outweighed by the losses on trips whose value is less than their resource costs."[6]

Despite the apparent attraction of reducing congestion, the economic case for subsidising public road-passenger transport is not a strong one.

19. Cross-subsidisation to avoid regional unemployment.

Cross-subsidisation involves the use of profits from one area of activity to subsidise the unremunerative aspects of other areas of activity. This technique has been extensively used in the coal-mining industry in order to combat the effects of regional unemployment. The 1967 White Paper explicitly condemned cross-subsidisation as a general principle, stating that "to cross-subsidise loss making services amounts to taxing remunerative services provided by the same undertaking and is as objectionable as subsidising, from general taxation, services which have no social justification".[7] Nevertheless, the

White Paper did concede that cross-subsidisation may be applicable in certain specific cases where it is justified on wider economic or social grounds.

Whether or not cross-subsidisation will be successful depends essentially on the inelasticity of demand in profitable undertakings, since price increases will only bring in further revenue if demand is inelastic. However, even where such demand inelasticity exists, cross-subsidisation still has the undesirable effect of retarding changes in industrial structure since the subsidised activity's demand will be artificially stimulated by its subsidised price. Moreover, this will lead in turn to a considerable pressure on the industry to direct its new investment to these depressed areas. Such a policy, if continued indefinitely, could lead to the growth of high-cost activities at the expense of low-cost activities, eventually endangering the existence of the entire industry.

Nevertheless, as a short-run policy, cross-subsidisation can play a considerable role in alleviating the problems of depressed areas until such time as new industries can establish themselves in these areas. In the last analysis the multiple effects of prolonged unemployment in an area may be more damaging than the structural effects of cross-subsidisation. It is important, however, that the use of cross-subsidisation as a short-run instrument to combat regional unemployment is accompanied by a positive policy of stimulating new industries to move into the area.

20. Subsidisation and the management of the economy. One of the major arguments in favour of subsidising the nationalised industries is that they have not been free to manipulate their pricing and investment policies in accordance with strict commercial principles. As a result they have suffered from three major aspects of interference:

(a) First, they have been subjected recently to severe price restraint which is damaging to profitability. This was due to the government's efforts to use their control over the public sector as a major weapon of anti-inflation policy.

(b) Secondly, the investment policies of the nationalised industries have similarly been used to combat the unemployment problem, sometimes to the detriment of the industries concerned.

(*c*) Finally, the industries have sometimes been forced to use high-cost inputs and to delay the closing down of high-cost operations. The Central Electricity Generating Board, for example, were subsidised for burning coal instead of oil in power stations, and the National Coal Board were compensated for delaying pit closures.

21. Evaluation of subsidies. The problem with general subsidies is not only that they encourage inefficiency and make the operation of a sound investment policy extremely difficult, but also that they involve the redistribution of income from the general tax-payer to consumers of the product. Even if deficits are financed by borrowing from the government, this eventually leads to subsidisation by the tax-payer as debts are written off. On the other hand, if subsidies are to be selective and separately financed, as suggested by the 1967 White Paper, there is the inevitable problem of defining which social obligation qualifies for a subsidy.

Of course, all these arguments against subsidies become largely irrelevant if one accepts the ideological position that the whole purpose of nationalisation is to control the "commanding heights of the economy" in a way that makes effective economic planning and control possible. If one accepts that the nationalised industries should be used as an instrument of macro-economic and social policy, the case for subsidisation is considerably strengthened.

HAVE THE NATIONALISED INDUSTRIES BEEN SUCCESSFUL?

22. How is success measured? The relative degree of success achieved by the nationalised industries is extremely controversial. The problem is that success can only be judged in the light of objectives, and as we have already observed, the enumeration of such objectives involves deep political and ideological convictions. Certainly the nationalised industries have achieved some degree of success in terms of rationalisation and economies of scale, of social achievement in terms of regional employment and social services, and of contribution to ideological motives in terms of control of the economy and public ownership.

However, economists are reluctant to make value judgments, and find it difficult to appraise industries in political and social terms. Moreover, the very acceptance of non-economic objectives makes it difficult to apply the usual yardstick of profitability as a measure of business efficiency. Continuous political interference with pricing and investment policies, considerations of the public interest and the monopolistic character of each nationalised industry invalidate the role of profits as the measure of economic performance.

Having down-graded the role of profits as a measure of economic performance, what do we put in its place? Pryke has suggested that in the nationalised industries labour productivity might be the appropriate measure to use. [8] With this yardstick, he has demonstrated that the nationalised industries have out-performed the private sector, particularly during the 1960s when more sophisticated management techniques were employed in the nationalised industries. Judged thus, the nationalised industries appear to be efficient. However, G. and P. Polanyi [9] take a substantially different view of the nationalised industries. They conclude that "the record of the nationalised industries compared with that of private industry, measured by any of the usually accepted indicators of efficiency, shows generally inferior performance" and that "there are no aspects of this performance which provide evidence of the inherent superiority of public ownership". This conclusion was based on evidence relating the losses made by the nationalised industries, their poorer net return on assets and lower value output per £100 of capital and labour as compared with private-sector manufacturing industry.

Which of these conclusions should we support? The answer surely lies in the fact that while nationalised industries possess a wide range of economic, social and political objectives, it is unlikely that any single statistical yardstick will provide an appropriate measure of comparison with the private sector.

PROGRESS TEST 9

1. In what ways do compensation payments affect the operation of the nationalised industries? (**4, 5**)
2. Explain the nature of the cost-allocation problem in the nationalised industries. (**6, 7**)

3. What are the objectives of the nationalised industries? Have these objectives been achieved?   **(9–12)**

4. What are the implications of marginal cost-pricing in decreasing-cost industries?   **(16)**

5. Assess the relative merits of the 1961 and 1967 White Papers.   **(13–16)**

6. Examine the case for and against the subsidisation of public road-passenger transport.   **(18)**

7. How can we measure efficiency in the nationalised industries? **(22)**

FURTHER READING

1. Webb, M. G., *The Economics of Nationalised Industries*, Nelson, 1973, p. 6.

2. Cmnd. 1337, *The Financial and Economic Obligations of the Nationalised Industries*, H.M.S.O., 1961.

3. Cmnd. 3437, *Nationalised Industries; A Review of Economic and Financial Objectives*, H.M.S.O., 1967.

4. Baum, H. J., "Free Public Transport", *Journal of Transport Economics and Policy*, January 1973.

5. Moses, L. N. and Williamson, H. F., "Value of Time, Choice of Mode, and Subsidy Issue in Urban Transportation", *Journal of Political Economy*, 1963.

6. Morgan, E. V., "Pricing, Investment Decisions and subsidies in Transport", *Manchester School of Economics and Social Studies* September 1974, p. 252.

7. Cmnd. 3437, *op. cit.*

8. Pryke, R., *Public Enterprise in Practice*, MacGibbon and Kee, 1971.

9. Polanyi, G. and P., *Failing the Nation*, Fraser Ansbacher Ltd. (Merchant Bankers), 1974.

10. Cmnd. 7131, *The Nationalised Industries*, H.M.S.O. 1978.

CHAPTER X

PRACTICAL PRICING PROBLEMS

INTRODUCTION

IN Chapter VIII we discussed the pricing problem of a firm selling a familiar product, to an outside market. There are situations, however, where complications arise that require special treatment.

(a) Transfer prices, i.e. the price charged by different divisions of the same firm for goods and services exchanged between them.

(b) The pricing of new products.

While the overall logic used in the last chapter is still essential, extra factors now need to be considered in deciding upon a price.

TRANSFER PRICES

1. Divisional organisations. As merger activity continues and concentration increases the U.K. industrial system is becoming increasingly composed of multi-product, multi-process companies. To facilitate greater efficiency and hence profitability it has been shown that the organisation of these large firms on a divisional basis (each division being a profit centre) is advantageous.

(a) It provides a systematic means of delegating a portion of the decision-making responsibility to personnel below top management.

(b) A manager can only make effective decisions concerning the allocation of scarce resources if he is responsible for profits, and this divisional responsibility brings decision-takers closer to the company's profit objectives.

(c) Managers' performance can be evaluated more precisely.

(d) It enables the contribution of each profit centre to the profitability of the firm as a whole to be measured.

2. Sub-optimising. For the advantages of divisional organisation to be obtained it is essential that sub-optimising should not occur, i.e. the economic decisions of the divisional manager should affect divisional profits consistently with company profits. There is a danger that because each division is a profit centre and each divisional manager knows that his performance is being evaluated on the basis of profit earned, he will attempt to increase his profits, possibly by increasing the price he charges (transfer price) to another division. The effect of this could be that, although his own division's profits may increase, company profits may fall.

All inter-profit-centre relationship systems, therefore, are compromises between allowing independent divisional decision-making and ensuring optimum overall decision-making. The degree of compromise should depend principally on the amount and type of inter-profit-centre transactions.

3. The need for transfer prices. If the establishment of transfer prices causes so much difficulty, why is it necessary? Why, particularly in a firm that is organised vertically, are prices needed at all? Would it not be easier to pass on products from one division to another and from one process to the next, and merely calculate total company profit? The answer here is an emphatic "no":

(*a*) Abolition of transfer prices prevents meaningful measurement of the profits of individual operating units.

(*b*) It also prevents accurate estimation of the earnings on proposed investment projects.

(*c*) Transfer prices give the divisional manager an economic base and incentive for correct decision-making, i.e. the allocation of scarce resources.

(*d*) It is a means of obtaining decentralisation, which most large firms seem convinced is the right thing to do.

4. Determining the transfer price. The actual transfer price chosen will depend upon:

(*a*) Whether a market price for the product already exists.

(*b*) The market structure under which the firm operates.

(*c*) Whether the separate divisions of the firm are independent or inter-dependent.

Inter-dependence is stronger if the firm is organised vertically, and if no outside supplier exists, or if an outsider supplier does exist and his supply of the relevant good is not reliable.

Transfer prices may therefore be determined by the following methods:

(a) Market prices.
(b) Negotiated or bargained market price.[1]
(c) Same-cost concept, marginal or full-cost.

5. Transfer price based on market price.

It is generally recognised[2] that if a market price exists and the market is competitive, i.e. no one producer can significantly affect market price by varying his output, then the market price should be the correct transfer price. This is so because the market price represents the relevant or opportunity cost to the firm concerned.

EXAMPLE 16: A firm is organised into two divisions: Division A is the buying division which eventually markets the product; and Division B is the selling division, which also manufactures the product. If Division A bought from Division B at a price lower than the existing market price, then it would be sub-optimising at the expense of Division B because its alternative source of supply is the higher market price, and the alternative market for Division B is the market price. The opportunity cost for Division B in selling at a price lower than market price to Division A would be the difference between the market price and the price charged to Division A, multiplied by the quantity transferred. If the opposite occurred, and Division B sold goods to Division A at a price which exceeded market price, then Division B would be sub-optimising at the expense of Division A and the firm as a whole. Division B would appear more profitable than it actually was, and there is a danger that because of this impression more resources would be channelled into that Division (capital investment).

The use of a market transfer price, where possible, will create the actual market conditions under which these divisions would operate if they were actually separate companies, rather than divisions of one organisation. Furthermore, to the extent that market prices can be established on the basis of outside forces, they form an excellent performance indicator because they cannot be manipulated by individuals who have an interest in the resulting profit calculations.

6. Difficulty of using market prices. Using and obtaining the necessary market prices is not always easy. Even in those industries where prices are published, care must be taken to ensure that:

(a) your product is comparable to the industry product in every way, i.e. size, quality, etc.;

(b) local conditions do not make different prices necessary, i.e. extra transportation or handling of the product;

(c) published prices reflect the current state of the market and are not affected by any time lag in obtaining and publishing the information;

(d) the current open market is a valid alternative for the intra-company buyer or seller, i.e. intra-company transactions may be so large in relation to the transactions in the open market that any attempt to obtain supplies there would drive prices up, and any attempt to sell them there would drive prices down.

Despite these provisos, if a market price can be established it is probably the best price to use for performance evaluation.

7. Transfer price based on negotiated or bargained market price. This method has been suggested by Joel Dean, and provided that each division of the firm is a profit centre and that the divisional managers have complete autonomy centrally in their operations, he suggests that transfer prices can be established between divisions, if three simple procedures are followed:

(a) Prices of all transfers in and out of a profit centre should be determined by negotiations between buyers and sellers.

(b) Negotiators should have access to full data on alternative sources and markets and to public and private information about market prices.

(c) Buyers and sellers should be completely free to deal outside the company.

Such a scheme has advantages over basing transfer price on market prices, particularly where establishing a correct market price is extremely difficult, if not impossible. It is also applicable where market price does not provide the true picture because selling costs to another division are so much lower than selling costs on the open market.

8. Transfer prices based on cost. Where no outside market exists and where a firm is organised vertically, a series of transfer prices will be required that will achieve *the best joint level of output*. This will also apply where, even though a market price exists, the firm for strategic or other reasons wishes to produce the majority of its own components.

> EXAMPLE 17: A firm is divided into three divisions, *A*, *B* and *C*. Division *A* produces components which are then further processed by Division *B* and then sold by the Marketing Division, *C*. Subject to the constraint that the firm feels for strategic reasons that it must produce the majority of its own components in order to maximise profits, it must solve the following problems:
>
> (*a*) What output should be achieved?
> (*b*) How are transfer prices to be determined between the divisions?
> (*c*) What level of profit is to be earned by each division?

Let us now look at how each of these questions should be answered.

9. Determination of output. The best joint level of output will be determined at that level of output where total marginal cost (TMC) is equal to marginal revenue. To obtain this output, each divisional manager should prepare a schedule of the respective *processing costs* for various levels of output. This will then give the marginal cost of producing each extra unit. These marginal cost curves can be added together to give a TMC curve, and by comparing the TMC curve with the MR curve the best joint level of output is obtained.

In Fig. 44 (*a*)–(*c*) the marginal cost curves of Divisions *A*, *B* and *C* are shown. *OX*, *MY* and *NZ* are the fixed costs incurred by each of the divisions. Figure 45 shows the TMC curve and the profit of the firm will be maximised where $TMC = MR$ at point *J* with output at OQ_1.

10. Determination of transfer prices. Now by looking at each of the divisional marginal cost schedules, the marginal cost of producing the Q_1th unit can be obtained, and transfer

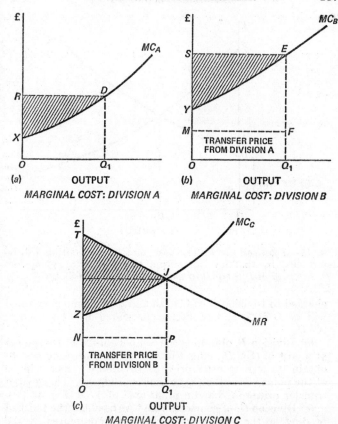

FIG. 44—*Marginal cost curves for divisions.* In determining inter-divisional prices at output OQ_1, each division will use as a transfer price the cost of producing the OQ_1th unit, i.e. Division A will charge OR for each unit sold to Division B.

prices between each Division will be built up in the following manner:

(a) For output OQ_1 Division A has incurred a total cost of $OXDQ_1$ (Fig. 44 (a)). It will use as a transfer price the marginal cost of producing the OQth unit, so, therefore, price

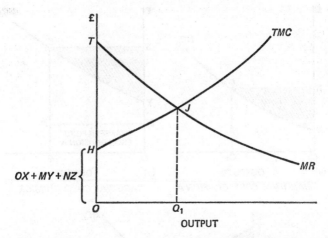

FIG. 45—*Total cost curve.* The best joint level of output will be determined by that level of output where total marginal cost (*TMC*) is equal to marginal revenue (*MR*).

charged to Division *B* will be *OR* and total revenue obtained will be *ORDQ₁* and profit is represented by the triangle *XRD*.

(*b*) Division *B*, obtaining the components from Division *A* at a cost of *ORDQ₁*, adds this cost to its processing cost to obtain its own transfer price to Division *C* which will be at the point where the *OQ₁*th unit is produced. This gives a transfer price of *OS* and a profit area of *YSE* (Fig. 44 (*b*)).

(*c*) Division *C*, of course, is faced with selling the finished product on the open market. Profit is represented by the area *ZTJ* (Fig. 44 (*c*)).

11. Profitability of each division. The over-riding aim should be to maximise the profits of the firm as a whole and as can be seen from Fig. 44, different levels of profit are earned by each division. It is extremely important that managers responsible for decision-taking should understand that it is not necessary for each division to earn the same profit. It is the maximisation of total company profits which is important and any attempt by a divisional manager to increase his profit at the expense of another division (sub-optimisation) would lead to total company profits falling.

In Fig. 46 we have assumed that the manager of Division A has deliberately overstated his costs so as to increase the transfer price he charges to Division B and therefore increase his profit. The result of this falsification is that central

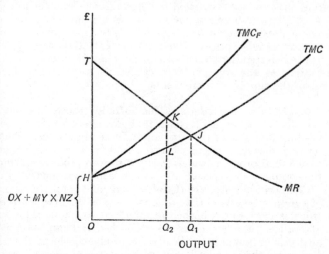

FIG. 46—*Overstatement of costs to increase divisional profits.* The result of overstatement is to create a false TMC curve, TMC_F. The firm now believes that profit maximising output is OQ_2. The result is that total profit falls by an amount LKJ to area $HLKT$.

management will derive a different TMC curve than previously, namely TMC_F. This curve is higher than the original TMC curve and cuts the MR curve at output OQ_2 which is to the left of OQ_1. The result, of course, is that total company profits fall from being equal to the area HTJ to area $HTKL$, a fall of LKJ.

12. Use of transfer prices in practice. Most large firms organised on a divisional basis produce a number of products that require many different components. The conditions in the market for each of these components varies enormously, and the firm will find itself purchasing and selling components under market conditions that range from near-perfect competition to monopoly. The calculation of the correct transfer price between divisions, therefore, can be straightforward in the case where a ready market already exists or extremely difficult where marginal cost curves and marginal revenue curves have to be constructed to determine the transfer price.

Accepting these varied conditions, central management in practice must develop some guidelines for the divisions to calculate transfer prices. One such system[3] divides all products transferred between divisions into one of four categories, according to the sourcing restrictions, i.e. restrictions that exist in the supply of components.

(a) *Category 1 products*. This includes those products transferred between divisions that are likely never to be produced outside of the company. These are products that for such reasons as quality control, secrecy, or relative value to the final product, management wishes to produce within the company irrespective of economic considerations.

Competitive prices are therefore unavailable for this type of product because of its uniqueness, and in practice the transfer price is established at standard cost plus a profit allowance. Standard costs are established and agreed on by all divisions (not only by the division producing the product). By using the standard cost as a base, any actual cost incurred which is higher than standard cost must be absorbed by that division. It is not allowed, in other words, to pass on its inefficiency to another division which is a captive customer. The profit allowance is a negotiated figure based upon capital employed, percentage return earned by similar products, and average percentage return earned by other products in the firm.

(b) *Category 2 products*. These are products that management may be willing to purchase from outside sources, but only on a relatively long-term basis, because their manufacture requires a significant investment in facilities and skills.

These products should be priced at estimated long-run competitive prices. By definition, the source of these products is likely to be changed only infrequently because of the amount of special equipment or special expertise required. Consequently, short-term price fluctuations only confuse the situation.

The source of such products should be changed only after a study of the total impact of such a change on the company profits. It should not be made unilaterally, even by the divisions directly involved.

(c) *Category 3 products*. These are products that can be produced outside the company without any significant disruption to present operations. They will be relatively small in volume and produced with general-purpose equipment. No problem arises in pricing them, because a ready market exists with prices clearly established.

(d) *Category 4 products*. These are products that can be bought and sold within and outside the company. Establishing a transfer price as in (c) above is relatively easy because of the existence of an established outside market.

This has been only a brief introduction to a very difficult practical problem but the student should be aware of the difficulties as the majority of people working in industry now belong to firms which are organised on a divisional basis, with each division trading, to some degree, with each other. There is no question that from a position of optimising profits and resource-allocation the use of market prices (if they exist) is to be desired. Given the multi-plant, multi-product complications of the real world, coupled to the fact that profit-maximisation is not the only objective pursued by firms, some practical guidelines (as in (a)–(d) above) are essential to aid divisional managers. These guidelines unfortunately depart from the strict logic of economics, yet the lack of adequate cost and revenue data and practical necessity make this departure inevitable.

PRICING NEW PRODUCTS

Business men are always short of information that will enable perfect decisions to be made, and this problem is particularly acute in the case of pricing a new product. There is no past information on which to establish trends or to determine consumer reactions. One therefore has to categorise one's product by asking a number of questions and then choose what appears to be the appropriate strategy.

13. What is meant by "new"? A product may be new because it is new to the firm producing it, but not new to the market in general because similar products are already being produced by competitors. A product may also be new because it is a new-product concept and is therefore new to the firm and new to the industry. Except for certain cases, which will quickly become clear, the pricing strategies discussed here are more applicable to a new-product concept.

14. Maintaining distinctiveness. The fact that a firm is producing a new product which is new to the industry means that, if handled correctly, the firm can possibly earn very good profits as a result of its uniqueness. Competitors will constantly be alert to new profit opportunities and therefore the distinctiveness of a new product is very temporary. How quickly a product loses its distinctiveness depends upon the following factors.

(a) Total sales potential.
(b) Investment required for rivals to manufacture and distribute the product.
(c) Strength of patent protection.
(d) Alertness and power of competitors.

The price chosen can have the dual role of keeping competitors at bay and earning good profits for the firm over the life of the product. The price chosen, however, must make a profit and must succeed in getting the product accepted.[4]

15. Choice of strategy. The length of life of a product and the speed of competitors' reactions are vital to the choice of pricing strategy, and keeping in mind the incremental cost of the product and the psychological effect of the price on the consumer (*see* Chapter IV, 20), the firm can choose to implement two strategies.

(a) *Skimming pricing.* Achieving the maximum contribution to profit in the shortest possible time by charging the highest possible price that the market will bear.

(b) *Penetration pricing.* Achieving the maximum market penetration by charging a low price to create large-volume sales.

Let us look at these two strategies in detail to establish the circumstances under which they would be adopted.

16. Skimming strategy. For products that represent a drastic departure from accepted ways of performing a service or filling a demand, a strategy of high prices coupled with large promotional expenditures in the early stages of market development has frequently proved successful. Skimming pricing is likely to be successful under the following conditions:

(a) Where the life cycle of the product is expected to be short—a feature of markets with a high rate of innovation incidence, e.g. fashions.

(b) With new-product concepts where the buyer has no measuring rod for comparisons of value and utility.

(c) Where sales seem relatively inelastic to price, but responsive to information promotion.

(d) Where one can take the cream of the market at a high price before attempting to penetrate the more price-sensitive areas. This measure can get more money from those who do not care how much they pay, while building up experience to fill the mass market with lower prices.

(e) Where one wishes to feel out demand. It is frequently easier to start with a high refusal price and later reduce it when the facts relating to demand become known, than to set a low price initially and then boost it to cover unforeseen costs.

(f) Where a fund is required to finance the product through its costly initial phases of introduction.

(g) Where future product modifications and improvements to meet changing consumer concepts of utility can be incorporated without price changes.

(h) Where the company has limited manufacturing facilities to produce the product or a small sales force to promote it, operation in a small but highly profitable segment of the market in the premium area may be most economic for the company.

17. Penetration strategy. This strategy is likely to be desirable under the following conditions:

(a) Where a high degree of price elasticity exists even in the early stages of introduction.

(b) Where high-volume sales will tend to give economies of large-scale production.

(c) Where the product is faced with threats of strong potential competition very soon after introduction. Such a policy tends to discourage competitive entry into the market as short- to medium-term profits will appear to be low and if a high level of investment is required in plant, labour and other production facilities.

(d) Where there is no "elite" market, i.e. a body of buyers who are willing to pay a much higher price in order to obtain the latest and best.

(e) In certain conditions a low price may penetrate an important section of the market not yet tapped by existing high-priced products.

18. Competitors' reactions. It is the speed with which competitors react and attempt to bring out a substitute that is really the prime factor to be taken into consideration when deciding on a policy of skimming or penetration. A skimming strategy can be turned into a penetration strategy at any stage in a product's life cycle, but a close watch must constantly be kept on one's competitors. A high initial price might have spurred one into making some initial investment with the intention of competing, and the fact that a firm later lowers its price might not deter a potential new entrant if he has proceeded to a certain point in his investment programme.

19. Conclusion. The pricing of a new product is logically no different from that of pricing any product. The first step for any firm is to calculate the incremental cost to the firm of producing it at all. This step is made more difficult in the case of a new product because new production processes may be in operation, heavy promotional expenditure may be required in the early life of the product and research and development expenditure may be particularly heavy to facilitate product improvement and the evolution of second-generation products.

The second step is to determine how far above incremental cost the price will be (how much of a mark-up on incremental cost). This question can only be answered by considering:

(a) Competitive reaction to the various prices that could be charged.

(b) The total economic situation and future trends. The economic situation in the overall market in addition to that within the specific market must be thoroughly and continuously evaluated.

(c) The influence of what the company requires the product to achieve in subjective terms of image and prestige, as well as in the objective terms of contribution to company profitability.

PROGRESS TEST 10

1. Why is it necessary to create profit centres when a divisional organisation is established? **(1)**

2. What is meant by sub-optimising? **(2)**

3. If transfer prices are difficult to calculate, why are they used? **(3)**

4. What problems exist in obtaining a market price to use as a transfer price? **(6)**

5. Why is the joint level of output obtained at the position where total marginal cost is equal to marginal revenue? **(8–11)**

6. Why is it not necessary for each division of a firm to earn equal profits? **(11)**

7. What additional difficulties exist in pricing a new-product concept from pricing a product for which substitutes already exist? **(13, 14)**

8. When would you choose to implement a penetration strategy? **(17)**

FURTHER READING

1. Dean, J., "Decentralization and Intracompany Pricing", *Havard Business Review*, Vol. 33, No. 4, July/August 1955, pp. 65–74.

2. Hirshleifer, J., "On the Economics of Transfer Pricing", *Journal of Business*, Vol. 29, No. 3, July 1956, pp. 172–84.

3. Dearden, J., *Cost Accounting and Financial Control Systems*, Addison-Wesley, 1973.

4. For further detail, *see* Davies, J. R. and Hughes, S., *Pricing in Practice*, Heinemann, 1975.

CHAPTER XI

INVESTMENT DECISIONS—PRIVATE ENTERPRISE

NATURE OF THE INVESTMENT DECISION

1. Introduction. For the continued growth and prosperity of the U.K., a high level of capital investment is essential. The U.K.'s poor performance in recent years as compared to her competitors on the world market has in no small way been attributable to her poor record of investment in new and more efficient equipment. Perhaps there are many reasons that explain this poor record, but the most important must be the uncertainty with which firms in the U.K. view their future. Various techniques are available that attempt to incorporate uncertainty into the investment decision (*see* **12** below) yet it is true to say that they do not provide the complete answer to the firm's problems.

Investment decisions are important because the whole idea of investment is based upon the principle of sacrifice today for gains in the future and in order to calculate these future gains all the elements within the firm must be brought together.

The investment decision is an integrating topic because all that has gone before in this book must be brought together to solve the investment problem. The steps taken in making an investment decision are as follows:

(*a*) The firm must be clear as to the objectives it is pursuing, i.e. profit-maximisation, growth-maximisation, market dominance, satisficing, etc. (*see* Chapter I).

(*b*) The initial capital cost must be estimated, and the outlays required during the life of the project. For this forecast a full understanding of cost behaviour is necessary (*see* Chapters V and VI).

(*c*) Demand forecasts are necessary to enable the future flow of total revenue into the firm to be calculated (*see* Chapters III, IV, VIII and X).

(*d*) By deducting (*b*) from (*c*) and estimating for taxation and capital allowances, the net cash flow into the firm over the life of the project can be obtained.

(*e*) This net cash flow is discounted at the firm's cost of capital (*see* Chapter XIII) to determine whether the sacrifice is justified.

This Chapter brings together all the concepts and techniques introduced in this book, and the important concept of incremental analysis is as important as ever. It is the additional costs incurred and revenues received that need to be appraised in the investment decision. Costs incurred through past decisions are of no relevance. Careful appraisals of capital expenditure proposals are almost a rarity in the smaller company, yet it is important that all capital expenditure projects should be considered very carefully since an operational mistake can be rectified relatively quickly at no great cost whereas a mistake in capital expenditure could involve the company in heavy direct losses. One of the reasons why many companies are not earning a sufficient return on capital invested is because they either used no method of appraisal of capital projects in the past or because they employed inaccurate or misleading methods. This gave rise to unsound investment decisions which resulted in an insufficient return on the investment or led them to overlook profitable investment opportunities.

The use of unreliable and inaccurate methods of appraisal can be as bad as conducting no appraisal at all. In these days of intense world competition no firm can afford to ignore the need.

2. Decision categories. Perhaps the most difficult problem for the firm is the generation of ideas that require an investment decision to be taken. Investment decisions can fall into a number of categories:

(*a*) Replacement.
(*b*) Expansion of existing equipment.
(*c*) Expansion into new product lines by the purchase of machinery not previously used.
(*d*) Lease or buy.
(*e*) Make or buy.
(*f*) Take-overs and mergers.

This categorisation is not comprehensive, but although somewhat arbitrary it indicates the type of decisions that must be taken within the firm that involve sacrifice today (the outlay of money) in the anticipation of cash flows in the future. The degree of risk attached to each category can very significantly—with (b), for example, if the machinery has been used in the firm for some time, then detailed records exist that will give output per hour, maintenance costs, variable costs and future demand patterns. Decision (c), however, can be an unknown quantity because if the firm is entering a field in which it has no previous experience, data on costs and revenues will be absent and estimation and guesswork will have to fill the void.

MODERN TECHNIQUES OF INVESTMENT APPRAISAL

3. Discounting and the time value of money. The notion that an investment decision involves a sacrifice today brings out the fact that money has a time value; modern methods of discounting are simply the inverse of compounding. Forgetting inflation for the time being, a given sum £z invested today at a rate of interest r per cent per annum will be worth £z $(1 + r)$ in 1 year's time. Now if this amount is allowed to remain invested for another year, it will earn r per cent interest per annum on £z $(1 + r)$ which at the end of the 2nd year will become £z $(1 + r)^2$. If the original sum is invested for n years it will accumulate to £z $(1 + r)^n$. It is this principle that forms the basis of discounting and investment appraisal, because one should always prefer £100 today to £100 in 1 year's time.

> EXAMPLE 18: If you made a loan to a person of £100 and the rate of interest is currently 10 per cent per annum, and he returned that £100 in 1 year's time, you would actually have sacrificed £10 because if you had not made that loan you could have invested the £100 and it would have accumulated to £110 in the same time period. Given the rate of interest, therefore, you should be indifferent to £100 today or £110 in a year's time or £121 in 2 year's time (i.e. £110 reinvested in the 2nd year at 10 per cent per annum).

Compounding tells us the value in the future of a given sum invested today at a given rate of interest for a given period, while discounting tells us how much a sum accruing in the future is worth in present-day terms.

If compounding equals

$$£z \times (1 + r)^n = £z(1 + r)^n$$

then discounting equals

$$\frac{£z(1 + r)^n}{1} \times \frac{1}{1(1 + r)^n} = £z.$$

We can always discover what a given sum at the year end is worth in present-day terms by discounting by a factor $1 + r$. Further, we can equate a given sum at the end of two years with its present value by discounting by a factor $(1 + r)^2$. From this technique we can develop a discounting formula that discounts all future cash flows back to their present-day value.

$$\sum_{m=0}^{m=n} \frac{Cm}{(1 + r)^m} = \text{gross present value } (GPV)$$

where m = number of years of project.

C = net cash flow (this will be fully explained in **9** below).

$(1 + r)$ = the cost of capital (this will be the subject of Chapter XIII).

When all expected net cash flows have been discounted and summed, we obtain the gross present value, GPV.

4. Discount tables. Tables A and B in Appendixes II and III provide us with the relevant discount rates for our calculations. Table A provides us with the present value of £1 for combinations of years and interest rates. The present value of £1 on money received in 3 years when the rate of interest is 10 per cent is 75·1p (0·751) and if £200 is expected in that year, its present value will be £200 × 0·751 = £150·2.

The present value of £1 received in 1 year's time at a rate of interest of 10 per cent is 0·909. This is obtained simply by dividing £1 by $(1 + r)$, i.e. $\frac{1}{1·10} = 0·909$.

The Table therefore saves us a lot of laborious mathematics because by looking up the relevant year and interest rate we can obtain the discount factor.

EXAMPLE 19: In Table XVIII, an investment by a firm results in a cash flow into the firm for the next 5 years. If the cost of capital is 10 per cent, the gross present value is obtained by multiplying the cash inflow in each year by the relevant discount factor obtained from Table A.

TABLE XVIII: CALCULATING GROSS PRESENT VALUE

(i)	(ii)	(iii)	(iv)
Year	Net cash inflow	Discount factor	Present value (ii × iii)
1	50	0·909	45·45
2	60	0·826	49·56
3	70	0·751	52·57
4	80	0·683	54·64
5	40	0·621	28·84
	300		GPV = 227·06

In some projects, the net cash flow will be equal from year to year and Table B can now be used to save further time. Table B in Appendix III shows the present value of £1 received annually for n years. If a project yields a net cash inflow of £300 for 3 years when the cost of capital is 10 per cent, the GPV is obtained by multiplying the £300 by 2·487, which equals £746. One calculation is necessary instead of four, i.e. three multiplications and one addition. The discount factor 2·487 can be obtained from Table A by adding together present value of £1 for the 1st, 2nd and 3rd years, as in Table XIX.

TABLE XIX: CALCULATING DISCOUNT FACTOR

Year	Net cash inflow	Discount factor	Present value
1	300	0·909	273
2	300	0·826	248
3	300	0·751	225
	900	2·486	746

5. Net present value. In 3 and 4 above our discounting resulted in establishing the gross present value of the cash inflow. The initial outlay has so far been ignored. To determine whether a project is worthwhile, it is necessary to compare the gross present value with the initial capital outlay, and this final step produces the net present value (NPV) which is the first of the modern methods of investment appraisal we shall look at. A slight addition to the formula produced in 3 above provides us with the formula for calculating the net present value of a project.

$$\sum_{m=0}^{m=n} \frac{Cm}{(1+r)^m} - C0 = NPV,$$

where $C0 =$ initial cash outlay.

Where the NPV of a project is positive it means that by undertaking this project the firm immediately increases its present wealth by the value of the NPV and the rate of return on the project exceeds the cost of capital. It means that in addition to the original outlay the firm could borrow the value of the NPV at its cost of capital, distribute this sum in dividends and the proceeds of the project would yield sufficient funds to repay the initial capital sum borrowed plus the additional borrowing to the value of the NPV.

EXAMPLE 20: Table XX should clarify this last point. Firm XYZ Ltd., by investing £1,000 now, will receive net cash inflows for 3 years of £450 per annum. The cost of capital is 10 per cent.

TABLE XX: INVESTMENT OF XYZ LTD.

Year	Net cash inflow	Discount factor	Present value
0	(1,000)	1·000	(1,000)
1	450	0·909	409·05
2	450	0·826	371·70
3	450	0·751	337·95
	350		$NPV = 118·70$

The project has a NPV of £118·70 and the firm could now proceed as in Table XXI, borrow £1,118·70 and with the cash inflow of £450 per annum repay the entire loan plus interest by the end of the 3rd year.

TABLE XXI: REPAYMENT OF LOAN BY XYZ LTD.

Years	Opening balance	Interest at 10%	Total debt outstanding at year-end	Cash flow	Closing balance
1	1,118·70	111·87	1,230·57	450	780·57
2	780·57	78·05	858·62	450	408·62
3	408·62	40·86	450·00	450	—

In Table XX the initial outlay has been placed in Year 0
and the cash inflows are assumed to commence 1 year after
the initial investment. It is obviously possible in practice
for cash flows to commence before a period of 1 year has
elapsed and also for them to commence after a longer period
than 1 year has elapsed, e.g. 18 months. Our methods of
discounting can quite adequately deal with these variations
when they arise. In Example 21 we will again take the
figures in Example 20 but assume that it takes 18 months
for the first £450 to be received and that receipts arrive
thereafter at intervals of 1 year.

EXAMPLE 21:

(£1000)

Because the cash flows are of even quantities we can use
Table B and multiply £450 by 2·487 to obtain a present
value of £1,119 (approximately). This discount factor,
however, has only given us the present value to within
6 months of the commencement of the project, Point A. To
complete the discounting we need to multiply the £1,119 by
5 per cent for 1 year (5 per cent because it is half a year
when the cost of capital is 10 per cent. If the cost of capital
had been 8 per cent and we were 9 months short we would
have to discount at 6 per cent to establish finally a present
value figure), £1,119 × 0·943 = £1,055·2 which gives an
NPV for this project of £65·62.

EXAMPLE 22: In this case, using the same figures as in
Example 20, the first cash inflow of £450 occurs 6 months
after the initial expenditure of £1,000.

(£1000)

Multiplying £450 by 2·487 over-discounts the present value
by 6 months, it gives us the present value at Point B, which
is 6 months before the initial capital outlay. To redress the
balance, we need to multiply the £1,119 by $\left(1 + \dfrac{r}{2}\right)$ which
in our present example would be 1·05, giving a final present

value of £1,175 and a NPV of £175. If we had over-discounted by 3 months we would redress the balance by multiplying by $\left(1 + \dfrac{r}{4}\right)$.

6. A further short cut. Cash inflows in practice might appear as in Table XXII. In the first 3 years the cash flow is irregular but in years 4 to 10 the cash flow is regular. By using the following technique, the number of calculations necessary to provide the NPV can be considerably reduced. Cost of capital is 8 per cent.

TABLE XXII: CALCULATION OF NPV

Years	Cash inflow	Discount factor	Present value
0	(300)	1·000	(300)
1	30	0·926	27·78
2	40	0·857	34·28
3	50	0·794	37·70
4–10	60	4·133	248·04
	540		347·80

$$\text{NPV} = 47\cdot80$$

The discount factor 4·134 was obtained by multiplying together (a) the discount factor 5·206 from Table B that gave the present value of 7 years' of cash flows at £60 per annum (this discounted the cash inflow in years 4–10 to a present value expressed in year 3) and (b) the discount factor 0·794 which is taken from Table A and is the present value of £1 for 3 years at 8 per cent.

7. The internal rate of return or yield (IRR). This is the second of the two important discounting methods of investment appraisal. The IRR is the rate of interest that will discount the expected stream of net cash inflows into equality with the capital cost of the project. The formula for NPV is amended as follows:

$$\sum_{m=0}^{m=n} \frac{Cm}{(1 + r)^m} = C0$$

where r is the rate of interest that discounts

$$\sum_{m=0}^{m=n} Cm$$

into equality with $C0$. Therefore, r is the rate of return which is earned on the capital outstanding at the end of each year of the project's life. It is the true profit over and above the full recovery of the capital.

Establishing r is therefore a matter of trial and error. If there is a negative value after discounting at a certain rate of interest, then too high a rate has been used, while if a positive value exists the discount rate used has been too low. The internal rate of return when finally established must then be compared with the firm's cost of capital. If it is above it, then the firm can accept the project, while if it is below it, the project must be rejected.

EXAMPLE 23: A project which requires an initial outlay of £500 has the net cash inflows shown in Table XXIII. The current cost of capital to the firm is 12 per cent.

TABLE XXIII: ESTABLISHING INTERNAL RATE OF RETURN

Years	Net cash inflow	Discount factor 20%	Present value	Discount factor 30%	Present value
0	(500)	1·000	(500·0)	1·000	(500)
1	300	0·833	249·9	0·769	230·7
2	200	0·694	138·8	0·591	118·2
3	100	0·578	57·8	0·455	45·5
4	150	0·482	72·3	0·350	52·5
5	100	0·401	40·1	0·269	26·9
	350		58·9		−26·2

Discounting at 20 per cent gives us an NPV of £58·9, indicating that the discount rate used is too low (i.e. the IRR is higher than 20 per cent). When we discount by 30 per cent it is clear by the £−26·2 that we have used a discount rate which is too high (i.e. the IRR is less than 30 per cent). The IRR can now be established through interpolation.

NPV at 20%   58·9
NPV at 30%   −26·2

Difference   85·1

The correct IRR lies $\frac{58\cdot9}{85\cdot1}$ of the way between 20 and 30 per cent, which is in fact 26·9 per cent.

The cost of capital being 12 per cent, the IRR on this project is way above the acceptance level.

8. NPV and IRR. In Example 24 and Fig. 47, the relationship between NPV and IRR can be seen.

EXAMPLE 24: We assume a project with an initial investment of £1,000 and the cash inflow over a number of years is such that the NPV can be calculated for various rates of interest. The difference between the present-value curve and the

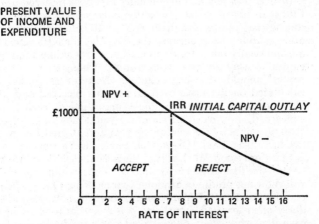

FIG. 47—*The relationship between NPV and IRR.* The difference between the present value curve and the initial capital outlay gives the NPV. The intersection of the present value curve with initial capital outlay gives the IRR.

initial capital outlay gives the NPV. The intersection of the present value curve and the initial capital outlay gives the IRR. If the company's cost of capital is less than the IRR, the project would add to the firm's worth and should be accepted. If it is higher than the IRR, the project should not be accepted.

9. The nature of the cash flows. So far in this Chapter we have merely mentioned net cash flow without explaining what this term should include or exclude. The costs and revenues to be included in the analysis of an investment decision should only be those costs and revenues that are directly affected by that decision. Incremental analysis applies with equal force here.

(a) *Capital outlay.* This should include the actual expenditure incurred to purchase capital equipment (buildings, machinery, etc.) or working capital for the project in question. If such equipment is not bought but is merely transferred from one use in the firm to this particular project then the cost incurred is the opportunity cost (i.e. the worth to the firm of using these assets in the most profitable alternative employment).

(b) *Net cash flows.* This includes revenues received during the year less expenses actually incurred. Taxation paid during that year is also deducted (*see* **10** below) and depreciation is added back because the formulae for NPV and IRR automatically allow for depreciation by including the initial capital outlay in the calculations. Changes in working capital should also be included. Accounting profits are calculated on the basis of total revenue received and total costs incurred during any one year; so far as cash flow is concerned, however, all debtors would not have cleared their accounts by the end of the year and all creditors would not have been paid. Given that money has a time value, it is therefore essential that it is the actual cash flow into and out of the firm that is calculated. The accounts of a firm will show net profits in any one year as being $(TR - TC)$ — corporation tax. Corporation tax is paid, however, with a delay of at least 12 months so it is essential to show in the cash flow when the money is paid. Any residual value from the equipment or working capital should be included but of course net of any dismantling costs.

10. Taxation. It is important that taxation is included in the calculation of the IRR or NPV, otherwise the actual gain to the firm from undertaking the project will be exaggerated. Further, taxation must be included in the cash flow at the time it is paid and not in the year of assessment of the profits. The time value of money makes this important. In Table XXIV we assume a corporation tax rate of 50 per cent and show profits as shown in an accounting statement and as the cash flow should be shown for investment appraisal purposes.

Although the money value of profits and tax are the same by both methods—£1,650 and £825—the discounted values of the profits after tax are different because of the timing of the actual tax payments. The accounting statement gives a discounted value of profits after tax as being £619·4, while the investment appraisal statement gives a discounted value of £675·8.

TABLE XXIV: ACCOUNTING FOR TAXATION

Accounting statement Year	1969	1970	1971	1972	1973	1974	1975
Profit before tax	200	400	500	350	200	100	
Tax	100	200	250	125	100	50	
Profit after tax	100	200	250	125	100	50	
Discounted at 10% to 1968 at 0		90·9	165·2	187·7	85·4	62·0	28·2
Investment appraisal statement Profit before tax	200	400	500	250	200	100	
Tax	—	100	200	250	125	100	50
Net cash flow	200	300	300	—	75	—	(50)
Discounted at 10% to 1968 at 0	181·8	247·8	225·3	—	46·5	—	(25·6)

The various capital allowances available must also be
included in the analysis of net cash flow, because they reduce
the profits on which corporation tax is paid and therefore
they are equivalent to a cash inflow. The capital allowances
available vary from budget to budget. From 12th November
1974, the initial allowance on new industrial buildings, for
example, was 50 per cent of the cost of the buildings plus a
writing-down allowance of 4 per cent per annum on the original
cost of the buildings. No allowance was to be given after the
25th year and the total allowances could not exceed the
qualifying cost of the building. On disposal of the building
within 25 years of its construction, a balancing allowance may
be given if the sale price is less than the residual value of the
building. If the sale price exceeds the residual value a
balancing charge is levied.

EXAMPLE 25: This includes capital allowances and corporation
tax and is therefore more complicated and realistic than the
simple examples used up to now. The student is strongly

advised to work his way through it, making sure he under-stands each step and the origin of each figure.

The information below relates to the Wizzo Co., which is contemplating the investment expenditure shown in Table XXV.

TABLE XXV: WIZZO CO. EXPENDITURE

	1975	1976	1977	Total
Buildings	20,000	40,000		60,000
Working Capital	5,000	15,000	10,000	30,000
	25,000	55,000	10,000	90,000

Corporation tax will be 50 per cent.
The firm's cost of capital is 10 per cent.
Capital allowances on buildings as in **10** above.
Buildings are to be sold in 1984 at an expected value of £10,000.
The working capital will be released at the end of the project in 1984.
The cash income will be as in column (*ii*) of Table XXVI.

TABLE XXVI: WIZZO CO. CASH FLOWS

Year	Investment	Net cash income	Tax on previous year's income	Tax reduction for capital allowances	Net cash flow
	(*i*)	(*ii*)	(*iii*)	(*iv*)	(*v*)
1975	(25,000)				(25,000)
1976	(55,000)	15,000		5,400	(34,600)
1977	(10,000)	15,000	(7,500)	11,200	8,700
1978		15,000	(7,500)	1,200	8,700
1979		20,000	(7,500)	1,200	13,700
1980		20,000	(10,000)	1,200	11,200
1981		10,000	(10,000)	1,200	1,200
1982		10,000	(5,000)	1,200	6,200
1983		10,000	(5,000)	1,200	6,200
1984	40,000*	10,000	(5,000)	1,200	46,200
1985			(5,000)		(5,000)
	(50,000)	125,000	(62,500)	25,000	37,500

* *Proceeds of the sale of buildings* (£10,000) *plus release of working capital* (£30,000).

Table XXVI shows the main cash flows relevant for this investment appraisal between the years 1975 and 1985. Most of the information in the columns is quite self-explanatory, except perhaps for column (*iv*) "Tax reduction for capital allowances". Table XXIX demonstrates how the figures in column (*iv*) of Table XXVI were calculated. Table XXVIII calculates the total allowances available on the new building for each year of the project. In year 1, for example, total allowances amount to £10,800, £10,000 being the 50 per cent initial allowance of the total cost of the new building plus 4 per cent of £20,000, the annual writing-down allowance. Table XXIX extracts the total allowances available in each year from Table XXVIII and applies the assumed rate of corporation tax to the figures to calculate the saving obtained.

Having established the net cash flow in each year in column (*v*) of Table XXVI, we now only need to discount these cash flows at the current cost of capital of the firm to produce the NPV. This is done in Table XXVII. The NPV as calculated is £−2013·8, which means that the firm should reject this project because the acceptance of it would result in a net loss to the firm of £2013·8. The IRR calculated through trial and error is 9·75 per cent and comparing this return with a cost of capital of 10 per cent indicates to the firm the same conclusions as the negative NPV above, i.e. that the project should not be accepted.

TABLE XXVII: DISCOUNTING CASH FLOWS AT CURRENT COST OF CAPITAL

Year	Net cash flow	Discount factor 10%	Present value
1975	(25,000)	1·000	(25,000)
1976	(34,600)	0·909	(31,451·4)
1977	8,700	0·826	7,186·2
1978	8,700	0·751	6,533·7
1979	13,700	0·683	9,357·1
1980	11,200	0·621	6,955·2
1981	1,200	0·564	676·8
1982	6,200	0·513	3,180·6
1983	6,200	0·466	2,889·2
1984	46,200	0·424	19,588·8
1985	(5,000)	0·386	(1,930)
	37,500		NPV = −2013·8

The student is invited to calculate the IRR for the project.

TABLE XXVIII: BUILDING ALLOWANCES

Year	1975	1976	1977	1978
Value	20,000	9,200 40,000	26,800	24,400
Initial allowance	10,000	20,000		
Annual allowance 4%	800	2,400	2,400	2,400
w/d value	9,200	26,800	24,400	22,000

Year	1979	1980	1981	1982
Value	22,000	19,600	17,200	14,800
Initial allowance				
Annual allowance 4%	2,400	2,400	2,400	2,400
w/d value	19,600	17,200	14,800	12,400

Year	1983	1984		
	12,400 2,400	10,000		
	10,000			
Realisation		10,000		
Balancing charge		nil		

TABLE XXIX: CALCULATING TAX REDUCTION FOR CAPITAL ALLOWANCES

Year	Allowances	50% tax	Year utilised
1975	10,800	5,400	1976
1976	22,400	11,200	1977
1977	2,400	1,200	1978
1978	2,400	1,200	1979
1979	2,400	1,200	1980
1980	2,400	1,200	1981
1981	2,400	1,200	1982
1982	2,400	1,200	1983
1983	2,400	1,200	1984
1984			
	50,000	25,000	

ADDITIONAL PROBLEMS

Up to this point, many of the difficult problems that arise in practice have been omitted, to enable us to concentrate on the basic techniques of NPV and IRR. Having explained the logic that lies behind NPV and IRR and having looked in detail at a comprehensive example it is now time to introduce those problems. In Example 25 we automatically assumed that the forecasts of future revenue and costs are perfectly accurate; that the company has an unlimited supply of money; and that inflation does not exist. It is obvious that in practice this is not the case.

11. Inflation. If we take account of inflation, it becomes clear that discounting by the firm's cost of capital is no longer sufficient to indicate the desirability of accepting a project. If the cost of capital is 10 per cent, £110 received in 1 year's time has a present value of £100. Without inflation the firm should be indifferent between £100 now or £110 in one year, but if inflation has been running at 5 per cent during the year the spending power of that £110 in one year's time is only equal to £104·72 and discounting at 10 per cent gives a present value of £95·19. The discount rate must therefore be adjusted to allow for inflation and in addition to this the cash flows must also be adjusted to show their future inflated value. Projects will otherwise continually be made to look less desirable than they actually are. The formula for this adjustment is:

$$\sum_{m=0}^{m=n} \frac{(\text{money value of net cash flows})^m}{(\text{money rates of interest})^m}$$

An alternative way of dealing with inflation is to reduce the money value of the net cash flow to real values and then discount by the cost of capital. This alternative, however, involves additional calculations, and therefore the first method is preferred.

12. Risk and uncertainty. Example 25 showed that the actual appraisal using either NPV or IRR is merely the final stage of the procedure. The greatest problems of investment appraisal involve obtaining demand and cost forecast that enable one accurately to calculate the cash inflows and outflows. The figures that are produced for analysis are based, in most cases, upon past records which have been extrapolated into the future, so, therefore, no certainty exists and it is possible, depending upon the assumptions made, for a number of different forecasts to be produced. Before one now proceeds with the analysis it is necessary to determine the probability of these various outcomes occurring. Under conditions of risk it is possible to allot probabilities to the various outcomes but under conditions of uncertainty this is not possible and, therefore, other techniques must be used.

(a) *Risk.* If we are operating under conditions of risk, the procedure may be as in Example 26.

EXAMPLE 26: A firm is appraising a certain project, the cash flows of which are not certain, nor is the actual capital cost that will be incurred. The expected value of the project is £600, which is the weighted average of the different cash flows and the probability of their occurrence. Project life is expected to be 5 years.

TABLE XXX: EXPECTED VALUE OF PROJECT

Cash flow	Probability	Weighted cash flow
500	0·3	150
600	0·4	240
700	0·3	210
Expected value =	1·0	600

The probable capital costs are as in Table XXXI.

TABLE XXXI: CAPITAL COSTS

Capital outlay	Probability	Weighted capital cost
1,500	0·6	900
2,000	0·4	800
Expected value =	1·0	1,700

We therefore expect the cash flow over the 5-year life of the project to be £600 per annum and the capital costs £1,700.

These figures, however, now need to be further qualified by comparing the firm's cut-off rate for acceptable investment opportunities to confidence limits established from the probabilities already derived of various combinations of cash inflow and capital outlay. Table XXXII includes all the

TABLE XXXII: CAPITAL COSTS AND IRR

Cash flows	1,500 (0·6)	2,000 (0·4)
500 (0·3)	(0·18) 20%	(0·12) 13%
600 (0·4)	(0·24) 29%	(0·16) 20%
700 (0·3)	(0·18) 37%	(0·12) 22%

figures used in this analysis, together with the probabilities attached to them. Also included are the IRR for each combination of cash flow and capital cost, e.g. the probability of the capital cost being £2,000 and the annual cash flow £600 is 0·16, which is derived by multiplying together the probabilities of the two separate events 0·4 × 0·4. If the company has a cut-off rate of 18 per cent, i.e. any project offering a rate of return of less than 18 per cent will be rejected, we can say from Table XXXII that there is an 88 per cent confidence level on the project achieving a rate of return that exceeds 18 per cent. It is only the combination of £2,000 capital costs and annual cash flow of £500 that fails to meet this criterion.

When one is comparing projects, it is important that the expected value of each project is qualified by a calculation of its standard deviation, otherwise choice of project will be distorted, e.g. two projects can have the same expected value yet have very different standard deviations; the higher the value of the standard deviation the higher the risk to the investor.

EXAMPLE 27: Compare the two projects A and B in Table XXXIII; the total value of expected cash receipts is the same, but the expected value of Project B exceeds the expected value for Project A. Project B, however, is not necessarily the best one to choose, because the standard deviation of Project B's cash flow is seven times greater than the standard deviation of Project A's cash flow.

Whether a project is accepted or rejected depends on whether a firm is a risk-taker or not. It might prefer a

TABLE XXXIII: STANDARD DEVIATION OF CASH FLOW

	Project A				Project B	
(i) Cash receipts	(ii) Prob-ability	(i) × (ii)		(iii) Cash receipts	(iv) Prob-ability	(iii) × (iv)
20	0·25	5		16	0·3	5
22	0·50	11		40	0·4	16
24	0·25	6		10	0·3	3
—	—	—		—	—	—
66	Expected			66	Expected	24
—	value	= 22		—	value	=

lower expected value and low standard deviation to a project that offers a high expected value but also a high standard deviation. Also it might not accept the project in Table XXXII even though the confidence limit is 88 per cent, because its attitude to risk might demand a confidence limit minimum of, say, 95 per cent.

It is possible to allow for risk by increasing the discount factor, but care must be taken here to adjust the risk factor over time because the allowance for risk increases over time as the risk premium grows.

(b) *Uncertainty.* The problem of uncertainty is particularly difficult, because no probabilities can be assigned to the values and therefore other approaches must be adopted, such as sensitivity analysis and decision theory. The student wishing to follow this is referred to the specialist literature on the subject in the Further Reading section at the end of this Chapter.[1]

No method has yet been established that will solve all the problems created by the existence of risk and uncertainty. The same techniques will provide different answers depending upon the psychological make-up of the decision-maker and his attitude to risk.

13. Capital rationing. It will generally be the case in practice that a firm will not have all the capital it requires at any one time, and therefore in its choice of projects some form of ranking must take place to ensure that the scarce resource is utilised in such a way as to increase the net wealth of the firm by the greatest amount. There are a number of reasons why situations of capital rationing exist, some external and outside the control of the firm, others internal.

(a) The non-availability of finance, which has been brought about by policies pursued by the Bank of England on behalf of the government.

(b) The opinion of the money market that the projects the firm are contemplating are too risky, and rather than raise the interest rate to compensate for this risk they refuse to lend altogether.

(c) The firm in question may already be heavily in debt and the money market will refuse to lend, despite the fact that the project contemplated would in normal circumstances obtain finance.

(d) Management may be reluctant to obtain external finance for expansion, particularly if this might result in a dilution of ownership and control.

(e) There may be a shortage of another vital factor of production, e.g. management expertise, and it is felt that the rate of growth generated by the new investment could not be adequately handled.

In (a), (b) and (c) above the rationing was imposed by the market, while in (d) and (e) the rationing has been self-imposed. In handling the problem of capital rationing it is essential to distinguish between single-period and multi-period rationing.

14. Single-period rationing. In this case, the future net cash flows can be discounted at the long-run marginal cost of capital in the usual way, since capital rationing lasts only one period, and therefore all profits can be reinvested at the company's long-run marginal cost of capital. The discount rate is therefore established in the normal way (*see* Chapter XIII, 9–15). The decision to accept projects that have been ranked according to their NPVs must, however, be modified and ranking should be based upon NPV per £1 of outlay. Ranking according to absolute values of NPV will not necessarily maximise the profits of the firm, as can be seen from Example 28.

EXAMPLE 28:

TABLE XXXIV: VALUE OF NPV AND PROFIT FOR THE FIRM

Project	Outlay	NPV	NPV per £ outlay
1	1,000	1,500	1·5
2	500	800	1·6
3	500	900	1·8

Project 1 has an NPV of £1,500 but Projects 2 and 3 between them have an NPV of £1,700 for the same money outlay. NPV per £1 of outlay provides a better guideline to project acceptance, and the ranking of projects according to this criteria would be 3, 2 and 1.

15. Multi-period rationing. When rationing exists over more than one period, it is no longer correct to use the long-run marginal cost of capital as the discount rate. The fact that a scarcity of capital exists and a choice must be made between projects, possibly all of which are profitable, means

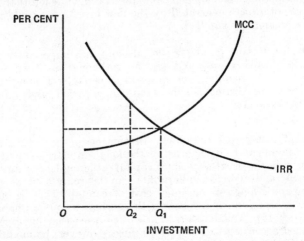

FIG. 48—*The optimum level of investment.* The logic of marginalism applies equally to the investment decision as to the output decision. Providing funds are available, the firm should continue to invest until MCC is equal to the IRR.

that the discount rate applied should be the opportunity cost of capital, i.e. the rate of return that could be earned on the next best project after the selection of the optimal plan. The investment decision is basically no different from any other economic decision, in the sense that the firm should move to that position where marginal revenue is equal to marginal cost (in the case of an investment decision, where the marginal cost of capital is equal to IRR (Fig. 48)).

In a situation of multi-period capital rationing the constraint on capital means that the firm is never allowed to reach point Q_1, and this is why the discount rate used should be that of the opportunity cost of capital. If a firm is faced with choosing between the four projects R, S, T and U in Fig. 49, and the capital available is only £30,000, then R, S

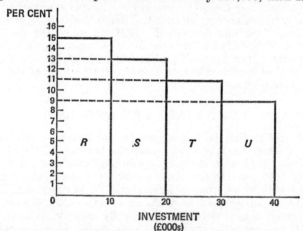

FIG. 49—*Multi-period capital rationing*. In such a situation where there is a limit on the availability of capital (£30,000), the discount rate to use is the opportunity cost of capital which in this case is 9 per cent.

and T will be chosen and the discount rate will be 9 per cent, i.e. the rate of return that could be earned on the next best project after the optimal selection has been made. Making the optimal selection of projects, however, is impossible without the use of programming techniques because we find ourselves in a "chicken and egg" situation, in that the firm cannot derive the correct discount unless it knows the projects that should be undertaken, and it does not know what projects should be undertaken unless it knows the rate of discount.

16. Replacement decisions. These decisions are a little more difficult than straightforward expansion decisions, because the firm already possesses an asset which is working and is justifying its existence. The problem hinges on the timing of the replacement. Should one continue to run the existing asset to the end of its life, or should it be replaced before the end of its life? The decision becomes one of balancing the sacrifice of spending to replace now against the extra cash flow generated (or cash saved) by that new asset. Replacing now rather than later will generate a different pattern of cash flows in the future and it is the difference in these incremental cash flows that need evaluating. Merrett and Sykes [2] have developed the optimal replacement method (ORM) to make the decision easier. This makes allowances for investment grants, annual allowances, tax rate and project life, and through the use of optimal replacement charts simplifies the problem of replacement decisions.

COMPARING NPV AND IRR

Accepting that discounting methods of investment appraisal are necessary, is it necessary to choose between NPV or IRR? Do they both offer the same operational advantages and will they both provide the same answer? On technical grounds, most authorities seem to agree that NPV is superior to IRR and therefore they advocate the use of NPV. Others[3] however, while agreeing that NPV is technically superior prefer to use IRR because of its operational advantages. Both techniques need to be mastered and the case for and against each one stated below (**17, 18**) should be noted because the truth is that in practice, depending upon the problem to be solved, the methods can be used to complement one another.

17. The case against IRR (or for NPV).

(a) *Mutually exclusive projects.* Where a firm has a choice to make between, for example, two methods of producing a given product, i.e. the projects are mutually exclusive, the NPV and IRR methods can provide different answers. The reason for this is that the IRR method gives a measure of the return relative to the outlay required for a project and ignores the absolute size of the return.

EXAMPLE 29: (*see* Table XXXV). Projects X and Y have different capital outlays although they have the same life. The IRR method advises one to accept Project Y, while the NPV method advises one to accept Project X.

The solution here is to calculate the NPV and IRR on the incremental cash flows that exist between Projects X and Y. If this rate exceeds the firm's cost of capital, then Project X is to be preferred because it offers as much as Project Y plus a return on the extra investment of £250 of 12·28 per cent. In this incremental form, the IRR and NPV methods will always provide the same results.

TABLE XXXV: NPV AND IRR FOR A PROJECT

Project	Capital cost	Annual cash flow	Life	NPV 10%	IRR
X	500	230	3	70·4	18·00%
Y	250	125	3	60·0	23·35%
$X - Y$	250	105		10·4	12·28%

If, when comparing two mutually exclusive projects, the lives of the projects differ, it is essential to consider the action that would be taken by the company when the project with the shorter life finished. If further capital outlays would have occurred then these need to be taken into account, together with the cash flows generated, in calculating the incremental cash flows.

(*b*) *Pattern of cash flows.* It is possible for differences to arise between NPV and IRR where cash outlays are identical but the pattern of cash flows is different. This difference reflects the difference in the rate of recovery of the investment and hence the differences in the average level of investment over time. Incremental analysis, as in (*a*) above, will provide the IRR with the correct solution.

(*c*) *Project profitability.* The IRR assumes that the project's profitability does not vary over time and variations in the cost of capital over the life of the project cannot be allowed for. Using the NPV method the future cash flows can be discounted at the cost of capital one desires.

(d) *Multiple positive roots (MPR)*. If negative capital exists during a project, then multiple positive roots (MPR) occur, and this means it is possible for a number of discount rates to provide a zero value for the NPV. Hawkins and Pearce [4] suggest applying a simple test to determine whether MPR of r exists:

"First find a solution rate for r. Then add up the discounted value of the cash flow year by year. If at any point this value is greater than the initial investment, then negative capital exists at that solution rate of return. Once negative capital has been found we know that the simple IRR method is invalid since one of two things must be true:

(a) either there will be MPR of r; or
(b) there will be a unique but 'economically meaningless' value of r."

It is possible to overcome this problem of negative capital by using the *extended IRR* method. The basis of this is to get rid of the negative cash flows by discounting them back at the firm's cost of capital into earlier years. Discounting the negative cash flow into earlier years continues until it has been absorbed. Finally, discount the new pattern of cash flow to 0 and that IRR is the true IRR for the project.

EXAMPLE 30: (*see* Table XXXVI). The negative cash flow in year 3 is discounted at the firm's cost of capital (15%) to year 2 (£$-70 \times 0.869 =$ £61 approximately) and therefore the adjusted cash flow in year 2 is £89 (£150 − £61).

TABLE XXXVI: DISCOUNTING NEGATIVE CASH FLOW

Year	0	1	2	3	4	IRR
Cash flow	−100	100	150	−70	50	
Adjusted cash flow	−100	100	89	—	50	

The firm should be indifferent now between the two cash flows because the extra £61 in the original cash flow can be invested at 15 per cent to yield £70 the following year which is sufficient to meet the outflow of £70.

18. The case for IRR.

(a) The IRR method is preferred by management because, by quoting the return on the project as a percentage of capital outstanding in the project, it can, by comparing this with the cost of capital, immediately see the profitability offered. Informing managers of the NPV of a project has less impact.

(b) In some respects, the IRR provides an indication of the margin of safety that a project possesses by comparing the IRR with the possible risk attached to a project.

It must also be remembered that in a pure accept/reject situation the IRR and/or NPV methods will both provide the same answer.

TRADITIONAL METHODS OF INVESTMENT APPRAISAL

Research[5] has indicated that the majority of investment decisions in business are taken by using methods which are different from those described above. In practice, what are collectively described as the traditional methods of investment appraisal are very commonly used, because the development and use of discounting methods is relatively new. We shall now briefly describe two of these and highlight their deficiencies.

19. The pay-back method. Firms normally set an objective that the only investment projects that will be accepted will be those that will repay the initial capital outlay within a stated number of years. e.g. 3 or 4 years. Three main criticisms can be made of this method:

(a) It neglects the total cash flow that arises over the life of a project. In Fig. 50, Project X repays the initial capital outlay (£4,000) within 3 years and is to be preferred over Project Y, yet over the life of the project, Project Y yields a greater overall cash flow—£10,000 compared to £6,000.

(b) It neglects the timing of the receipts, which as we have seen is extremely important. In Fig. 51, Project X and Y both yield £4,000 after 5 years, yet Project X has recovered 75 per cent of the initial capital outlay after only 2 years while Project Y has recovered only 25 per cent of the initial capital outlay after 4 years.

(c) The method can lead to underinvestment, because for a project to satisfy a 4-year pay-back criterion it would have

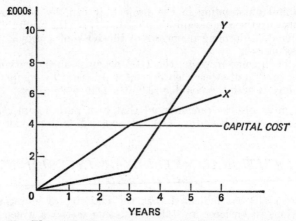

FIG. 50—*The pay-back method.* The pay-back method neglects the total cash flow over the life of the project. Project *Y* yields £10,000 over the life of the project as opposed to the £6,000 of Project *X*. Using a pay-back criteria of 3 years would mean that *X* would be chosen in preference to *Y*.

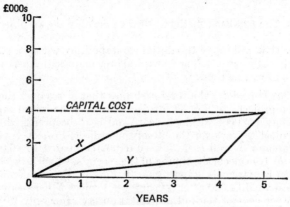

FIG. 51—*The pay-back method and the neglect of timing of receipts.* Both Projects *X* and *Y* pay-back the initial investment after 5 years. Project *X* is to be preferred, however, because 75 per cent of the investment is recovered after 2 years.

to achieve an annual cash flow over these years of 25 per cent of initial capital costs. How many low-risk projects could offer this return is questionable, and this theory also goes against the logic of accepting projects and investing up to the point where the marginal cost of capital is equal to the IRR.

The pay-back method, therefore, has serious deficiencies, although a number of authorities recognise situations in which it can be useful.[6]

20. Rate of return method. With this method the measurement of profits can take into account taxation and investment allowances and these are compared with the capital outlay. The comparison of these two variables, however, is not entirely straightforward because one has to decide whether the value for profit is to be the total profit earned in the lifetime of the project, the average profit earned in each year of the project's life, or the profits earned in the first year. Similarly, should profits (however defined) be compared with the initial capital outlay, or the average capital commitment over the life of the project? It is possible that use of different definitions, and the resulting profit ratio obtained, will point both to accepting and rejecting a given project. In addition to this problem of definition, the rate of return method is subject to two other criticisms:

(a) Like the pay-back method, it ignores the timing of the cash flows.

(b) It cannot cope adequately with the problem of comparing two investment projects whose lives are of different length, e.g. it cannot compare a project that has a rate of return of 15 per cent for 10 years with one that has a rate of return of 13 per cent for 15 years.

21. Conclusions. The discounting techniques described in **3–18** above are far superior to the traditional methods of investment appraisal which most firms in practice apply. This is not to say, however, that the discounting techniques are perfect. They have their faults and limitations, but provided these are kept in mind they are the best methods of investment appraisal we currently have.[7] Discounting itself is easy, it is the supply of information to produce the cash flows that is difficult. No matter how superior a technique seems to be, it is only as good as the information it can work on, so, as we have previously emphasised, full understanding of Chapters I–X is as essential as an understanding of this Chapter if correct investment decisions are to be achieved.

PROGRESS TEST 11

1. What is meant by the "time value of money"? **(3)**

2. Define the following terms:
   (a) Gross present value.
   (b) Net present value.
   (c) Internal rate of return.
   (d) Net cash inflow. **(3–8)**

3. Why is it unnecessary to allow for depreciation when calculating the net cash flow? **(9)**

4. How is it possible to allow for inflation when discounting future cash flows? **(11)**

5. What is the difference between risk and uncertainty? **(12)**

6. Is it correct to say that in a situation of multi-period rationing the correct discount rate to use is the firm's marginal cost of capital? **(15)**

7. What are the disadvantages of IRR? **(17)**

8. In making a choice between Projects R and T below, would the NPV and IRR methods provide different answers? The projects are mutually exlusive. **(17 (a))**

Years	0	1	2	3	4
Project R	25,000	2,000	4,000	6,000	8,000
Project T	15,000	4,000	4,000	4,000	2,000

Years	5	6	7	IRR	NPV
Project R	5,000	5,000	5,000		
Project T	2,000	2,000	2,000		

9. How does one handle the problem of multiple positive roots? **(17 (d))**

10. A haulage contractor is considering purchasing four extra lorries, two 10-tonners, one 5-tonner and one 3-tonner. The price of these lorries is £12,000, £8,000 and £6,500 respectively. According to his calculations they will between them earn £3,500 net of running costs per annum. The lorries are expected to have a life of 9 years and will be sold for scrap at an estimated total price of

£2,750. If the cost of capital to the contractor is 12 per cent, should he purchase the additional lorries? (Example 20, **5**)

11. An existing business is considering replacing an old machine which at present can be sold for scrap at £500. The new machine costs £15,000 and its use will save the firm £2,000 per annum in labour costs. It will have an effective life of 10 years, after which it is assumed it will realise £250 for scrap.

(a) Corporation tax—50 per cent.

(b) Capital allowances—equal to 80 per cent in the first year and 25 per cent of the reducing balance in subsequent years.

(c) Wages will increase by 15 per cent per annum.

What is the IRR on this project and should the firm accept the project if its cost of capital is 16 per cent? (Example 25)

12. If the above example is appraised using the techniques of pay-back and rate of return, would the firm make the same decision? (Pay-back criterion 6 years.) (**19** (a)–(b))

FURTHER READING

1. Hirschleifer, J., "Risk, the Discount Rate and Investment Decisions", *American Economic Review*, May 1961, pp. 112–20.

Archer, S. H. and D'Ambrosio, C. A., *The Theory of Business Finance*, Macmillan, 1967.

2. Merrett, A. J. and Sykes, A., *Capital Budgeting and Company Finance*, Longman, 1971, Chapter 8.

3. Merrett, A. J. and Sykes, A., *op. cit.*, p. 114.

4. Hawkins, C. J. and Pearce, D. W., *Capital Investment Appraisal*, Macmillan, 1971, p. 32.

5. N.E.D.C., *Investment Appraisal*, H.M.S.O., 1965.

6. Hellings, J., "Technical Note. The Case for Pay Back Re-Examined", *Journal of Business Finance*, Spring 1972, pp. 99–102.

Adelson, R. M., "DCF, The Other Point of View", *Moorgate and Wall Street Review*, Spring 1971, p. 57.

7. Adelson, R. M., "DCF, Can We Discount It? A Critical Examination", *Journal of Business Finance*, Summer 1970.

CHAPTER XII

INVESTMENT DECISIONS—PUBLIC ENTERPRISE

COST/BENEFIT ANALYSIS AND PUBLIC EXPENDITURE

1. Introduction. Cost/benefit analysis is beginning to be applied to a wide variety of public projects in the U.K. The first major application was the M1 motorway study undertaken by the Road Research Laboratory. This was followed by a social cost/benefit appraisal of the Victoria Underground line, and more recently the technique has been applied to the proposed siting of the third London airport.

Cost/benefit analysis is essentially an investment appraisal technique which takes account not merely of the private costs and benefits of an investment project but also of the social costs and benefits. The increasing support for the application of cost/benefit analysis to public expenditure has arisen for two main reasons.

(*a*) The growth of the welfare state (free state provision in areas such as medical care, schooling etc., to ensure equal opportunity regardless of income), with its associated disinclination to apply commercial techniques of investment appraisal to areas such as health, education, etc., has rendered it difficult to evaluate the efficiency of resource allocation in these areas. The advocates of cost/benefit analysis hope that it will eventually provide an efficient guideline to public expenditure in such politically sensitive areas.

(*b*) It has always been accepted that public enterprise should operate in the "public interest". The major problem here has been the actual identification of the public interest in practice. Here again the supporters of cost/benefit analysis are confident that it could provide a more practical interpretation.

Nevertheless, a recognition of the potential advantages of cost/benefit analysis does not give it a mandate to be applied indiscriminately to all aspects of public expenditure. Indeed, public expenditure still tends to be allocated on an *ad hoc* rather than an economic basis, and where a cost/benefit study has been undertaken, its recommendations have not always been applied (as, for example, in the case of the siting of the third London airport where the results of the analysis weighed heavily upon the valuation put on noise and other intangibles enabling local pressure groups to persuade the government to abandon the project).

2. Limited utilisation. In practice, the application of cost/benefit analysis as an investment appraisal tool has been limited mainly to transportation projects in the U.K. It is true that academic economists have been making attempts to widen its scope to incorporate areas such as the social rate of return to education and the social costs and benefits of research and development. However, such ambitious projects have not yet become the basis of practical policy.

In this respect, it is worth noting that it was not until the 1967 White Paper [1] (*see* Chapter IX, **14**) that cost/benefit analysis was considered applicable to the nationalised industries, and even then it was assigned a limited role. The White Paper suggested that the nationalised industries should be expected to earn a discounted cash flow rate of return of 8 per cent (subsequently raised to 10 per cent) in the normal commercial manner, except where there were grounds for thinking that the social costs and benefits would diverge markedly from those associated with the alternative investments.

Cost/benefit analysis has therefore not yet emerged as a fully-fledged investment appraisal technique in the public sector. However, it is likely that as an economy develops, environmental problems and considerations of social welfare will become more equal combatants with economic growth. Whether such considerations will be dealt with by the application of techniques such as cost/benefit analysis, or simply by the application of micro-economic legislation remains to be seen. At this stage it is sufficient to recognise that social cost/benefit analysis is a topic worthy of further investigation and one which, with further refinement, may provide a valuable addition to the array of investment appraisal techniques outlined in Chapter XI.

COST/BENEFIT ANALYSIS COMPARED WITH CONVENTIONAL INVESTMENT APPRAISAL TECHNIQUES

3. Three differences. Cost/benefit analysis differs from conventional investment appraisal techniques in three main ways.

(*a*) Cost/benefit analysis includes not merely private costs and benefits but also social costs and benefits in the calculation of the annual cash flows of a project.

(*b*) The valuation of these costs and benefits is also significantly different, conventional techniques using market values while cost benefit/analysis often uses shadow prices.

(*c*) The discount rate used to discount these costs and benefits may also be different, conventional techniques using the cost of capital (NPV), the discounted cash flow rate (DCF) or some combination of these, while cost/benefit analysis generally uses some sort of social discount rate.

In 4–14 below we will consider each of these problems in turn.

4. What are social costs and benefits? If a company undertakes an investment project it is concerned only with its private costs and benefits. The private costs are represented by the cash outlays and the private benefits by the financial returns. For example, if conventional investment appraisal techniques had been used on the Victoria Underground line, the analyst would have been concerned only with the private cost of constructing and operating the line and the private returns received from fare-paying passengers. However, this would have ignored completely the benefit to society achieved by the reduction in road congestion in London that accrued as well. A private company would have ignored such a benefit, since there is no way in which it can charge for this service and consequently it receives no revenue from reduced congestion. It is the purpose of cost/benefit analysis to include such social costs and benefits, so that investments are appraised according to their benefit to society rather than their profitability to private enterprise.

5. Technological and pecuniary spillovers. Cost/benefit analysis answers this question by including all "technological spillovers" and excluding all "pecuniary spillovers". Technological spillovers represent real costs and benefits to society, whereas pecuniary spillovers merely represent financial gains and losses to various members of society. If we take, for example, the decision to build a motorway, a technological benefit may be represented by reduced congestion in town centres and on alternative roads, while a technological cost may be represented by the increased noise levels and reduced visual enjoyment received by householders in the vicinity. These represent real social costs and benefits, and should be included in the analysis. An example of a pecuniary benefit could be increased house values caused by better access to business centres, while conversely a pecuniary cost could be decreased house values because of the proximity of the motorway. These pecuniary costs and benefits obviously have distributional implications (*see* **15–16** below) but they are not real costs and benefits and should not therefore be counted in the analysis. In practice, of course, it is often difficult to disentangle technological and pecuniary spillovers since both may occur together. Nevertheless, relevant social costs and benefits have to be identified if cost/benefit analysis is to have value.

6. Valuation of social costs and benefits. Having successfully identified the relevant social costs and benefits of a project, the cost/benefit analyst is then faced with the momentous task of placing a social evaluation upon them. In the first place, even where the costs and benefits have an existing market price, it is likely that such a price does not reflect society's true valuation of the cost or benefit involved. Secondly, there may be no existing market price at all for a particular cost or benefit.

(*a*) *Inadequacy of existing market prices.* Existing market prices would provide a useful starting point for the valuation of costs and benefits only if such prices provided a true reflection of society's valuation of them; however, existing market prices are unlikely to provide a true social valuation. In the first place, in the absence of perfectly competitive markets, prices tend to become administered and hence do not give an accurate measure of the social cost or benefit involved. Secondly, even within a perfectly competitive environment, prices would tend to reflect marginal private cost not marginal social cost, since individuals would be concerned only with the costs and benefits to themselves rather than the costs and benefits to society.

In general, we would expect marginal social cost and benefit to be the relevant criterion for evaluation of costs and benefits, since such a measure reflects society's willingness to use resources in that particular manner. However, the problem is that not only do existing market prices provide an inadequate measure of marginal social cost and benefit, but also that the advent of a marginal cost pricing rule solely in public enterprise will increase the welfare of society. The latter problem arises because of the existence of "second best" considerations, whereby the introduction of marginal social cost pricing in public enterprise, but not in private enterprise, may reduce welfare.[2]

(b) *Evaluation in the absence of an existing market price.* Cost/benefit analysts have responded to the problem provided by the absence of existing market prices for particular costs and benefits in two main ways. In the first place, valuation is often attempted by indirect means. For example, estimates of the value of time saved by speeding up commuter traffic can be made by estimating the additional earnings that could be achieved in this time saved. A similar approach to the same problem could be by estimating the value which individuals appear to put on their own time when offered the possibility of a faster journey at a higher price. Indirect valuation of this type is common in cost/benefit studies.

A second approach to valuation of costs and benefits makes no attempt to place monetary values on certain kinds of intangibles. This approach opts for the contingency method, whereby monetary benefits are subtracted from monetary costs, and the decision-maker then decides whether the value of the intangibles is worth the difference. This method receives support from advocates who find it aesthetically distasteful to place a monetary valuation on, say, human life or the destruction of an ancient church.

7. Value of cost/benefit analysis. Cost/benefit analysis is an investment appraisal technique and it is essential that it is based on correct social cost/benefit valuation. This is extremely difficult to achieve because where market prices do not exist the problem of valuation often becomes insurmountable.

Road pricing demonstrates some of the difficulties involved, since cost/benefit analysis has so far been applied mainly to transportation problems, and road pricing provides a striking example of the inadequacy of investment appraisal techniques in the absence of a correct pricing rule. In the case of roads, the marginal social cost of road travel is considerably in excess of the marginal private cost, since each additional vehicle on the road imposes social costs on all other users in the form of congestion. (This, of course, ignores all other social costs such as pollution, noise, etc.) If the price charged for road use is considerably below the marginal social cost, then demand will be artificially stimulated, thus causing a further need for road investment. Thus the investment required is dependent upon the pricing rule used.

Road pricing provides a striking demonstration of the importance of correct valuation techniques to cost/benefit analysis. Valuation based upon marginal private costs and benefits are clearly inadequate, and some attempt must be made to estimate the marginal social cost and benefit involved.

Despite the difficulties in attempting to compute the marginal social cost, and despite the existence of the "second best" problem mentioned in 6 (a) above, the valuation of costs and benefits where market prices exist is considerably easier than the valuation of intangibles. The placing of monetary values upon intangibles such as human life, noise, pollution, etc. has raised considerable public outcry when such projects begin to reach the implementation stage. Moreover, when the value of such intangibles is high in relation to the size of the project, pressure-group politics is inevitably going to play a large role in its acceptance or non-acceptance.

Thus cost/benefit valuation is still very much at a controversial stage. Hard and fast rules have not been applied, and often cost/benefit valuations have ignored important spillover effects.

CHOICE OF DISCOUNT RATE

Of all the problems faced by the cost/benefit analyst, perhaps the most controversial is the choice of the appropriate rate of discount with which to discount the costs and benefits of the investment project.

Just as the discounted cash flow and net present value investment appraisal techniques in the private sector recognise the need to discount future costs and benefits into present-value terms, so also cost/benefit analysis recognises that social costs and benefits should be properly discounted into present-value figures. However, in the public sector there exists the crucial problem of what is the appropriate social rate of discount. Many alternatives have been suggested by both academic and practising economists and they in general fall into one of the following three categories—the social time preference rate (STPR), the social opportunity cost rate (SOCR) and a combination of these.

8. Social time preference rate (STPR). The STPR is a normative rate reflecting society's evaluation of the relative desirability of consumption at different points in time. It is unquestionable that individuals, on the whole, prefer consumption now to consumption in the future. Empirical evidence supports this proposition by demonstrating that individuals often choose jobs with high earnings at the start and relatively lower earnings in the future, as compared to employment which provides low incomes at the start and higher earnings in the future. Moreover, the consumption habits of individuals reveal that many borrow on the strength of future earnings in order to finance consumption now. Moreover, if future income is expected to be greater than current income, it is likely that the operation of diminishing marginal utility will give a positive preference for current as opposed to future consumption. The effects of a progressive income tax system will strengthen this preference. In any case, purely on a risk of death basis it has been argued that individuals prefer present to future consumption, just in case they will not be around to enjoy the future benefit.

However, the decision on an STPR is really a collective rather than an individual decision. Moreover, the STPR problem is analogous to that of a public good, in that individuals are unlikely to reveal their true preferences: the summation of individual time preference rates would be an inappropriate approach. Indeed, Pigou[3] has argued that present society possesses a "deficiency of the telescopic faculty" in that time preference rates reflect the irrational preferences of present society. The only way individuals reveal their preferences is through the ballot box.

9. Political manipulation. In practice, of course, the STPR would be set politically. This would open the door to party politics, since the lower the STPR selected the more public projects would be approved and the greater the degree of state intervention in the economy. To some extent this problem is inevitable, in that the government is the only body which assumes collective responsibility for future generations. Such responsibility is particularly important in areas such as industrial pollution, conservation, mineral exploitation, etc.

10. Criticism of STPR. However, the main argument against the use of the STPR as the sole rate at which to discount the future costs and benefits of a project lies not in the difficulties surrounding its calculation but in the fact that it completely ignores the social opportunity cost of funds. The use of an STPR alone has implications not merely for the overall current level of investment but also for its distribution between the public and private sectors. For example, the choice of a low STPR might mean that a public project is preferred which has lower *social* benefits than a private-sector project which is forced to use the higher commercial discount rate on its future revenue streams. Thus the STPR completely ignores the social opportunity cost of funds. It is for this reason that the STPR is an inappropriate rate at which to discount the costs and benefits of a public-sector project.

11. Social opportunity cost rate (SOCR). The SOCR of a public-investment project is the value to society of the best alternative use for the resources involved. Opportunity cost lies at the heart of the economic problem. Since resources are limited in relation to the demand for them, the use of such resources in a public-sector project inevitably involves their withdrawal from other potential applications.

Of crucial importance here is the alternative use to which such resources would have been put. If the resources were taken from an alternative private-sector investment project, then the social-opportunity cost is the social benefit that would have been reaped from this alternative project. How do we measure the social benefit that arises from a private-sector project?

(a) Even if we accepted the private rate of return as being a useful measure of the benefits arising from the project, there is still the problem that different companies have different rates of return.

(b) The private rate of return measures only the private costs and benefits, and consequently ignores the spillover effects so crucial to cost/benefit analysis. Moreover, all subsidies in the form of investment grants, etc. and all company taxes would have to be removed before one could obtain a reasonable approximation of the social rate of return from the project.

Moreover, it is possible that the funds used to finance the cost/benefit project may not have replaced an alternative private-investment project but may instead have replaced consumption expenditure. The government may finance the project by borrowing or by taxation. If these funds would have been spent on consumption in the absence of the project, then the opportunity cost is the amount of funds transferred. The government borrowing rate has often been used as a measure of the funds used in this way.

The problem then is that there is no single SOCR. Krutilla and Eckstein [4] suggested a special weighted average of market interest rates and company investment yields designed to recognise the incidence of taxation and to reflect funds withdrawn from both consumption and investment. This approach is likely to bring about a more accurate measure of the social opportunity cost of funds than would the application of a single SOCR.

12. Criticism of SOCR. Like the STPR, the major criticism of the SOCR does not lie in the problems surrounding its calculation. The major criticism of the SOCR approach is that it has concentrated upon the distribution of resources between the private and public sectors to the neglect of time-preference considerations. The discounting of the costs and benefits of a public project using an SOCR alone would ignore the government's role in providing for future generations. It is for this reason that many economists are coming round to the view that both STPR and SOCR are relevant to public-sector projects. Hence we must consider the arguments for combining both STPR and SOCR to calculate the social discount rate.

13. Discounting by combined STPR and SOCR. The funds used in a public project can be regarded as displacing other forms of expenditure such as private investment and consumption. Moreover, it can be argued that SOCR is best considered as the STPR discounted present value of the consumption stream that would have occurred if the public project had not been undertaken. Thus, the calculation of the SOCR would involve tracing the means of financing the public project. The proportion of funds that have come from current consumption would merely be discounted at the STPR, as this would indicate the relative value of consumption foregone in the present compared with benefits to be obtained from a public project in the future. However, the proportion of funds that have displaced alternative investment would first need to be converted into a stream of future consumption foregone by applying the SOCR. This stream of future consumption (which would have arisen from the alternative snvestment project) is then further discounted by the STPR iin order to obtain its present value. Thus, in so far as resources were taken from consumption, then discounting would be by the STPR only, whereas to the extent that resources were taken from investment, then discounting would take place first by the SOCR and then by the STPR.

14. Advantages of combination. This combination of STPR and SOCR has the great advantage that it takes account of both the community's rate of time preference for consumption over time and the opportunity cost of transferring funds from the private to the public sector. There are still, of course, many controversial issues to be resolved, particularly with regard to the actual calculation of STPR and SOCR. Nevertheless, many economists are coming around to the viewpoint that both STPR and SOCR are relevant to public-sector investment projects and further research in this area will hopefully provide the most likely solution to this problem.[5]

DISTRIBUTIONAL CONSIDERATIONS IN COST/BENEFIT ANALYSIS

15. Neglect of distributional considerations. Most cost/benefit projects which have been undertaken in the U.K. have proceeded according to the basic decision rule that costs and benefits are expressed in monetary units over the life of the project, and that these monetary units are discounted by a social rate of discount in order to obtain a net present value of social benefits. Such a procedure is concerned only with the magnitude and timing of the social benefits and costs, and takes no account of their distribution between the various sections of the community.

There are two reasons why cost/benefit analysts have tended to neglect distributional considerations:

(a) It is argued that many cost/benefit projects have *little effect upon the redistribution of income*, and that in any case the cumulative effect of many projects is likely to cancel each other out, i.e. the redistribution effects of one project are likely to be offset by redistribution effects in an opposite direction from another project. However, one could argue, against this, that major projects such as the siting of an airport are likely to impose severe social costs in one area, whereas the benefits are likely to be more widespread.

(b) The disinclination to see *investment appraisal techniques as the appropriate means* of achieving redistribution. Many cost/benefit analysts are of the opinion that redistribution is the prerogative of the government and is best achieved by methods other than cost/benefit analysis.

16. Problems of using cost/benefit analysis to aid distribution of income. While it is true to say that most cost/benefit projects have made no attempt to incorporate distributional considerations, many academics are beginning to press for the inclusion of such criteria in cost/benefit studies.[6] There are, however, two major problems involved in this procedure:

(a) The cost/benefit analysts will be required *to measure accurately the incidence of costs and benefits* on various sections of the community. This is likely to prove as difficult a problem as measuring the incidence of taxation.

(b) Decisions will have to be taken on the *weighting* to be attached to the costs and benefits which accrue to the various "deserving" or "undeserving" groups, the benefits and costs that fall on deserving groups receiving a higher weighting. A lower valuation would apply to benefits and costs falling on undeserving groups

Inevitably, such a weighting system will have to be based on other important criteria such as the marginal tax rates of the recipients, whether such groups receive other social benefits such as family allowances, subsidies, rate rebates, etc. Under such a system individuals with high marginal tax rates would be regarded as undeserving groups while those who receive social benefits such as family allowances would be regarded as deserving groups.

One could criticise such an approach, in that there are obvious imperfections in such a system—as, for example, the neglect of the role of indirect taxation or the assumption that marginal tax rates were devised purely for the purpose of achieving an equitable distribution of income.

It would appear that the role assigned to distributional considerations is becoming as controversial as many of the other areas of cost/benefit analysis. The authors are of the opinion that while there may be problems involved in incorporating distributional considerations into the analysis, the neglect of such considerations would be as undesirable as the acceptance of market prices as a valuation criterion for costs and benefits. The distribution of the social benefits is as important as their size, and this is particularly the case where social costs are concentrated in one locality. Continued use of cost/benefit analysis as an investment appraisal technique requires an acceptable solution to this problem.

RISK AND UNCERTAINTY IN COST/BENEFIT ANALYSIS

17. Can we exclude risk and uncertainty? The existence of risk and uncertainty provides yet another controversial area for the cost/benefit analyst. Some advocates argue that there is no need to make any special provision for the existence of risk and uncertainty, and two major arguments are used to support this standpoint:

(a) The government undertakes a number of investment projects, so that there is likely to be a *risk-pooling effect*, whereby the risk and uncertainty associated with various projects will cancel each other out.

(b) Since public projects are financed by the general tax-payer, the *risk will be spread among millions of tax-payers*, so that the risk for any one individual is likely to be negligible.

18. Reasons for including risk and uncertainty.

However, these arguments take no account of the effect upon the distribution of resources between the private and the public sector. The keenest supporter of the viewpoint that public projects should allow for risk has been Hirshleifer who argues that the absence of any allowance for risk would lead to a maldistribution of resources between the private and the public sectors, in that high-yield private-sector projects would be shelved in favour of low-yield public-sector projects.[7]

If allowance is to be made for risk and uncertainty in cost/benefit projects, then the same techniques may be used as in the private sector. Risk may be allowed for by adding a risk premium to the discount rate, by the use of certainty equivalents, or sensitivity analysis, while uncertainty may be treated by such decision rules as maximax, maximin, etc.[8]

19. Conclusion.

In the preceding sections we have discussed the main principles underlying the application of social cost/benefit analysis. As the reader will now be aware, many controversial issues still remain to create difficulties for the policy-maker. Nevertheless, to recognise the limitations of cost/benefit analysis is not to discard it, since economic theory has not produced a more appropriate investment appraisal technique to deal with public-sector projects which are likely to produce significant externalities, i.e. where the social costs and benefits are likely to be different from the private costs and benefits.

Such a judgment does not mean that the results of a cost/benefit study should be accepted unreservedly. Indeed, one could argue that cost/benefit analysis will only attain respectability when the government is willing to provide politically-determined criteria for such issues as shadow prices, the social rate of discount and the weighting to be given to social costs and benefits that fall on particular groups. Even then cost/benefit analysis will not relieve the decision-maker of critically important decisions. As Walsh and Williams put it, "the advantages of cost/benefit analysis lie not in making decision-making simpler, but in the possibilities for the systematic examination of each part of a problem in hand, for putting decisions on a par, and for following the logical consequences of a synoptic view. In short, it is a means of organising thought, not a means of avoiding it!" [9]

PROGRESS TEST 12

1. In what way does cost/benefit analysis differ from conventional investment appraisal techniques? (3)

2. Distinguish between technological and pecuniary "spillovers". Why is such a distinction important? (5)

3. In cost/benefit analysis what is a shadow price? Why are existing market prices likely to be inappropriate? (6)

4. What is an intangible? How is it valued? (6)

5. Distinguish between the social time preference rate and the social opportunity cost rate. Which, if any, of these would you use to discount the costs and benefits of a project? (8–14)

6. Argue for and against the inclusion of distributional considerations in a cost/benefit study. (15–16)

FURTHER READING

1. Cmnd. 3437, *Nationalised Industries: A Review of Economic and Financial Objectives*, H.M.S.O., 1967.

2. Lipsey, R. G. and Lancaster, K., "The General Theory of Second-Best", *Review of Economic Studies*, 1965.

3. Pigou, A. C., *The Economics of Welfare*, Macmillan, 1932.

4. Krutilla, J. and Eckstein, O., *Multiple Purpose River Development*, Johns Hopkins Press, 1958, Chapter 4.

5. Feldstein, M. S., "Opportunity Cost Calculations in Cost Benefit Analysis", *Public Finance*, 1964.

6. Maass, A., "Benefit-Cost Analysis: Its Relevance to Public Investment Decisions", *Quarterly Journal of Economics*, May 1966.

7. Hirshleifer, J., "Investment Decision Under Uncertainty; Choice-Theoretic Approaches", *Quarterly Journal of Economics*, November 1965.

8. Thierauf, R. J. and Grosse, R. A., *Decision Making through Operations Research*, J. Wiley, 1970.

9. Walsh, H. G. and Williams, A., *Current Issues in Cost Benefit Analysis*, C.A.S. Occasional Paper 11, H.M.S.O., 1969.

CHAPTER XIII

THE COST OF CAPITAL

INTRODUCTION

THE measurement of the cost of capital is not an easy task. Even when it is broken down into its individual capital components and when complications concerning the inter-relationships between these components are assumed away, its calculation is still beset by uncertainties concerning the rate of return on assets, tax changes which influence the cost of the various components, and, perhaps most important of all, the institutional framework which enables capital to be raised from a great variety of sources. Moreover, once we remove the assumption concerning the absence of inter-relationships between the individual capital components, then the calculation of the cost of capital and the optimum capital structure become even more controversial. The purpose of this Chapter is to examine the problems involved in the calculation of the cost of capital, and to make some observations on the controversy that surrounds the concept.

COST OF INDIVIDUAL CAPITAL COMPONENTS IN THE ABSENCE OF INTER-RELATIONSHIPS

1. The cost of debt. In its simplest form and in the absence of inter-relationships between the capital components, the cost of debt capital is the easiest cost of capital to identify. Debt capital represents a long-term loan to the company, and the reward of the lender is a legally-stipulated interest rate. This interest rate must be paid irrespective of the profits of the company, and represents part of the costs of the firm and is consequently subtracted from the company's earnings before profits are arrived at. If the long-term debt-holders do not receive their interest, then they can undertake proceedings to liquidate the company in order to recoup both their principal and interest. Thus the cost of debt to the company will be the legally-defined interest rate on the debt certificate. However, there are a number of issues that the student should bear in mind:

(a) *Tax complications.* The interest that the company pays on its long-term capital is tax-deductible, so that the cost of debt capital will be reduced. In this case, the after-tax cost of debt will be equal to the before-tax cost of debt multiplied by 1— the tax rate. Thus if the interest on the debt certificate was 10 per cent and the corporation tax rate on company profits was 50 per cent, then after-tax cost

$$= 10\% \times 1 - 0{\cdot}50$$
$$= 0{\cdot}10 \times 0{\cdot}50$$
$$= 5\%.$$

However, even in this simple case, the after-tax cost of debt will be influenced by variations in the corporation tax rate. If in the above example the corporation tax was 40 per cent, then the after-tax cost of the particular debt would be

$$= 10\% \times 1 - 0{\cdot}40$$
$$= 0{\cdot}10 \times 0{\cdot}60$$
$$= 6\%.$$

Thus, when a new issue of long-term debt is undertaken the company will not know the after-tax cost because of the variations in the corporation tax rate that are likely to take place over the life of the loan. It is partly for this reason that much of the literature defines the cost of debt as *the rate of return that must be earned on debt-financed investments in order to keep unchanged the earnings available to equity shareholders.*[1] Thus in order to maintain the earnings of the equity shareholders, assets financed by 10 per cent must be invested to earn 10 per cent.

EXAMPLE 31: If £100,000 of assets financed by 10 per cent debt were invested to yield 10 per cent, then the £10,000 earnings from the investment would equal the £10,000 interest, and there would be no tax complications since the tax on the earnings (£5,000 at a 50 per cent corporation tax rate) would be exactly offset by the tax allowance on the interest (£5,000).

(b) *Institutional complications.* The institutional complications in calculating the cost of capital arise primarily from the fact that not only are there a variety of sources from which long-term capital can be acquired but also that there are a variety of debt certificates which can be used. Different companies will face different rates of interest, so it would be a fallacy to attempt to identify one cost of debt.

In the U.K., long-term loans to companies are usually made in the form of *debentures*. There are three main types of debenture—mortgage debentures, debentures with a floating charge and convertible debentures. A mortgage debenture is secured by the mortgage of a particular fixed asset owned by the company, and is the most secure from the point of view of the lender, since he will be the first to receive payment from the sale of these particular assets in the event of liquidation. Debentures with a floating charge are also reasonably safe since, although they are not secured by any particular asset, they nevertheless have first claim on the assets of the company (other than those secured by mortgage debentures) in the event of liquidation. Convertible debentures reduce the uncertainties concerning the future of the firm, in that the holders can either retain them as debentures or convert them into ordinary shares before a specified date. Normally, convertible debentures will be issued at a lower rate of interest than ordinary debentures, since they enable the holders to convert into ordinary shares at a favourable price. It is clear that the rate of interest will differ not only according to the type of debenture issued, but also in line with the creditworthiness of the company making the issue.

2. Alternative sources of debt finance. Debt finance is not confined to debenture issues on the new issue market. There exist a whole host of financial institutions prepared to make long-term loans including Finance for Industry incorporating I.C.F.C. and I.F.C., and many other special-purpose institutions for particular industries. Moreover, the growth of the Euro-dollar and Euro-bond markets has continued the trend towards the internationalisation of interest rates and may yet prove an important source of funds for large companies.

The vital point is to realise that there is no one single rate of interest in existence. There are a whole host of interest rates dependent upon the type of client and the type of loan. Thus, even without introducing the complicating effects of the level of debt on the cost of other types of finance, the calculation of the cost of capital is not easy.

3. Cost of preferred stock. After creditors and long-term debt-holders, preference shareholders represent the next claim on company assets in the event of liquidation. Preference shareholders, as the name implies, are shareholders of the company, and consequently the remuneration they receive is dependent on the making of profits. Even though they are normally issued with a fixed rate of interest, the payment of this interest in principle depends upon the company making profits, and they cannot liquidate the company in the event of insufficient profits being made to cover the preferred dividend charge. However, in practice, so long as the company continues as a going concern, preference shareholders almost invariably receive their dividend payment, partly because non-payment would be likely to have undesirable repercussions on the stock market and partly because preference share dividend arrears would have to be paid in subsequent years before there could be any payment to ordinary shareholders. Thus the preferred dividend yield can be regarded as representing the cost of preferred stock. However, as in the case of debt finance, there are a number of complications in practice.

(a) *Tax complications.* Unlike the debenture-holder, preferred stock-holders represent part of the shareholders of the company and consequently any dividend they receive is regarded as part of the profits of the company and is therefore not treated as tax-deductible. Thus, assets financed by 10 per cent preference shares would need to yield at least 20 per cent before tax (with a corporation tax rate of 50 per cent) if the company is to benefit.

EXAMPLE 32: If £100,000 of assets financed by 10 per cent preferred stock were invested to yield 20 per cent, then the £20,000 earnings from the investment would equal the £10,000 preferred dividend plus the £10,000 tax payment on these extra earnings (corporation tax assumed to be 50 per cent). If the corporation tax rate had been 40 per cent, then the £20,000 earnings from the investment would have been greater than the sum of the preferred dividend (£10,000) and the extra tax payment (£8,000), so that the company would have benefited by £2,000.

It is clear from this that the corporation tax rate will affect the rate of return required on preferred stock-financed assets, and consequently the true cost of preferred stock so far as the company is concerned. In Example 32, with a corporation tax rate of 50 per cent the assets financed by 10 per cent preferred stock would have required a rate of return of 20 per cent; with a corporation tax rate of 40 per cent the assets financed by preferred stock would have required a rate of return of approximately 16·7 per cent; while assets financed by 10 per cent debt would have required a rate of return of only 10 per cent with either rate of corporation tax (*see* **1** (*a*) above).

(*b*) *The reverse yield gap.* It was in fact this effect of corporation tax which led in the second half of the 1960s to a situation known as the reverse yield gap. Traditionally, debt capital has always yielded a lower rate of interest than preferred stock, which in turn has yielded a lower rate of return than ordinary shares, due to the fact that debt capital has greater security for the holder than preferred stock, which in turn is much more secure than equity capital. However, the introduction of corporation tax in 1965 distorted this situation, in that so far as the company was concerned it was now much cheaper to issue debt capital which was tax-deductible than to issue ordinary or preference shares which received no tax concessions. This is borne out by Example 32. In contrast, it was now much cheaper for the investment institutions which were subject to corporation tax to hold investments which had already borne corporation tax (preference shares and equities) in preference to debentures, the interest on which would bear corporation tax in the hands of the investment institutions themselves.

Thus the effect of the introduction of corporation tax was to change the demand for, and supply of, various types of long-term capital, with a consequent distorting influence upon their yields. So far as debt capital was concerned there was an increased supply of debt from companies wishing to take advantage of the tax incentive, but a decreased demand for debt from investment institutions subject to corporation tax. These two effects inevitably raised the yield on debt capital. Conversely, and for similar reasons, there was a reluctance to issue preferred stock and equities by the company sector coupled with an increased demand to hold this type of certificate by the investment institutions. These two influences resulted in a reduced yield on preferred and equity capital and a reverse yield gap developed with low-risk debt carrying a higher yield than relatively high-risk equity. Although there was some revival of equity financing in 1968, the general trend towards debt finance continued so that by 1970 around 80 per cent of new issues by companies were debt financed. However, in 1971 there was a massive revival of equity financing with equity representing almost 70 per cent of new issues by the end of 1972. This was probably due to the fact that for many companies the excess of interest rates over dividend yields had become sufficient to offset the effects of tax discrimination, so that equity had become relatively attractive again to the borrower. However, in 1973–74 there was a substantial slump in activity in the new issue market. The reluctance to use the new issue market stemmed from the high cost of raising long-term funds. This rise in the cost of long-term borrowing was brought about by the substantial rise in yields which in turn was a reflection of the decline in the market prices of both fixed-interest securities and equities. During this period, companies in general chose to ignore the new issue market in favour of financing themselves by various expedients of a short-term nature. This situation continued until 1975 when the spectacular revival of share prices enabled companies to return to the new issue market and raise much needed long-term finance by means of equity issues. However, September 1981 saw another major collapse of share prices reflecting the underlying lack of confidence in the equity market. Moreover, the current average yield on equities (1981) is a mere $6\frac{1}{2}$ per cent compared to a yield on long-term Government stock of 16 per cent, representing a reverse yield gap approaching 10 per cent.

This is far from being an exhaustive analysis of the relative yields of various securities, but it does illustrate that the cost to the company of even a fixed-charged security, such as preferred stock, is not quite as simple as it might appear.

(c) *Institutional complications.* Several types of preferred stock also exist. A company may make more than one issue of preference shares and it then becomes necessary to stipulate which of these has priority either on an earnings basis, or on a redemption basis in the event of liquidation. Companies sometimes issue A and B or first and second pre-

ference shares. In some cases it may be possible for preference shareholders to participate in profits with the equity
shareholders up to a certain maximum amount. Participation, however, is not common. On the other hand, most
preferred-stock issues are cumulative, in that in the event of
non-payment of preferred-stock dividends over a number of
years, the full payment of arrears has to be paid before
equity shareholders can receive any dividends. If companies
get themselves into this situation, they may offer the
preference shareholders equity shares in exchange for writ-
ing-off the arrears of preference dividend outstanding. Preference shares also differ in the voting rights attached to
them. Preference shares are usually non-voting, although
the extent of this restriction will be laid down in the Articles
of Association of the company.

Once again there are institutional complexities which
make it difficult to identify a unique dividend rate for
preference-share finance. The preferred dividend will
depend upon the nature of the company and the particular
configuration of preferred rights and restrictions comprising
the issue.

4. Cost of equity capital. We have already seen that the true
cost of debt and preferred stock is somewhat obscured by tax
changes and other institutional obstacles. Nevertheless, their
true cost can be traced directly to the rate of interest on the
debt or share certificate. When we come to calculate the true
cost of equity finance, however, the situation is altogether
more complicated, since we have no legally-binding interest
rate on which to base our analysis. Equity shareholders have
no guaranteed rate of return, since their reward is entirely
dependent upon the profits of the company. Equity shareholders may also receive their return either in the form of
dividends or in the form of capital appreciation, or more
usually both. Indeed, the reward of the equity shareholders
may even be negative, since if the company makes a loss, even
though it may continue to pay a dividend, the drop in value of
of the shares on the stock market is likely to more than outweigh any dividend payment.

Thus it is clear that the calculation of the cost of equity
capital is likely to be much more complicated than that of
fixed-charged finance.

(a) *Uncertainties concerning the rate of return on capital*
When considering the cost of debt and preferred stock in
1–3 above, we were able to incorporate the effect of tax complications and move some way towards ascertaining the
true cost by finding out what the assets financed in these
ways would need to yield in order to break even, any higher
yield generating wealth for the company. In Examples 31
and 32 above, assets financed by 10 per cent debentures
would need to yield 10 per cent while assets financed by
10 per cent preferred stock would need to yield 20 per cent
(assuming a 50 per cent corporation tax rate) in order to
break even.

It is only in this way that we can define the cost of equity
capital—*the rate of return required on new equity-financed
assets in order to break even.* (Note that break even in this
section does not refer to the overall performance of the
company, but to the equation of the earnings of the new
assets with the cost of financing the new asset.)

There are two advantages in defining the cost of equity
capital in this way:

(*i*) it provides a common base for comparing the cost of
equity with other sources of long-term finance, and

(*ii*) it enables the company to compare its forecast rate of
return with the cost of new equity so that a correct investment decision can be made.

The great problem here, of course, is the difficulty of
forecasting accurately the rate of return. Although this
difficulty also applies to the other forms of long-term finance,
the problem is much more acute with equity.

In the case of debt and preferred stock, so long as the
company had knowledge of the corporation tax rate it would
know its interest and dividend charge, even though it would
only have estimates of the returns from the assets financed
in these ways. However, in the case of new equity capital,
the extent of participation in both profits and losses is not
limited to the rate of return on the new assets. If, for some
reason unconnected with the new equity, the overall rate of
return and hence profits of the firm suddenly rose, the new
equity shareholders would participate in these profits,
thereby reducing the profits available for the existing shareholders, so that the true cost of the new equity in this case
may be extremely high. On the other hand, if, for some

reason unconnected with the new equity, the overall rate of return and hence profits of the firm suddenly slumped, the new equity shareholders would also participate in any losses that were made, thereby reducing the burden on the existing shareholders, so that the true cost of the new equity in this case may be extremely low. It is these uncertainties concerning the rate of return on capital that make it extremely difficult to calculate in advance the cost of equity capital.

(b) *Tax complications*. So far as the Inland Revenue is concerned, equity shareholders represent the ownership of the company, and any profits generated are subject to corporation tax. Thus the same analysis applies here as in the case of preferred stock—equity-financed assets yielding 20 per cent before tax would give a return of only 10 per cent to the shareholders if we assume a 50 per cent rate of corporation tax.

EXAMPLE 33: If £100,000 of assets financed by equity were invested to yield 20 per cent, then the £20,000 earnings from the investment would give a return of only £10,000 (i.e. 10 per cent) to the shareholders after the Inland Revenue had taken its £10,000 (50 per cent of the profits).

It is clear from this that a reduced rate of corporation tax would increase the rate of return to the equity shareholders, while a higher rate of corporation tax would reduce the return to them. Thus the cost of equity, like the cost of preferred stock, will vary with the corporation tax rate: there will be a positive relationship between the rate of return required on equity-financed assets and the corporation tax rate, in order to yield a given after-tax return to the equity shareholders.

Equity finance, however, has an additional tax complication in that even after corporation tax has been levied on the profits of the company, there is the additional question as to whether or not these profits should be distributed. In the first place there are the liquidity effects of having to pay corporation tax in advance on distributions. Secondly, despite the intention of the new imputation system to treat distributions and retentions in the same way (*see* Chapter II, 15), the fact remains that dividends received by shareholders will be taxed to the extent that personal rates of tax lie above the basic rate.

If, on the other hand, the profits are retained in the firm, then the only other tax the shareholders will be subjected to will be the capital gains tax levied on the capital appreciation of the shares at the time of sale. Since the capital gains tax rate will, for most shareholders, be appreciably below their personal tax rates on unearned income, this will clearly affect the cost of retained earnings *vis-à-vis* other methods of raising equity finance. This issue will be considered further in **5–6** below.

(*c*) *Institutional complications.* In the case of equity finance, the major institutional complications arise first from the cost difference between internal and external finance, and secondly from the variety of methods available for the issue of shares.

5. Cost of internal finance. The major source of long-run internal finance comes from retained earnings, although depreciation provisions also make some contribution. The crucial question here is what determines the distribution between retained earnings and dividends.

If a firm has a 10 per cent rate of return on its assets, then presumably shareholders who receive dividends could reinvest these dividends in companies of similar risk and receive a 10 per cent rate of return, so that in the absence of any imperfections, this 10 per cent would represent the opportunity cost of retained earnings. However, in the real world, imperfections exist:

(*a*) Shareholders in higher tax brackets would have to pay any *additional tax* above the basic rate on the dividends they receive so that they may have considerably less left for reinvestment than if the earnings had been retained and reinvested internally;

(*b*) the shareholders will incur *brokerage costs* in reinvesting the distributed profits, which will also reduce the amount available for reinvestment.

We would therefore expect the cost of retained earnings to be lower than the cost of new issues. Moreover, if the distribution of dividends means that the firm has to issue new equity, then (*see* **7** and **8** below) the flotation costs involved and the possible underpricing of the issue would reinforce this argument. Indeed, one could logically argue from this that so long as the firm has a supply of investment opportunities yielding a rate of return in excess of the cost of equity capital, it should retain all its earnings.[2]

6. Arguments in favour of the distribution of earnings. There are, however, powerful counter-arguments against the line of reasoning set out in **5** above.

(a) It is argued that dividends contain a large element of *informational content* which can affect the share price. If a firm has stabilised its dividend pay-out ratio over a number of years, a sudden change of policy would have the effect of conveying to investors management's expectations about future profitability. It is for this reason that companies attempt to maintain their dividend pay-out ratios if a temporary fall in profits has taken place. A more prolonged fall in profits will clearly necessitate a change in the ratio.

(b) Some shareholders prefer a *current income* from their shareholdings. The proposition that this could equally well be achieved by the sale of shares is not really defensible in view of the transaction costs involved and the uncertainties regarding the share price at the time of sale.

It is clear that there are therefore a number of conflicting issues regarding the effect of dividend distribution on the value of the enterprise and hence on the true cost of retained earnings. The preference of investors for current income, the existence of transaction costs and uncertain share prices suggest that dividend distribution has a positive effect on share prices. On the other hand, the flotation and underpricing costs of new issues and the existence of a differential tax rate between dividends and capital gains tend to favour profit-retention. Whether the factors raising the costs of retention outweigh the factors lowering the cost of retention is uncertain. The empirical evidence is conflicting and omits a number of important variables, particularly growth and risk. Certainly companies behave as though dividends do affect the value of the enterprise.

The same analysis can equally well be applied to depreciation provisions. Once again, the conclusion must be that we are uncertain about the true cost of internal finance since we are uncertain concerning the value of the opportunity cost involved (i.e. the effect of dividend policy on the value of the enterprise).

7. Cost of external equity. The conceptual problems involved in finding out the true cost of new equity issues have already been highlighted in **6** above—the market discount cost involved in underpricing the new issue and the administrative and underwriting expenses involved in floating it. The situation is made even more complicated by the fact that there exist a variety of issue methods and therefore corresponding variations in market discount and administrative expenses. Nevertheless, these costs are important and the cost of new equity capital is positively related to the administrative expenses and market discount involved.

The administrative expenses involved vary significantly with the method of issue.

(a) *The rights issue* is the cheapest method, since the offer is made directly to the existing shareholders by means of a circular. Thus no expensive advertising nor allotment procedure is required, and normally very little commission has to be paid to the underwriters. The other methods of issue require much higher administrative expenses.

(b) *The Stock Exchange placing*, whereby the issuing house places the shares with its clients, requires a placing letter and other documents, and the publication of information concerning the issue.

(c) *The public issue by prospectus*, whereby the public are invited to subscribe at a fixed price, is even more expensive and includes the costs of printing and advertising the prospectus, the cost of allocating the shares in the event of oversubscription, the cost of underwriting the issue to ensure that all the shares will be taken up, in addition to the remuneration to the issuing house and to all other advisers to the issue.

(d) *The offer for sale*, whereby the issuing house sells the shares to the public involves similar costs as (c) above although in this case the expenses may be paid by the issuing house out of its remuneration.

(e) *The tender* method of issue is similar to the offer for sale, except that only a minimum price is stated in the prospectus and the public are invited to submit a tender indicating the price they are prepared to pay and the number of shares they are prepared to buy. The administrative expenses involved in the tender method are therefore similar to those of the offer for sale.

8. Market discount. Just as the rights issue involves the lowest administrative costs, it also eliminates the problems associated with market discount.

Market discount involves a cost to the company, since it involves the underpricing of an issue to the extent that the post-issue price is considerably above the pre-issue price—because the company is uncertain about the demand for the new issue, and in its efforts to ensure that the issue will be fully subscribed, it chooses underpricing. This obviously represents a loss to the company and the existing shareholders, since new shareholders will be coming into the company on preferential terms, and the price of the company's shares after the issue will be somewhere between the original price and the lower new-issue price. In the case of a rights issue, however, underpricing will be irrelevant since it is the existing shareholders who will enter at the preferential price, thus compensating for the loss in value on the existing shares. (Note that the existing shareholders can obtain their compensation by selling their rights if they do not wish to participate in the new issue.) It is for this reason that the Stock Exchange Council demands that issues of new equity for cash be offered to existing shareholders, unless the prior approval of these shareholders has been obtained at a general meeting.

Thus it is clear that with the exception of rights issues, underpricing involves a cost to the company whenever any of the other existing methods of issue are used. This is particularly so with the fixed-price methods of issue, and in this respect it is worth noting that it is only the tender method of issue that makes any attempt to estimate market demand in the hope of reducing market discount.

9. Empirical evidence. An extensive study of the cost of new issues has been provided by the work of Merrett, Howe and Newbould.[3]   Their analysis was based upon issues over the period 1959–63 and proved to be highly illuminating on the subject of new-issue costs.

(*a*) The study showed that there were significant advantages to be gained in the selection of advisers, in so far as the pricing of the shares in the issue was concerned, i.e. some advisers were much more efficient at minimising market discount than were others.

(b) The vast majority of issues by quoted companies were rights issues, and this method proved to be most efficient in eliminating the problem of underpricing and minimising the administrative costs of the issue, which averaged 1 per cent of the issue proceeds, although underwriting costs did average out at 1·8 per cent.

(c) The method of issue used by new companies seeking a Stock Exchange quotation had a significant effect on the costs of the issue, and the major element of this differential cost arose from underpricing rather than administrative expenses. Their analysis was particularly concerned with the comparison of the tender method of issue with the fixed-price methods of offers for sale and placings, and they found that the average total costs (comprising both market discount and adminstrative expenses) of tender issues were significantly and consistently lower than the similar average total costs of offers and placings. Indeed, in the extreme case of the comparison between the offers and tenders in 1963 up to a value of £500,000 they found that the average total cost including market discount was 60·8 per cent of the net proceeds in the case of offers and 17·2 per cent in the case of tenders. In other words, for every £1 raised, another 60·8p cost had been incurred for the offers and 17·2p for the tenders.

More recently, research undertaken by Davis and Yeomans[4] reached similar conclusions. Their analysis was based on a cross-section of 265 firms coming to the new issue market over the period 1965–71. Their statistical analysis came up with the following results:

(d) Firm size was important, and there was an inverse relationship between firm size and market discount.

(e) There was considerable variation in average discounts between methods of issue. Tender issues displayed the lowest average discount at 6·95 per cent of issue price, with levels of 8·88 per cent for offers for sale and 19·08 per cent for placings.

(f) In conditions of stock market uncertainty, there were increasing errors in new issue pricing, particularly with regard to placing. Moreover, the issuing houses frequently overpriced small-firm issues during pessimistic periods, causing under-subscription and a depressed market price.

The cost of new equity capital obviously therefore varies in relation to the efficiency of the advisers to the issue, the administrative costs involved and the amount of underpricing involved. In this respect, it is worth noting that the costs associated with the rights method of issue are significantly less than for any other method. However, for new companies coming to the market for the first time and consequently unable to use the rights method, the choice of method may be of paramount significance in relation to the costs involved.

10. Average cost of equity capital. Equity capital, as we have seen in 4 and 7 above, is itself derived from a variety of sources, and before we can include the cost of equity as part of the overall cost of capital we will need first to calculate the average cost of equity capital. This is achieved by simply averaging the cost of each source of equity in proportion to its use.

INTER-RELATIONSHIPS IN THE COST OF CAPITAL

11. Two opposing views. So far in this Chapter the entire analysis of the cost of the individual capital components has been conducted on the assumption that the cost of each individual capital component is not influenced by the cost of any other. To complete our analysis we must now remove this assumption, and allow inter-relationships to exist.

The question of inter-relationships between the capital components is an extremely controversial one and is fundamental to the choice of an optimum capital structure. Two opposing views have been expressed. One view, the traditional approach, is that the inter-relationships are such that changes in the composition of finance will affect the overall average cost of capital and hence the optimum capital structure. The opposing view, held by Modigliani and Miller (*see* 13 below), is that the inter-relationships are such that changes in the composition of the capital structure will not affect the average cost of capital, so that capital structure decisions are irrelevant.

2. Traditional approach. The major part of the financial literature supports the traditional approach, which argues as follows. The cost of each individual capital component will depend in the main upon the risk attached to it. Thus, we would except debt to be cheaper than preferred stock, which in turn will be cheaper than equity (note, however, the reverse yield gap, **3** (*b*) above). However, there will be inter-relationships, in that the amount of equity employed will affect the risk attaching to debt. The larger the equity base, the less risk will attach to any debt issued by the firm, and this will tend to reduce the cost of debt. Conversely, the smaller the equity base and the larger the amount of debt already issued, the greater the risk attached to any new debt issued, and the cost of debt will rise. A similar type of risk analysis applies to equity. When there is very little fixed-charge capital in the capital structure, the risk to equity will be low, so that only a relatively low yield will be required by equity shareholders. Conversely, as the debt ratio increases, the risk attached to equity increases and the corresponding cost of equity will rise.

This analysis suggests two opposing trends. On the one hand, debt generally costs less than equity, so that the increasing use of low-cost debt will reduce the average cost of capital. On the other hand, the increasing use of debt increases risk both for debt-holders and equity-holders, and this tends to raise the average cost of capital. The traditional approach believes that the combination of these two influences works in such a way that there is an optmum capital structure. In Fig. 52, the cost of debt rises after a while, demonstrating the higher risk involved as more debt is used. Similarly, the cost

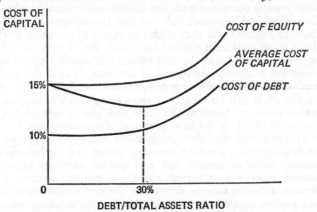

FIG. 52—*The cost of debt.* The traditional approach to the determination of an optimum capital structure, where the use of low-cost debt initially lowers the cost of capital.

of equity, although it too may remain constant for a time, eventually rises as the debt ratio increases. The traditional approach, however, argues that initially the use of low-cost debt will more than offset the extra cost from the greater risk involved, so that the average cost of capital falls. However, eventually, as the use of debt increases, the rising cost of both debt and equity from the higher risk involved will more than offset the use of lower-cost debt, so that the cost of capital rises. Thus there will be a minimum cost of capital associated with an optimal capital structure.

Note that the optimum capital structure for the firm will depend upon the risk involved. The more stable and less risky the industry, the more likely it is that the optimum capital structure will be at a higher debt ratio.

13. Modigliani–Miller approach.[5]

The Modigliani–Miller theory is based upon the same principles as the traditional theory, i.e. that the increased use of low-cost debt will on the one hand reduce the average cost of capital (because of the combination of low-cost debt with relatively high-cost equity) but that on the other hand the increased use of debt will raise the average cost of capital (because the increased risk raises the cost of equity capital). However, here the Modigliani–Miller theory parts company with the traditional approach; whereas the traditional approach believes that the relative strength of these two effects will vary with the degree of leverage, so that there is an optimum capital structure, the Modigliani–Miller approach argues that the two effects will exactly cancel each other out whatever the degree of leverage, so that the cost of capital will be completely independent of the debt/equity mix. In Fig. 53 it can be seen that the average cost of capital remains constant because the increased use of low-cost debt is exactly offset by the increased cost of equity capital.

The proof of the Modigliani–Miller theory is based on an *arbitrage process*, whereby they argue that in a perfect capital market firms of similar risk and similar earnings potential cannot receive a different valuation simply because they possess different capital structures. However, the assumption of a perfect capital market is unreal, and the arbitrage process breaks down once we introduce the complications of brokerage fees, capital gains tax and other imperfections of the capital market. Indeed, if tax allowance on debt interest is introduced

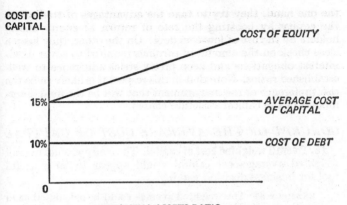

DEBT/TOTAL ASSETS RATIO

Fig. 53—*The Modigliani–Miller theory.* There is no unique optimal capital structure in the Modigliani–Miller approach, since the use of low-cost debt is offset by the rising cost of equity capital.

into the model, then the Modigliani–Miller theory leads to the conclusion that the cost of capital continuously declines with increased debt. Thus it is unlikely that the assumptions of the Modigliani–Miller theory will hold in the real world, and hence one must have grave reservations about the conclusions of their model.

14. Empirical evidence. The empirical studies on optimal capital structure have been inconclusive. Modigliani and Miller have produced evidence claiming to support their theory, while others have produced evidence claiming to support the traditional approach. However, most of these studies have been statistically biased, particularly in omitting important variables. In any case, the fundamental problem is that evidence of a declining capital cost with increased debt is consistent with both the traditional approach and a tax-adjusted Modigliani–Miller approach. It is only in the unlikely event of finding evidence of a firm which has gone beyond its optimal capital structure to the point where excessive debt raises the cost of capital that the traditional theory can be said to have been proved.

Whatever the academics may claim, firms continue to behave as though there is an optimum capital structure. On

the one hand, they try to take the advantages of trading on
the equity by boosting the rate of return to equity shareholders by the use of low-cost debt. On the other, they keep a
close check on the amount of earnings required to cover fixed-
interest obligations and keep pretty strict adherence to well-
established ratios. Note that in this respect it is likely to be the
risk preference of the management that will be the final determinant of the capital structure chosen.

CONCEPT OF THE AVERAGE COST OF CAPITAL

15. Overall weighted cost of capital. The concept of an overall
weighted average-cost capital would appear to be a useful
tool for business decision-making.

EXAMPLE 34: The weighted average could be calculated as in
Table XXXVII, a 50 per cent corporation tax rate being
assumed.

TABLE XXXVII: WEIGHTED AVERAGE COST OF CAPITAL

(i) Capital	(ii) Total	(iii) % of total	(iv) After tax cost	(v) Column (iv) × column (iii)
10% debt	£30	30%	5%	0·0150
10% preferred stock	£10	10%	10%	0·0100
Equity	£60	60%	12%	0·0720
				0·0970 = 9·7%

The average weighted cost of capital can be seen to be
9·7 per cent.

However, it is questionable as to whether one should talk
about "the" average cost of capital. As this Chapter has
demonstrated, capital is raised from many sources and at
varying cost. It is important, therefore, that any business
decisions to be undertaken include a calculation of the true
cost of the particular source of funds so that a correct decision
may be taken.

16. Conclusion. Despite the variety of sources of funds, the
institutional and tax complications, the varying degrees of

credit-worthiness and corresponding interest charges that exist and the inter-relationships that occur between the cost of the individual capital components, the calculation of the correct cost of capital for business decision-making purposes is not impossible. The crux of the problem is to ensure that new investments undertaken are based upon marginal rather than average considerations and that the financing decision is based upon comparisons of the new source of funds with the expected returns from the investment. These considerations are far more important than any detailed deliberations concerning the overall weighted average cost of capital.

PROGRESS TEST 13

1. Estimate the effect of corporation tax changes on the cost of debt capital, preferred stock and equity. (**1** (*a*), **3** (*a*), **4** (*a*))

2. Explain the term "reverse yield gap". What circumstances brought it into existence? (**3** (*b*))

3. Why is it so difficult to calculate the cost of equity capital? (**4–9**)

4. Is the dividend policy of a company irrelevant? (**5, 6**)

5. Explain what is meant by the "market discount" cost of issue. Explain the performance of rights issues, tender issues and offers for sale according to this criterion. (**8**)

6. Is there an optimal capital structure? (**11–14**)

7. Discuss the relevance of a weighted average cost of capital. (**15, 16**)

FURTHER READING

1. Weston, J. F. and Brigham, E., *Managerial Finance*, Holt, Rinehart and Winston, 1969.

2. Gordon, M., *The Investment, Financing and Valuation of the Corporation*, Irwin, 1962.

Modigliani, F. and Miller, M., "Dividend Policy, Growth and the Valuation of Shares", *Journal of Business*, October 1961.

Walter, J., "Dividend Policy; its influence on the value of the enterprise", *Journal of Finance*, May 1963.

3. Merrett, A. J., Howe, M. and Newbould, G. D., *Equity Issues and the London Capital Market*, Longman, 1967.

4. Davis, E. W. and Yeomans, K. A., "Company Finance and the Capital Market", *Department of Applied Economics Occasional Papers*, No. 39, Cambridge University Press, 1974.

5. Modigliani, F. and Miller, M., "The Cost of Capital, Corporation Finance and the Theory of Investment", *American Economic Review*, June 1958.

CHAPTER XIV

CORPORATE STRATEGY

DEFINITION

1. Objectives and resource-allocation. The concept of
corporate strategy is a relatively old concept which has
recently re-emerged, both as a crucial guide to company
decision-making and as a topic worthy of academic investigation on its own merits. Nevertheless, despite the new
popularity surrounding the concept there is still considerable
confusion as to how far company decision-making should be
affected by it. It appears to be generally agreed that corporate
strategy includes the deployment of the firm's resources in
pursuit of its objectives, but there is some disagreement as to
whether the choice of company objectives is itself also included.

We are inclined to the viewpoint that the concept of corporate strategy includes both these elements, i.e. both the
choice of objectives and the deployment of resources in pursuit
of them. Company objectives themselves are not formulated
in a vacuum and must be responsive to environmental feedback so that the observed success or lack of success of the
chosen strategy during the process of implementation may
itself cause company objectives to be revised. Similarly, the
revision of company objectives will lead to a new deployment
of resources: the inter-dependence between the choice of
objectives and the resource-allocation process is a two-way
flow which makes it undesirable to separate them.

Thus we believe that effective strategic planning requires
that the corporate planning process includes both the choice
of company objectives and the allocation of resources necessary
for carrying them out. Such a definition of corporate strategy
also overcomes the methodological problems of defining terms
such as goals, policies, objectives, etc., since these are all now
incorporated within the strategic plan.

2. Long-run strategic decision-making. To have a more clear-cut understanding of the concept of corporate strategy, it is necessary to distinguish between strategic and operating decisions.

Strategic decisions are concerned with the long-run development of the company, and these are the decisions which corporate strategy centres upon. These decisions are concerned with the growth path of the firm through time, the kinds of businesses in which it will wish to participate, and in particular, the kinds of product mix the firm will produce and the kinds of market it envisages for its products. It is essentially these kinds of long-run strategic decisions with which corporate strategy is concerned.

Operating decisions, on the other hand, are concerned with issues requiring day-to-day decision-making within the company. Such decisions are concerned with the supervision of performance, week-to-week price changes, optimum level of inventories, etc., so that a maximum performance is obtained from the product mix established by the strategic plan. Corporate strategy would be concerned only indirectly with such short-term operational activities, in so far as they provide feedback for the overall strategic plan.

3. What strategy demands of a company. It is important, as Andrews says, that "the identification of strategy captures the present and projected character of the organisation".[1] Corporate strategy requires that the firm should define its products and clearly indicate the markets for them. Sources of finance must be clearly designated and the degree of risk-aversion specified. Most important, the kind of organisation structure required to achieve the company's objectives must be indicated. Strategy therefore demands that a company knows in which direction it intends to go, what sort of financial constraints exist, and what kind of organisational structure is likely to be most successful in meeting its objectives.

IS STRATEGIC PLANNING NECESSARY?

4. Advantages claimed. There have been a number of reasons suggested as to why the clear specification of a corporate plan is likely to be desirable. The main arguments put forward are as follows:

(a) It is *insufficient merely to state objectives in terms of maximisation of profits*. In the first place, profitability is seldom the only objective, as was demonstrated in Chapter I. In any case, even if profitability were the only criterion, such an objective would not show us how the profit is to be earned, what products should be produced, what markets should be penetrated, what organisational structure is best suited to satisfy the firm's objectives, etc. It is to generate answers to questions of this kind that a statement of objectives and plans, more detailed and more specific than a mere adherence to profit-maximisation, is required.

(b) Forward planning is beneficial to all companies, in that a *more rational allocation of resources* is possible than that determined by decisions taken on the spur of the moment. Moreover, planning ahead is absolutely essential in some companies where projects have long lead times between the conception of an idea and its eventual launching on the market, which may be years later. With some projects new product development takes years, and where distribution and marketing costs are likely to be heavy, it is essential that such projects be subject to long-range planning.

(c) The *possibility of influencing*, rather than merely adapting to changes in, *the business environment*. Professor Galbraith [2] was one of the first to realise the power of the large corporations, and he pointed out that they recognised the need not merely to respond to demand but to create and influence it. The power of some of these large organisations with their huge advertising and marketing expenditures have cast doubt upon the principle of "consumers' sovereignty", so prevalent in the economic literature. Faced with such competition, the modern corporation cannot afford to stand still and wait for the environment to change in its favour. Forward planning coupled with an active research and development department can help the modern corporation to carve out a niche for itself, rather than wait for a favourable environment. Moreover, the rapidly-changing environment makes it essential that the company possess an explicit strategy. It is inadequate simply to extrapolate the past performance of the company into the future. It is essential that industrial trends, competitors' behaviour and other essential elements of environmental change be closely monitored and used as a guide to corporate decision-making.

(*d*) The *identification of a specific corporate strategy* with well-defined objectives acts as a focus of organisational effort. Tilles[3] points out that as companies become larger it is more and more difficult to reconcile co-ordinated action and entrepreneurial effort without an explicit statement of strategy, and that this becomes particularly important where companies are divisionalised. We will return to this question in Chapter XV when we consider some of the problems of successfully implementing the chosen strategy.

5. Reservations. The concept of corporate strategy has not been accepted without reservations, particularly in an imperfect world where often management is committed heavily to operational considerations. The following are some of the criticisms that have been made of the strategic planning process.

(*a*) Company strategy is *too important to be revealed* to the entire organisation, and indirectly to competitors. Most of the early pioneers of strategic planning in the business world were of the opinion that it conveyed a unique competitive advantage to the firm and that to make corporate strategy explicit would undermine this. Thus, prior to the 1950s, when companies employed a strategy it was regarded as something private to be shared only by top management. The problem with this approach is that the advantages demonstrated in **4** (*d*) above are lost, namely that many of the key employees involved in the implementation of strategy will have no clear guidelines as to what contribution they should make. In recent years, much of the literature has come increasingly to the view that the advantages gained from explicit strategy formulation outweigh the disadvantages of increasing the information available to competitors.

(*b*) The argument that many firms succeed without an explicit strategy raises the fundamental question of how large, complex, business firms can possibly achieve *co-ordination of effort and successful implementation of policy* without an explicit strategy. Ansoff suggests that the answer to this lies in the nature of the firm's growth. When the environment, technology and competition change only slowly in an orderly manner, then strategy changes only slowly, so that managers are able to adapt to the changes using their accumulated knowledge and experience. Thus "given deliberate extrapolative growth, an explicit strategy is not essential to co-ordinated adaptive growth". However, where the environment, technology or state of competition change rapidly, then the established organisational structure will find it extremely difficult to cope with the new conditions. "Under these conditions . . . without the benefit of a unifying strategy, the chances are high that different parts of the organisation will develop different and contradictory responses."[4] Thus under such conditions of rapid change, strategic planning becomes essential to guarantee survival.

(c) The danger that concentration on a specific strategy may lead to an *inability to take up better opportunities as they arise*. The argument here is that the uncertainties of the environment and the inability to obtain correct information about the future mean that unforeseen opportunities will arise as time proceeds which may be by-passed because of over-dedication to the strategic plan, which was formalised when less information was available. However, it could equally well be argued that a good strategic plan should be flexible enough to incorporate these unforeseen opportunities—indeed we would expect the strategic plan to be continually revised as information about environmental change became more readily available.

(d) Strategic planning is extremely complex, indeed so complex that it can become *prohibitively expensive* to operate. The introduction of strategic planning into a business organisation may require massive upheavals in organisational structure as interested parties try to maintain the *status quo*. Most business organisations are lacking in the managerial skills required for successful strategy formulation. The implementation of strategy poses problems of developing motivational and incentive systems geared to the strategy chosen.

We will consider some of these problems in Chapter XV. It is sufficient to say here that strategic planning has its costs as well as its benefits, and it is not surprising that in view of the administrative skills it demands, companies have been reluctant to rely heavily upon it.

EMPIRICAL EVIDENCE

6. Will strategic planning bring about a better organisational performance? There is very little empirical evidence on this. However, what we do have seems to suggest that strategic planning does improve organisational performance. Ansoff and his colleagues,[5] in a study of American mergers and acquisitions, have demonstrated that financial performance was much better where the acquisition was part of a pre-planned strategy. A similar conclusion was reached by Thune and House[6] in their study of the effectiveness of long-range planning on company performance.

STRATEGY FORMULATION—GENERAL CONSIDERATIONS

7. Strategic plan. The formulation of a strategic plan is a complex process, particularly for large companies where the number of opportunities available are virtually unlimited and the problem of choice extremely difficult. Consequently, it is essential that companies have some kind of analytical framework which will aid them in their search for a rational strategy. Intuition and experience suggest that companies should undertake the following activities when devising their strategic plans:

(a) *A rigorous analysis of its environment*, with a view to possible exploitation of environmental opportunity or anticipation of environmental threat. The environmental forces which affect a company may emanate from rapid technological change, from a changing economic environment or from social and political change. Extreme political change could, of course, have the most adverse effect upon a company, but normally the main pressure comes from technological and economic factors. Rapidly changing technology may offer exceptional opportunity, but on the other hand also threatens its very existence if it is slow to adapt to the new opportunities created. Similarly, major economic changes such as the growth of multi-national firms, increased industrial concentration, the industrialisation of the under-developed countries, the enormous increase in world commodity prices, etc., also make it essential that economic changes are closely monitored and used to the company's advantage. Major social changes, such as the movement towards consumer durables or the more recent concern with the protection of the environment pose opportunities and threats which a company would be unwise to ignore.

(b) *An analysis of company strengths and weaknesses* to ensure that environmental opportunity is matched with corporate competence. There would be little point in a company attempting to take advantage of an outstanding environmental opportunity if it did not, and is unlikely to be able to, possess the technological knowledge and company organisation required to see the project through. It is essential, therefore, that the company tries to identify what it is good at and also what weaknesses it has. It is important that strengths and weaknesses are recognised, and that an attempt is made to build upon strengths, and where possible to eliminate weaknesses.

It is possible, of course, that environmental opportunity for a particular company is limited because none of the company's areas of strength can exploit it. However, in most cases, there is likely to be some talent or skill which the company can make use of. As Ansoff [7] has pointed out, most corporate strategies have a *synergy component* which enables companies to obtain the maximum performance potential out of any given strategy. Synergy is commonly known as the $2 + 2 = 5$ effect—the sum of the whole is likely to be greater than the sum of the parts. The combined performance of two operations between which synergy exists will thus be greater than that of the performance of the two activities undertaken separately. Ansoff argues that it is possible for this synergistic effect to be negative, i.e. it is possible that the conglomeration of strengths and skills involved in one type of operation may be so different from those required for another activity that a strategy which tried to combine the two would fail; the two operations would be more efficiently performed if they were undertaken separately. A movement from defence/space hardware into production of a fast-moving consumer good such as cigarettes, would be likely to have negative synergy.

Company strengths and weaknesses and the synergy component, therefore, are both likely to constrain the company's ability fully to capitalise on a potential environmental opportunity.

(c) *A clear recognition of the personal values and aspirations* of the chief executive and the key managers in the business. In small companies it is only the personal values of the chief executive which are likely to be important, whereas in large organisations there may be a considerable number of key executives whose viewpoints must be taken into account if strategy formulation is to be effective. It is extremely important that such personal values should harmonise with the adopted strategy otherwise successful strategy cannot be implemented. It is, of course, true that strategies unacceptable to the key management may be implemented, but in such cases it is unlikely that more than mediocre effort will be expended in their implementation. We will return to this question in Chapter XV.

(d) *A careful consideration of the ethical aspects* of the strategic choice. Some companies are concerned with this problem because they want to be, others are concerned with it because they have to be. Some companies recognise that they have obligations to elements of society other than shareholders (*see* Chapter I) and regard themselves as providers of good jobs, fair prices, reasonable dividends, etc., with a healthy regard for the interests of the community. Other companies recognise that if they do not respond to socially sensitive issues then there is always the threat of legislation in the background. Issues such as fair prices, employee exploitation, pollution, etc., have forced many companies to have a long hard think about the ethical considerations of their various strategies.

STRATEGY FORMULATION—ECONOMIC ISSUES

In **7** (*a*)–(*d*) above, we have considered some of the most important aspects that strategic planners should concern themselves with. However, these general considerations do not answer certain crucial questions: Where do we start from—the internal strengths of the company or environmental opportunities? What happens if an analysis of internal strengths and environmental opportunities leads in different directions? Do we limit ourselves to a particular set of environmental opportunities, or do we consider all conceivable ones? We hope to provide tentative answers to some of these questions.

8. Scope of environmental opportunity. There is considerable disagreement in the literature regarding the extent to which the company should probe the external environment. Should such a search for environmental opportunities be limited to the industries in which the firm is already operating, or should there be a general search? If one supports the latter approach then this raises the fundamental question of whether the company has the requisite resources to undertake such a search, and if great detail is required the answer is likely to be negative. On the other hand, if the former approach is advocated then it is likely that the company will miss out on profitable opportunities for expansion which do not fall within the scope of search

9. Narrow definition. The first approach is to take a narrow definition of the firm's business (such as railways or newspapers); strategy formulation is then based strictly upon this definition. With this approach there are three major steps in strategy formulation.

(a) The identification of the crucial *economic and technical characteristics* of the industry in which the company operates, and an analysis of any trends which suggest future economic or technical change.

(b) The identification of the *type of competition* within the industry and an analysis of that type of competition which is likely to be successful in the industry in the future, i.e. price, marketing, quality, etc.

(c) The identification of any *political and social developments* which are likely to influence the choice of strategy.

This narrow definition of the firms' business has the advantage of concentrating on specific industrial trends for which statistics are usually available, and also identifies the essential competitive elements and the specific requirements for competitive success in the business. However, this approach has received considerable criticism in the literature.

Simmonds points out that the definition itself is usually inadequate—a firm could define its function by a single-word description, such as "movie business", but such a business serves both entertainment and communication needs, and therefore serves more than one industry. Most firms have more than one product, and even if it produces only one, such as boots, it may still be satisfying a range of consumer needs—status, economy, fashion, etc.—for different customers.

To quote Simmonds: "The fallacy of a single-word approach lies in trying to force multi-dimensional opportunity into a one-dimensional model. A firm is a complex entity in a complex environment and it would be unusual if there were not a number of directions for profitable development."[8]

10. Ansoff's definition. Ansoff rejects the one-word description as inadequate. However, he still believes that the company needs a "common thread—a relationship between present and future product-markets which . . . [enables] outsiders to perceive where the firm is heading, and the inside management to give it guidance".[9]

(a) The *common thread* is specified in terms of the two dimensions of product and market, the product–market scope; a description of this often needs to be made in terms of sub-industries which contain product–markets and technologies with similar characteristics. This product–market scope defines the scope of search.

(b) The *direction of expansion* within this scope is classified into four possible directions:

(i) market penetration, expansion through the increase of market share for the present product markets;

(ii) market development, new missions are sought for the firm's products;

(iii) product development, the creation of new products to replace current ones; and

(iv) diversification, both products and missions are new to the firm.

(c) *There is a competitive advantage element*, where the firm attempts to identify the characteristics of outstanding opportunities within the area defined by the results of (a) and (b) above. These specifications describe "the firm's search for inherently profitable opportunities in the external environment. The first sets the scope for the search, the second the directions within the scope, and the third the characteristics of outstanding opportunities".

Ansoff's approach to environmental search has received similar criticism to that outlined in 9 above. Although his approach is broader, it has still been criticised for chaining the company's product policy to the choice of one common thread. Simmonds questions the fact that there need only be one common thread for expansion purposes, and does not believe that a many-dimensioned entity can be chained to one dimension of growth. Ansoff has since recognised the limitations of building upon company strengths. This leads us on to Simmonds's own approach.[10]

11. The multi-dimensional definition. Simmonds argues that the company should explore environmental opportunity along all the dimensions in which it has contact with its environment. He suggests an analysis of the customer, distributive, product and production characteristics of the product-market, and proposes seventeen dimensions for such analysis:

Customer characteristics
  Age
  Sex
  Loyalty
  Income bracket
  Social class

Product characteristics
  Size of item
  Material
  Design

Order characteristics
  Size of order
  Time of year
  Credit arrangements

Production characteristics
  Technology required
  Skills employed
  Machines used

Outlet characteristics
  Type
  Size
  Location

The task of the corporate planner is to identify the strengths the firm has along any particular dimension. Moreover, as the strategist moves from the consideration of strengths towards specific proposals, he begins to examine more and more dimensions. A new class of customer may become the focus of attention, or a new type of technology may be needed, etc. In effect, "the separate examination of individual dimensions of existing activity has been a vehicle for arriving at actions which must become fully specified in all dimensions if action is to be taken on them".

The great advantage of the multi-dimensional approach is that analysis of environmental opportunity is not limited to any one particular direction, so that all potential opportunities are examined. Moreover, the approach lends itself to the application of strengths and weakness analysis which we will now consider.

ENVIRONMENTAL OPPORTUNITY v. CORPORATE COMPETENCE

12. Inside-out or outside-in? We now have to examine the fundamental question of whether corporate planning begins with an analysis of environmental opportunity, or of company strengths and weaknesses. In other words, should the strategic planning process be based upon what consumers need or on what the company is good at producing?

These two basic approaches to strategy formulation have been termed the "outside-in" and "inside-out" approaches respectively, the former emphasising the shaping of the company to meet environmental opportunity, the latter emphasising the internal strengths of the company and the search for environmental opportunities which exploit these strengths.

There is considerable support in favour of both these approaches. The marketing-orientated approach has been most forceably put by Levitt, who argues that "An industry begins with the customer and his needs, not with a patent, a raw material or a selling skill. Given the customer's needs, the industry develops backwards".[11] The emphasis in this approach is on forecasting customer needs and restructuring the organisation to facilitate the fulfilment of them. Note that in this respect, environmental opportunities are not limited to the present customers of the company, and it may be that environmental trends suggest that the company seek a new class of customers with a different set of needs.

13. Advantages of outside-in.[12]

(a) It is claimed that the marketing approach engenders alertness and aggressiveness among management who become characterised by a restless discontent which makes them more dynamic.

(b) Emphasis on the marketing approach equips management with a broader view of environmental opportunities than would be acquired by taking a narrow view of current organisational activities.

(c) The emphasis is always upon the meeting of future customer needs, so ensuring that the search for technical perfection is pursued only in so far as it contributes towards the fulfilment of these needs.

(d) The rapidly changing business environment and the dynamic nature of the marketing approach ensure that management is not tempted to stay with a good product or a growth industry for too long.

14. Dangers of outside-in.

(a) First, and perhaps most important, is the great weight placed upon forecasting ability. Forecasting has always been a complex process and has become even more so with the rapid growth of inter-industry competition. The extent of diversification among many large firms is making it even more difficult to forecast future trends with any degree of reliability (see Chapters III, 1–30 and IV, 1–18).

(b) There is also the likelihood that many firms will try to cash in on the same environmental opportunities, so that the potential profits after entry may be considerably lower than those forecast before the entry of other firms.

15. Inside-out.
The alternative inside-out approach to strategy formulation emphasises expansion based upon company strengths, or occasionally growth designed to remove important weaknesses in the organisation. The emphasis is generally on building upon strengths. The general philosophy behind this approach is that any strength or advantage which the company possesses over other companies should be utilised if possible, and that the company should expand in areas where it has a competitive advantage. Such a strength may lie in any part of the firm's activities, such as its physical assets, distribution system, customer contacts, etc. This strategy-from-strengths approach has found an ardent advocate in Simmonds who argues that "right at the start of the

marketing process, the orientation is towards assets rather than customer needs. Strategy from strengths is the emphasis".[13] Nevertheless, this is not to say that customer needs are ignored in setting strategy, or indeed that the customers will be the ones currently supplied by the firm. It may be that the firm's customers may represent one of the strengths of the company.

16. Advantages of inside-out. This approach, too, has its pros and cons.[14]

(a) A major factor in its favour is the advantageous effect it has upon employee morale, in that the organisation becomes involved in projects which employees have already demonstrated they can handle efficiently.

(b) The approach facilitates entry into new areas which are eminently suitable for the kinds of talents the company possesses. As Clemens points out: "Any market reasonably accessible to the firm in which price is greater than marginal cost constitutes an invitation to invade. It is not necessary that the market be related to the firm's existing ones".[15]

17. Disadvantages of inside-out.

(a) A major disadvantage of the inside-out approach is that it places an extra weapon in the hands of those executives who want to keep on doing the same old things simply because it makes for a quieter life.

(b) A related danger is that the existing strengths of the company may become out of date and less powerful in the future, so that it may be unwise to build upon them. Moreover, it is likely that executives will be reluctant to pursue courses of action that involve radical organisational changes.

(c) It is imperative that any approach does not ignore the influence of the environment. In the last analysis the firm must be able to sell the product, even accepting the notion that the large companies of today can often create a demand for a product with the aid of a judicious marketing programme.

18. Combination to suit each firm. Which, then, of these approaches to strategy formulation do we choose? It is unquestionable that different strategies will suit different companies. In this repect, it is important to note that the outside-in approach does not ignore corporate competence, nor does the inside-out approach ignore environmental opportunity. It is simply that the ability of the organisation to carry through the projects appears at a later stage in the former, as does demand forecasting in the latter.

The important point is that a strategy is chosen which suits each particular company. As Ewing points out: "If a strong marketing orientation happens to be the real strength of the organisation, that is indeed the correct place to begin thinking and discussions".[16] Similarly, a strategy based on the development of particular strengths can be regarded only tentatively until demand forecasts have been made. In any case, the strengths of the company will be based on past marketing successes so that the two approaches are not as conflicting as they appear at first sight.

PROGRESS TEST 14

1. How would you define the term "corporate strategy"? (1–3)

2. What are the advantages and disadvantages associated with strategic planning? Is strategic planning always desirable? (4–6)

3. What considerations would you take into account when formulating a strategic plan? (7–18)

4. Explain the term "strengths and weakness analysis". How important do you consider it to be? (7–18)

5. Discuss the relative advantages of the "inside-out" and "outside-in" approaches to strategic planning. Which, if any, of these two views do you support? (12–18)

FURTHER READING

1. Andrews, K. R., *The Concept of Corporate Strategy*, Dow-Jones Irwin, 1971.

2. Galbraith, J. K., *The New Industrial State*, Hamish Hamilton, 1967.

3. Tilles, S., "Making Strategy Explicit", *Harvard Business Review*, 1968.

4. Ansoff, H. I., "Strategy as a Tool for Coping with Change", *Handbook of Strategic Planning*, ed. Taylor, B. and Hawkins, K., Longman, 1971.

5. Ansoff, H. I., Avner, J. L., Brandenburg, R. G., Portner, F. E. and Radosevich, H. R., "A Study of Acquisition Behavior of U.S. Manufacturing Firms during the Period 1946–65", *Hand-*

book of Strategic Planning, ed. Taylor, B. and Hawkins, K. Longman, 1971.

6. Thune, S. S. and House, R. J., "Where Long Range Planning Pays Off", *Business Horizons*, reprinted as Chapter 7 of *Handbook of Strategic Planning*, ed. Taylor, B. and Hawkins, K., Longman, 1971.

7. Ansoff, H. I., *Corporate Strategy*, Penguin Books, 1968.

8. Simmonds, K., "Removing The Chains From Product Strategy", *Journal of Management Studies*, February 1968.

9. Ansoff, H. I., *op. cit.*, Penguin Books

10. Simmonds, K., *op. cit.*

11. Levitt, T., "Marketing Myopia", *Harvard Business Review*, August 1960.

12. Ewing, D. W., *The Practice of Planning*, Harper and Row, 1968, Chapter 4.

13. Simmonds, K., *op. cit.*, p. 34.

14. Ewing, D. W., *op. cit.*, Chapter 5.

15. Clemens, E. W., "Price Discrimination and the Multiple Product Firm", *Review of Economic Studies*, 1950–51, p. 2.

16. Ewing, D. W., *op. cit.* p. 63.

CHAPTER XV

IMPLEMENTATION OF STRATEGY

THE MAJOR PROBLEMS

THE successful implementation of strategy is an even more arduous task than that of strategy formulation, and the path to successful implementation is beset with difficulties for the unprepared corporate planner. Problems such as distinguishing between the need for strategic or operating decisions, or of obtaining the appropriate organisational response at the correct time, or of co-ordinating the conflicting objectives of organisational participants, can only be solved by provision of the appropriate administrative structures essential to the strategy. Thus successful strategy implementation must overcome the following problems:

1. Over-emphasis on operating decisions. It is natural that most business firms will spend much the greatest part of their executives' time on fairly routine decision-making, concerned with the efficient conduct of current operations. Whether the organisation is a simple one-man business or an extremely complex multi-product, multi-national firm, it is inevitable that the greatest volume of decision-making will be of the current operating kind.

This of course is a natural result of events, and it would indeed be unusual if this were not the case. However, the great danger is that the sheer volume of such operating decision-making will leave little time for anything else, so that strategic decision-making may become completely ignored, or at best attended to only when there is sufficient respite from the burden of day-to-day activities. Such an approach to strategic decision-making is likely to be extremely dangerous in that it will be attended to only when everything is running smoothly. The executives of the firm are most likely to be concerned with improving the operating efficiency of the organisation when the firm is not doing well. The danger is that they will be over-burdened with their efforts to improve operating efficiency at the very time when it is strategic decisions that are required. The likelihood is that the firm is not doing well because of the character of its product mix or the unsuitability of its markets. Efforts to improve operating efficiency will thus have only a marginal effect, which will be more than offset by the diversion from the real need to alter drastically the product policy. It is essential, therefore, that proper attention is given to strategic decision-making at all times. Such attention can only be ensured by the provision of the appropriate administrative structure.

2. Goal conflict within the organisation. To be successful, strategy must be able to harness the resources of the organisation in pursuit of its objectives. The problem here is that it is the individuals within the organisation rather than the organisation itself who possess objectives. It would thus be surprising if these individuals did not have a variety of objectives, many of which are in conflict with one another.

Unless some sort of broad agreement is made concerning objectives, then it is unlikely that strategy will be implemented successfully. Cyert and March[1] regarded such conflict as being partially resolved by making side-payments to various members of the organisation whose goals do not altogether coincide with the negotiated outcome. Note that such payments may be either financial or policy commitments, and are needed to maintain the decision-making nucleus in the firm. However, even within this small decision-making nucleus there are likely to be a variety of objectives put forward, so that goal conflict will never be completely resolved.

As well as the existence of conflict in the selection of the goals and strategy, there is the additional problem of implementing the strategy chosen, particularly when such implementation involves members of the organisation whose views and aspirations do not accord with that decided upon. This problem can be resolved partially by involving the more influential executives with the selection of strategy, and also by the setting up of an administrative structure capable of properly motivating and retraining participants in the organisation to achieve the desired objective. We will discuss such solutions in **7–12** below.

3. Achieving administrative efficiency. Making sure that the correct information is available in the right place at the right time is one of the most complicated tasks in a large industrial organisation. Delays in the feedback of important marketing information or a bureaucratic organisational hierarchy which imposes time delays on important administrative decisions can place the firm at a grave disadvantage *vis-à-vis* its competitors. The problems of co-ordinating the vast inflow and outflow of information represent the administrator's chief function, and it is important to the success of the organisation that such co-ordination is achieved quickly and effectively. Once again these problems impose restraints on the administrative hierarchy of the firm which we will consider in **5–10** below.

4. Motivating the organisation. It has never been doubted that the success of a business depends not merely on the choice of a good strategy but also upon the effort of the organisation in achieving the desired strategy. An excellent strategy implemented with mediocre effort is likely to be no more successful than a less desirable strategy implemented with the full backing of the organisation. In this respect, of course, the motivation of certain key executives is likely to be more important than other members of the organisation, since such executives will be in a crucial position to implement strategy. It is extremely important that the personal values and aspirations of such key executives accord with the ethical values of the chosen strategy if implementation is to be successful. Moreover, the organisation must be equipped with the right type of motivation and incentive systems geared to inspire maximum effort from its members.

RELATIONSHIP BETWEEN STRATEGY AND STRUCTURE

5. Suitable administrative structure. It is extremely important that the administrative structure a company adopts is suitable to the business strategy it has chosen. Chandler made a study in 1962 of the largest companies in the U.S.A. and noticed that since 1918 many of them had changed from a functional to a multi-divisional structure.[2] The functional structure was one in which the organisation was divided up into a series of specialised functions such as marketing, finance, manufacturing, etc., the co-ordination of such functions being undertaken by the chief executive. As its name suggests, the functional structure is organised along functional lines.

In contrast, a multi-divisional structure is one in which the organisation is divided into a series of autonomous multi-functional divisions. These divisions were usually product divisions although divisions organised along geographical lines were not uncommon. While these divisions were responsible for operations, broad strategic decisions were undertaken by a general office which monitored and co-ordinated the performance of the divisions. Thus, in the multi-divisional structure it is the product division rather than the functional division which is responsible for operating decisions.

6. Changing administration. Chandler observed that these administrative changes were mainly the result of changed strategy in the companies concerned, arguing that structure follows strategy and that the most complex type of administrative structure is the result of several basic strategies. It is unquestionable that a new strategy creates new administrative needs, since expansion through geographical dispersion, vertical integration and product diversification adds new resources and new activities to the company. Although the old administrative set-up could still be used to administer the new activities, it is likely to become increasingly inefficient as the company becomes more diversified.

Channon has shown that British companies have tended to follow much the same course as those in the U.S.A., although in the U.K. product diversification and structural change was much more gradual and came very much later than in the U.S.A. It was not until after 1950 that British companies began to undertake product diversification on a large scale. Moreover, structural change was also much slower in the U.K. and the change from a functional to a multi-divisional structure was often achieved by a more gradual transition, first to a type of holding company structure and eventually to the ultimate adoption of the multi-divisional system.[3]

DESIGNING APPROPRIATE ADMINISTRATIVE STRUCTURES

7. Overcoming problems. In order to overcome the problems listed in **1–4** above, it is important that the administrative structure of the organisation be well suited to tackle them.

There is no one administrative structure which is suitable for all organisations at all times. Which organisational structure will be most suitable will depend upon the corporate strategy chosen by the organisation. Andrews illustrates this point admirably when he states that "the nature of the corporate strategy must be made to dominate the design of the organisational structure and process. That is, the principle criterion for all decisions on organisational structure and behaviour should be that they are relevant to the achievement of organisational goals and objectives".[4] In this respect, it is worth recalling that in both Chandler's and Channon's analyses it was extreme changes in corporate strategy which promoted the changes in administrative structure which eventually brought the replacement of the functional structure by the multi-divisional structure in highly-diversified firms.

Most theorists would now agree that although the unitary functional structure is eminently suitable for small single-product concerns, it is likely to be less successful in large multi-product concerns where the multi-divisional structure comes into its own (see **8–12** below). Nevertheless, such a broad generalisation should not obscure the fact that even where diversification does take place within companies the particular type of multi-divisional structure they would like to adopt would depend upon the unique strategy chosen.

Why does retention of the functional structure become more difficult as the company opts for a more diversified strategy? Much of the answer to this question rests upon the ability of the multi-divisional structure to provide more appropriate solutions to the problems posed in **1–4** above. If we now return to these problems we will be in a position to examine to what extent this statement is justified.

8. Over-emphasis on operating decision-making. The great advantage possessed by the multi-divisional structure in relation to its ability to provide adequate time and attention to strategic decision-making emanates from its divorce of operating decisions from the overall strategic decision-making process. Under the multi-divisional structure, operating decisions are taken by the product division chiefs, whereas strategic decisions are undertaken by the executives in the general office, whose function it is to monitor the performance of the product divisions and make general entrepreneurial decisions regarding the allocation of the company's resources among them. Obviously in many companies the product division chiefs will participate extensively in the product planning of their respective divisions. Nevertheless, the existence of the general office means that there is a team of general executives not responsible for operating decisions who can devote all their time to strategic decision-making. There is little danger of these general executives being swamped by operating problems, and consequently strategic decision-making becomes a continuous process, rather than something resorted to only in times of dire emergency or when spare time is available.

This is in marked contrast to the functional type of organisation, where rapid growth of the company and the increasing complexity caused by product diversification forces the chief executive to bring functional division chiefs into the strategic decision-making process. However, these functional division chiefs spend most of their time upon operating problems so that there is a danger that strategic decision-making will still be subservient to the operating needs of the company. As Ansoff points out, strategic decisions make no automatic claims upon top management attention and unless specific provision is made for strategic decision-making, then it is likely to be neglected.[5] In complex organisations, the multi-divisional structure is likely to provide a better solution to this problem than the functional structure.

9. Goal conflict. As stated in **1–4** above, the problem of goal conflict within an organisation is unlikely ever to be completely resolved. Individuals will always have different conceptions of what an organisation should be doing, and the real issue here is the effect different organisational structures will have upon selecting the best strategy from the conflicting objectives, and also in obtaining adherence to the strategy once it has been chosen. In both these respects, the multi-divisional structure is likely to be more successful than the functional structure.

In so far as the selection of the best strategy is concerned, the multi-divisional structure provides a general office consisting of general executives who will have little or no preference for the conflicting claims of each product division. Chandler regards these general executives as performing the entrepreneurial function of allocating resources between the product divisions, the allocation process being based upon the overall strategy of the company as decided by the general office.

By contrast, the allocation process in the functional structure will be determined by the strategic decision-making unit which in this case consists not only of the chief executive but also, as the company becomes more complex, of the functional division chiefs. The result is that these functional division chiefs will favour strategies which are to their own particular advantage. Williamson has developed a managerial utility model of the firm, and argues that the managerial behaviour postulated by his model is likely to be more readily applied in functional organisations, where the functional division chiefs have been brought into the strategic decision-making process, since "such a move will bring about a ... bias in favour of staff expenditures and a permissive attitude towards slack".[6] In other words, the danger is that the functional division chiefs will put forward the claims of their own departments until the overall strategy of the company becomes subservient to departmental demands. This is unlikely to happen in the multi-divisional structure, where the general-office executives are unlikely to benefit from pushing the claims of a particular product division, since they have no operating responsibilities.

The multi-divisional structure is also likely to be more successful than the functional structure in obtaining adherence to the strategy once it has been chosen. There are a number of reasons for this, well illustrated by Williamson. In the first place, in the multi-divisional structure it is relatively easy to remove product division chiefs who do not accede to general-office policy, whereas in the functional structure it is rather more difficult, since they themselves will be involved in this crucial decision-making process. The allocation of resources between product divisions in the multi-divisional structure can also be used to reward those product divisions conforming, and to deter those divisions not conforming, to general-office policy, since the product divisions can be compared in terms of a common yardstick such as profit; since the divisions are semi-autonomous there are unlikely to be any spillover effects between them.

Such use of a carrot and stick policy in order to obtain conformity to overall strategy is likely to be much less successful in the functional structure, partly because of the immense difficulty of comparing the performance of separate functions such as manufacturing and marketing, and partly because the functions are inter-dependent and resources taken away from one function will produce an adverse effect upon the whole organisation. It is this superior ability of the multi-divisional structure to treat product divisions as profit centres which is the crucial element in obtaining greater conformity to corporate objectives.

10. Administrative efficiency. Williamson contends that the multi-divisional structure is also likely to be more efficient than the functional structure because co-ordination within and between functions is likely to involve a communication flow across fewer hierarchical levels and consequently less distortion of information. The more hierarchical levels, the greater the problems of information distortion and co-ordination, since much of the data needs to be interpreted and synthesised as it moves up the organisation in order to relieve the burden on top management. However, the question of adopting a multi-divisional structure really rests upon the strategy of the company. The important issue from the point of view of efficient implementation of the strategy is, as Andrews points out, identification of the key tasks of the company in terms of its unique strategy. Once these key tasks have been identified the organisational structure can then be geared towards their efficient performance. The design of an efficient information system capable of communicating strategy to the organisation, and the development of an effective co-ordination system to enable information and material to be available at the right time, represent the most difficult administrative tasks faced by the firm and pose problems common to all administrative structures.

11. Motivating the organisation. Motivation is another key aspect in strategy implementation and cannot be left to chance. Indeed, as we noted in Chapter XIV, 4 (d), one of the advantages of making strategy explicit was that it served as a focus of organisational effort and facilitated the identification of the crucial aspects of the strategic plan so far as the various parts of the organisation were concerned.

However, successful motivation needs more than simply a

clear communication of the strategy to be adopted. It requires also that the views of the various participants in the organisation accord with those inherent in the chosen strategy, and that the motivation and incentive systems within the organisation are sufficiently attractive to overcome any discord which may arise.

To some extent, of course, this is analogous to the Cyert and March concept of side-payments to resolve goal conflict within the organisation. However, in the implementation of strategy some executives are likely to play a more crucial role than others and it is particularly important that the personal and ethical views of these key personnel coincide with the strategy of the organisation. To some extent this can be achieved by including such personnel in the strategy-formulation process. In the last analysis, the optimal strategy for an organisation does not merely reside in the physical resources and capacities of the company but also in the response of the executives whose drive and effort is likely to be tempered by the extent of their acquiescence or non-acquiescence in the chosen strategy. An acceptable strategic choice coupled with an attractive incentive system is likely to have a generally stimulating effect upon its implementation.

12. Evaluation of performance. Related to this problem of obtaining the desired motivation, there is the analogous problem of controlling the behaviour of members of the organisation. In this respect the evaluation of the performance of certain key executives is crucial. The great danger here is that of evaluating such performance on the basis of attractive short-run accounting results instead of on the longer-term and more subjective basis of contribution towards the desired strategic objective. Such evaluation of performance in terms of long-run objectives is extremely difficult, yet it is essential to the successful implementation of strategy. It is because of the problems involved in such evaluation that many large companies have introduced the system known as "management by objectives", whereby an executive's objectives are agreed upon with his superiors and the evaluation of his performance is based upon his ability to overcome problems of known magnitude

In so far as controls over members of the organisation are concerned, incentive systems are generally regarded as being

more desirable than restraints upon behaviour, since the
policing system required by the latter is likely to have adverse
effects upon the morale and motivation of all members of the
organisation, irrespective of their sense of commitment to the
company.

13. Conclusion. The extent to which a company's strategy
will be implemented successfully depends upon the relationship
between the organisational structure of the company and the
strategy it has adopted. It cannot be over-emphasised that the
organisational structure of the company must be designed so
as to suit the particular needs of the strategy adopted. Once
this is achieved, the major problems become those of motivation and commitment and the design of incentive systems and
evaluation criteria to achieve these ends. Neglect of organisational aspects is likely to impair seriously any new strategy
the company may undertake.

PROGRESS TEST 15

1. Distinguish between strategic and operating decisions. What
is the importance of the distinction? **(1–4, 8)**
2. Why does goal conflict arise in an organisation? In what ways
may this problem be overcome? **(1–4, 9)**
3. What kinds of administrative problems are likely to arise in
a business firm? How may they be tackled? **(1–11)**
4. How important is motivation to strategy implementation?
What methods are available to foster motivation? **(1–4, 11, 12)**
5. Assess the contribution of divisionalisation to strategy-
implementation in large multi-product firms. **(5–13)**

FURTHER READING

1. Cyert, R. and March, J. G., *A Behavioural Theory of the
Firm*, Prentice-Hall, 1966.
2. Chandler, A. D., *Strategy and Structure*, Massachusetts
Institute of Technology Press, 1962.
3. Channon, D. F., "Corporate Strategy and Organisation
Structure in British Industry", *Journal of Business Policy*, Vol. 3,
No. 1, 1973.
4. Andrews, K. R., *The Concept of Corporate Strategy*, Dow-Jones
Irwin, 1971.
5. Ansoff, H. I., *Corporate Strategy*, Penguin Books, 1968.
6. Williamson, O. E., "Managerial Discretion, Organisation
Form and the Multi-Divisional Hypothesis", *The Corporate
Economy*, ed. Marris, R. and Wood, F., Macmillan, 1971.

APPENDIX I

EXAMINATION TECHNIQUE

FOR success in examinations, effective preparation in the months before the examination is essential. This preparation involves acquiring the discipline to set aside a number of hours a week for study in a particular subject. Reading a Chapter per week, or attending a lecture, are not sufficient on their own. The student must think about the subject, spend time questioning the logic of the techniques and the ideas used, and must always attempt the homework that is set. Homework is vital for a number of reasons.

(a) Preparation for homework involves a much greater concentration of effort than merely reading a Chapter to keep up to date.

(b) This preparation will reveal to the student his own weaknesses, and if he cannot resolve them himself he should make a note to consult his teacher on such points.

(c) Through submitting homework the teacher can identify weaknesses in the student's understanding and take steps where necessary to rectify such weaknesses. Homework is the touchstone that brings student and teacher together. Without demonstrating what you know or don't know, the teacher is in a weaker position to help you.

(d) By taking your own homework attempts and your teacher's comments, a set of model answers can be built up which will prove invaluable during final revision.

Final revision should commence as early as possible and it would be wise for the student to set out a detailed table of revision a few weeks before the examination for all the subjects to be studied. In this way, just like budgeting, you can judge your own progress; at this stage time is important and you want to ensure you are allocating enough time to cover all you intend. Although different people have different ways of revising, it would be wise to remember that it is extremely difficult to concentrate effectively for more than two hours; greater dividends can be obtained by having frequent short breaks than by "pressing on", as diminishing returns are bound to set in. The student will also find it refreshing to switch from one subject to another after a number of hours, particularly from a numerical subject to a more literary one.

On the day of the examination, the student should follow the points listed below, many of which seem obvious, but are nevertheless ignored by candidates year after year.

(*a*) Arrive at the examination centre in plenty of time.

(*b*) Read the examination paper carefully, double-checking on how many questions you have to attempt and from which sections of the paper they are to be taken.

(*c*) Select a question, and on scrap-paper jot down the main points you intend making. Always write legibly and show a good command of English.

(*d*) Structure your answer so that it is logical and reads well. So many candidates, on recognising a question they can attempt, pour their knowledge on to the paper in a series of unconnected points, leaving the examiner to decide whether the question has been answered.

(*e*) Do not spend an over-proportionate amount of time on a question just because you have a great deal to say. This can backfire towards the end of the examination as time runs out.

(*f*) Attempt the number of questions required. This is absolutely vital; in most examinations candidates are sacrificing 20 per cent of the total marks by answering only four questions instead of five.

(*g*) If time is running out then complete your answer in point form. Do not waste time on lengthy explanations of points already made. Make sure the examiner knows you are aware of all the points that should be made.

(*h*) If possible, check your answers before handing in the paper, so that corrections can be made.

TABLE A: PRESENT VALUE OF £1

Years hence	1%	2%	4%	6%	8%	10%	12%	14%	15%	16%	18
1	0·990	0·980	0·962	0·943	0·926	0·909	0·893	0·877	0·870	0·862	0·8
2	0·980	0·961	0·925	0·890	0·857	0·826	0·797	0·769	0·756	0·743	0·7
3	0·971	0·942	0·889	0·840	0·794	0·751	0·712	0·675	0·658	0·641	0·6
4	0·961	0·924	0·855	0·792	0·735	0·683	0·636	0·592	0·572	0·552	0·5
5	0·951	0·906	0·822	0·747	0·681	0·621	0·567	0·519	0·497	0·476	0·4
6	0·942	0·888	0·790	0·705	0·630	0·564	0·507	0·456	0·432	0·410	0·3
7	0·933	0·871	0·760	0·665	0·583	0·513	0·452	0·400	0·376	0·354	0·3
8	0·923	0·853	0·731	0·627	0·540	0·467	0·404	0·351	0·327	0·305	0·2
9	0·914	0·837	0·703	0·592	0·500	0·424	0·361	0·308	0·284	0·263	0·2
10	0·905	0·820	0·676	0·558	0·463	0·386	0·322	0·270	0·247	0·227	0·1
11	0·896	0·804	0·650	0·527	0·429	0·350	0·287	0·237	0·215	0·195	0·1
12	0·887	0·788	0·625	0·497	0·397	0·319	0·257	0·208	0·187	0·168	0·1
13	0·879	0·773	0·601	0·469	0·368	0·290	0·229	0·182	0·163	0·145	0·1
14	0·870	0·758	0·577	0·442	0·340	0·263	0·205	0·160	0·141	0·125	0·0
15	0·861	0·743	0·555	0·417	0·315	0·239	0·183	0·140	0·123	0·108	0·0
16	0·853	0·728	0·534	0·394	0·272	0·218	0·163	0·123	0·107	0·093	0·0
17	0·844	0·714	0·513	0·371	0·270	0·198	0·146	0·108	0·093	0·080	0·0
18	0·836	0·700	0·494	0·350	0·250	0·180	0·130	0·095	0·081	0·069	0·0
19	0·828	0·686	0·475	0·331	0·232	0·164	0·116	0·083	0·070	0·060	0·0
20	0·820	0·673	0·456	0·312	0·215	0·149	0·104	0·073	0·061	0·051	0·0
21	0·811	0·660	0·439	0·294	0·199	0·135	0·093	0·064	0·053	0·044	0·0
22	0·805	0·647	0·422	0·278	0·184	0·123	0·083	0·056	0·046	0·038	0·0
23	0·793	0·634	0·406	0·262	0·170	0·112	0·074	0·049	0·040	0·033	0·0
24	0·788	0·622	0·390	0·247	0·158	0·102	0·066	0·043	0·035	0·028	0·0
25	0·780	0·610	0·375	0·233	0·146	0·092	0·059	0·038	0·030	0·024	0·0
26	0·772	0·598	0·361	0·220	0·135	0·084	0·053	0·033	0·026	0·021	0·0
27	0·764	0·586	0·347	0·207	0·125	0·076	0·047	0·029	0·023	0·018	0·0
28	0·737	0·574	0·333	0·196	0·116	0·069	0·042	0·026	0·020	0·016	0·0
29	0·749	0·563	0·321	0·185	0·107	0·063	0·037	0·022	0·017	0·014	0·0
30	0·742	0·552	0·308	0·174	0·099	0·057	0·033	0·020	0·015	0·012	0·0
40	0·672	0·453	0·208	0·097	0·046	0·022	0·011	0·005	0·004	0·003	0·0
50	0·608	0·372	0·141	0·054	0·021	0·009	0·003	0·001	0·001	0·001	

able A cont.

20%	22%	24%	25%	26%	28%	30%	35%	40%	45%	50%
0·833	0·820	0·806	0·800	0·794	0·781	0·769	0·741	0·714	0·690	0·667
0·694	0·672	0·650	0·640	0·630	0·610	0·592	0·549	0·510	0·476	0·444
0·579	0·551	0·524	0·512	0·500	0·477	0·455	0·406	0·364	0·328	0·296
0·482	0·451	0·423	0·410	0·397	0·373	0·350	0·301	0·260	0·226	0·198
0·402	0·370	0·341	0·328	0·315	0·291	0·269	0·223	0·186	0·156	0·132
0·335	0·303	0·275	0·262	0·250	0·227	0·207	0·165	0·133	0·108	0·088
0·279	0·249	0·222	0·210	0·198	0·178	0·159	0·122	0·095	0·074	0·059
0·233	0·204	0·179	0·168	0·157	0·139	0·123	0·091	0·068	0·051	0·039
0·194	0·167	0·144	0·134	0·125	0·108	0·094	0·067	0·048	0·035	0·026
0·162	0·137	0·116	0·107	0·099	0·085	0·073	0·050	0·033	0·024	0·017
0·135	0·112	0·094	0·086	0·079	0·066	0·056	0·037	0·025	0·017	0·012
0·112	0·092	0·076	0·069	0·062	0·052	0·043	0·027	0·018	0·012	0·008
0·093	0·075	0·061	0·055	0·050	0·040	0·033	0·020	0·013	0·008	0·005
0·078	0·062	0·049	0·044	0·039	0·032	0·025	0·015	0·009	0·006	0·003
0·065	0·051	0·040	0·035	0·031	0·025	0·020	0·011	0·006	0·004	0·002
0·054	0·042	0·032	0·028	0·025	0·019	0·015	0·008	0·005	0·003	0·003
0·045	0·034	0·026	0·023	0·020	0·015	0·012	0·006	0·003	0·002	0·001
0·038	0·028	0·021	0·018	0·016	0·012	0·009	0·005	0·002	0·001	0·001
0·031	0·023	0·017	0·014	0·012	0·009	0·007	0·003	0·002	0·001	
0·026	0·019	0·014	0·012	0·010	0·007	0·005	0·002	0·001	0·001	
0·022	0·015	0·011	0·009	0·008	0·006	0·004	0·002	0·001		
0·018	0·013	0·009	0·007	0·006	0·004	0·003	0·001	0·001		
0·015	0·010	0·007	0·006	0·005	0·003	0·002	0·001			
0·013	0·008	0·006	0·005	0·004	0·003	0·002	0·001			
0·010	0·007	0·005	0·004	0·003	0·002	0·001	0·001			
0·009	0·006	0·004	0·003	0·002	0·002	0·001				
0·007	0·005	0·003	0·003	0·002	0·001	0·001				
0·006	0·004	0·002	0·002	0·002	0·001	0·001				
0·005	0·003	0·002	0·002	0·001	0·001	0·001				
0·004	0·003	0·002	0·001	0·001	0·001					
0·001										

TABLE B: PRESENT VALUE OF £1 RECEIVED ANNUALLY FOR N YEARS

Years n	1%	2%	4%	6%	8%	10%	12%	14%	15%	16%	18%
1	0·990	0·980	0·962	0·943	0·928	0·909	·0893	0·877	0·870	0·862	0·8
2	1·970	1·942	1·680	1·833	1·783	1·736	1·690	1·647	1·628	1·605	1·5
3	2·941	2·884	2·775	2·673	2·577	2·487	2·402	2·322	2·283	2·246	2·1
4	3·902	3·808	3·630	3·465	3·312	3·170	3·037	2·916	2·855	2·798	2·6
5	4·853	4·713	4·452	4·212	3·993	3·791	3·605	3·433	3·352	3·274	3·1
6	5·795	5·601	5·242	4·917	4·625	4·355	4·111	3·889	3·764	3·685	3·4
7	6·728	6·472	6·002	5·582	5·206	4·868	4·564	4·288	4·160	4·039	3·8
8	7·652	7·325	6·733	6·210	5·747	5·335	4·968	4·639	4·487	4·344	4·C
9	8·566	8·162	7·435	6·802	6·247	5·759	5·328	4·946	4·472	4·607	4·3
10	9·471	8·983	8·111	7·360	6·710	6·145	5·650	5·216	5·019	4·833	4·4
11	10·366	9·787	8·760	7·887	7·139	6·496	5·966	5·453	5·234	5·029	4·6
12	11·255	10·575	9·385	8·856	7·536	6·814	6·194	5·660	5·421	5·197	4·7
13	12·134	11·343	9·986	8·653	7·904	7·103	6·424	5·842	5·583	5·342	4·9
14	13·004	12·106	10·583	9·285	8·244	7·387	6·628	6·002	5·724	5·468	5·0
15	13·865	12·849	11·118	9·712	8·559	7·606	6·811	6·142	5·647	5·575	5·0
16	14·718	13·578	11·652	10·106	8·851	7·824	6·974	6·265	5·954	5·669	5·1
17	15·562	14·292	12·166	10·477	9·122	8·022	7·120	6·373	6·047	5·749	5·2
18	16·398	14·992	12·659	10·828	9·372	8·201	7·250	6·467	6·128	5·818	5·2
19	17·226	15·678	13·134	11·158	9·604	8·365	7·366	6·550	6·198	5·877	5·3
20	18·046	18·051	13·390	11·470	9·818	8·514	7·469	6·623	6·259	5·939	5·3
21	18·857	17·011	14·029	11·764	10·017	8·649	7·562	6·687	6·312	5·973	5·3
22	19·660	17·658	14·451	12·042	10·201	8·772	7·645	6·743	6·359	6·011	5·4
23	20·456	18·292	14·857	12·303	10·371	8·883	7·718	6·792	6·399	6·044	5·4
24	21·243	18·914	15·247	12·550	10·629	8·985	7·784	6·895	6·434	6·073	5·4
25	22·023	19·523	15·622	12·783	10·675	9·077	7·843	6·873	6·464	6·097	5·4
26	22·795	20·121	15·983	13·003	10·810	9·161	7·895	6·906	6·491	6·118	5·4
27	23·560	20·707	16·330	13·211	10·935	9·237	7·943	6·935	6·514	6·136	5·4
28	24·316	21·281	16·663	13·406	11·051	9·307	7·984	6·961	6·534	6·152	5·5
29	25·066	21·844	16·983	13·591	11·158	9·370	8·022	6·983	6·551	6·166	5·5
30	25·808	22·396	17·292	13·765	11·258	9·427	8·055	7·003	6·566	6·177	5·5
40	32·835	27·355	19·793	15·046	11·925	9·779	8·244	7·105	6·642	6·234	5·5
50	39·196	31·424	21·483	15·762	12·234	9·915	8·304	7·133	6·681	6·246	5·6

ble B cont.

20%	22%	24%	25%	26%	28%	30%	35%	40%	45%	50%
0·833	0·820	0·806	0·800	0·794	0·781	0·769	0·741	0·714	0·690	0·667
1·526	1·492	1·457	1·440	1·424	1·392	1·361	1·289	1·224	1·165	1·111
3·106	2·042	1·901	1·953	1·923	1·868	1·816	1·896	1·589	1·495	1·407
2·589	2·494	2·404	2·362	2·320	2·241	2·166	1·997	1·849	1·720	1·605
2·991	2·884	2·745	2·689	2·635	2·532	2·436	2·220	2·035	1·876	1·737
3·326	3·167	3·020	2·951	2·885	2·759	2·643	2·385	2·168	1·983	1·824
3·605	3·410	3·242	3·161	3·083	2·937	2·802	2·508	2·263	2·057	1·883
3·837	3·619	3·421	3·329	3·241	3·076	2·925	2·598	2·331	2·108	1·922
4·031	3·786	3 566	3·463	3·366	3·184	3·019	2·665	2·379	2·144	1·948
4·197	3·923	3·682	3·571	3·465	3·269	3·092	2·715	2·414	2·168	1·955
4·327	4·035	3·776	3·656	3·544	3·335	3·147	2·752	2·458	2·185	1·977
4·439	4·127	3·851	3·725	3·606	3·387	3·190	2·779	2·456	2·196	1·985
4·533	4·203	3·912	3·780	3·656	3·427	3·223	2·799	2·486	2·204	1·990
4·611	4·265	3·962	3·824	3·695	3·459	3·249	2·814	2·477	2·210	1·993
4·675	4·315	4·001	3·859	3·726	3·483	3·268	2·825	2·484	2·214	1·995
4·730	4·357	4·033	3·887	3·751	3·503	3·283	2·834	2·489	2·216	1·997
4·775	4·391	4·059	3·910	3·771	3·518	3·295	2·840	2·492	2·218	1·998
4·812	4·419	4·080	3·928	3·786	3·529	3·304	2·844	2·494	2·219	1·999
4·844	4·442	4·097	3·942	3·799	3·539	3·311	2·848	2·496	2·220	1·999
4·870	4·460	4·110	3·954	3·808	3·546	3·316	2·850	2·497	2·221	1·999
4·891	4·476	4·121	3·963	3·816	3·551	3·320	2·852	2·498	2·221	2·000
4·909	4·488	4·130	3·970	3·822	3·556	3·323	2·853	2·498	2·222	2·000
4·925	4·499	4·137	3·976	3·827	3·550	3·325	2·854	2·499	2·222	2·000
4·937	4·507	4·143	3·981	3·831	3·562	3·327	2·855	2·499	2·222	2·000
4·948	4·514	4·167	3·985	3·834	3·564	3·329	2·856	2·499	2·222	2·000
4·956	4·520	4·151	3·988	3·837	3·566	3·330	2·856	2·500	2·222	2·000
4·964	4·524	4·154	3·990	3·839	3·567	3·331	2·856	2·500	2·222	2·000
4·970	4·528	4·157	3·992	3·840	3·568	3·331	2·857	2·500	2·222	2·000
4·975	4·531	4·159	3·994	3·841	3·569	3·332	2·857	2·500	2·222	2·000
4·979	4·534	4·160	3·995	3·842	3·569	3·332	2·857	2·500	2·222	2·000
4·997	4·544	4·166	3·999	3·846	3·571	3·338	2·857	2·500	2·222	2·000
4·999	4·545	4·167	4·000	3·848	3·571	3·338	2·857	2·500	2·222	2·000

SPECIMEN TEST PAPERS

1. Economic analysis based on an assumption of profit-maximisation, in itself, cannot fully explain the behaviour of the large corporation operating in the private sector. (*Polytechnic Certificate in Accountancy, Lanchester 1975*)

2. "It is by no means obvious that action intended to maximise the utility of a company's shareholders is consistent with maximising the utility of its action-takers, i.e. management" (R. Marris). Discuss the implications for an economic theory of business behaviour. (*B.A. Hons. (Business Studies), Part III, Economics of the Firm, Lanchester 1972*)

3. Discuss the major problems facing small firms in manufacturing industry in Britain today. (*H.N.C., (Business Studies), Part I, Applied Economics, Lanchester 1975*)

4. Explain why supply generally increases if price rises, but why it may not. (*I.C.S.A., Economic Theory, 1974*)

5. "In the long-run all costs are variable." Discuss the meaning and importance of this statement. (*I.C.S.A., Economic Theory, 1974*)

6. "Variable costing methods provide more meaningful cost information for decision-making purposes than full (absorption) costing methods." Give a critical analysis of this statement. (*I.C.S.A., Management Accounting, 1976*)

7. "All monopolies operate against the public interest." Discuss. (*D.M.S., Part I, Economics, Lanchester 1975*)

8. Compare and contrast the monopolist and the competitive producer from the point of view of their freedom to decide their price policies. (*D.M.S., Part I, Economics, Lanchester 1973*)

9. Outline and criticise the expressed objectives of U.K. governments towards the nationalised industries, and the extent to which these objectives have been pursued. (*H.N.D., (Business Studies), Part II, Economics, Lanchester 1975*)

10. Some nationalised industries have made fairly consistent losses since their inception in the late 1940s. Should one necessarily conclude from this that the public sector has been less efficient than its private counterpart? (*B.A. (Econ.), (Hons.), Part I, Business, Lanchester 1972*)

11. What factors should a firm take into account when choosing sources of finance? (*H.N.C., (Business Studies), Part I, Applied Economics, Lanchester 1973*)

12. "Firms should always choose the cheapest source of finance." Discuss. (*H.N.C.*, (*Business Studies*), *Part I, Applied Economics, Lanchester 1973*)

13. How does a producer maximise profits? (*I.C.S.A, Principles of Economics, 1975*)

14. Write a report to your works manager explaining why techniques applicable to the problems of joint product costing should not be used for managerial decisions regarding whether a product should be used as it stands or be further processed before sale. (*I.C.M.A., Management Accountancy, 1, 1974*)

15. From the data given you are required to:

(*a*) construct a profit volume chart showing:

(*i*) the budget contributions of each product to the total budget profit; and

(*ii*) the actual contributions each product achieved in the overall profit earned in the month.

(*b*) comment briefly on three useful management points which could be used from the chart.

Data for the month of April 1975 were as follows:

BUDGET

Product	Sales volume in units	Selling price each	Contribution % of selling price
W	8,000	30	25
X	12,000	20	15
Y	6,000	10	30
Z	4,000	25	10

Fixed overhead for month: £40,000

ACTUAL

Product	Sales volume in units	Selling price each	Contribution % of selling price
W	6,000	34	30
X	14,000	15	negative 10
Y	8,000	15	30
Z	3,000	24	8

Fixed overhead for month: £35,000

(*I.C.M.A., Management Accountancy, 2, 1975*)

16. Why do people generally buy more of a product when its price falls? (*I.C.S.A., Principles of Economics, 1975*)

17. Companies from time to time find it necessary to reappraise their product pricing policies. You are required to prepare notes for a report outlining the way in which customers, competitor costs and other major factors can influence product pricing decisions. (*I.C.M.A., Management Accountancy, 2, 1972*)

18. Why do marginal costs fall and/or rise? (*I.C.S.A., Principles of Economics, 1975*)

19. A company is considering investing £260,000 in a new plant which will take one year to build. It is estimated that profit after depreciation, but before corporation tax, will be:

			£
in years 1 and 2	..	..	50,000 per year
in years 3 and 4	..	..	20,000 per year
in year 5	..	..	10,000 per year.

The plant will not be required after the fifth year.

You are required, using the data given, to calculate the discounted cash flow (D.C.F.) return for the project.

DATA

Item	Amount invested	Depreciation, straight line basis	Capital allowances for tax	
			First year	In subsequent years on the reducing balance
	£000s	%	%	%
Plant	160	12½	50	10
Buildings	50	10	20	5
Working capital	50	Nil	Nil	Nil

Residual value: plant will be 25 per cent of original cost; buildings will be the written-down book value.

Corporation tax rate is to be taken at 50 per cent.

All tax payments are made in the year following that in which the profit was earned. Other parts of the existing business make sufficient profits overall to absorb any capital allowances as they arise.

It may be assumed that residual value and working capital are recovered at the end of the fifth year and that any tax balancing charges and allowances are due in that year.

(Calculations should be correct to one decimal place of £1 with D.C.F. calculations to nearest whole number.) (*I.C.M.A., Management Accountancy, 2, 1974*)

20. From the following information, you are required to draw a graph illustrating the relationship between net present values of a capital expenditure proposal and discount rates used from 7 per cent to 15 per cent. From the graph read:

(a) the D.C.F. rate of return for the proposal;
(b) the net present value of the scheme at:

(i) 7½ per cent;
(ii) 12½ per cent.

FIXED CAPITAL

	£
Cost of plant and machinery	100,000
Residual value of plant and machinery after five years working	NIL

WORKING CAPITAL

	£
Additional required at commencement of the scheme	10,000
Additional required one year later	10,000
Refund at end of year five	Cr.20,000

ANNUAL COST SAVINGS BEFORE TAX

	£
Year 1	20,000
Year 2	40,000
Year 3	45,000
Year 4	45,000
Year 5	15,000

ESTIMATED EFFECT ON COMPANY'S TAX PAYMENTS:

Year	Saving	Additional payment
	(£)	(£)
1	50,000	—
2	—	10,000
3	—	20,000
4	—	22,500
5	—	22,500
6	—	7,500

(*I.C.M.A., Management Accountancy, 1, 1975*)

21. As management accountant of a large multi-product company you are required to make a major contribution to the decision-making process by providing management with cost and

revenue information which is relevant to product pricing decisions.
A product management system is in operation and each product
manager is responsible for developing marketing plans for his
own group of products. He controls sales promotion, advertising,
packing, pricing, product improvement and consequently product
profit.

List the kind of problems facing a product manager and
indicate how you, as management accountant, can assist him with
product pricing decisions. (*I.C.M.A., Management Accountancy,
1, 1974*)

22. Distinguish between short- and long-run cost curves.
Initially they both slope downwards from left to right. Why?
(*D.M.S., North Staffordshire Polytechnic, 1973*)

23. It is always important to remember that for any decision
the costs to be considered are the "relevant costs". Describe
what is meant by "relevant cost" and give examples of costs
that in one case need to be considered and in another are not
relevant to a decision. (*D.M.S., North Staffordshire Polytechnic,
1973*)

24. What is the "identification problem" and why does it
cause problems for those estimating the demand for a product?
(*D.M.S., North Staffordshire Polytechnic, 1974*)

25. Advertising is sometimes referred to as a factor of revenue
because it increases the quantity bought at a certain price. Can a
firm always rely on advertising expenditure shifting its demand
curve to the right and thus increase profitability? (*D.M.S., North
Staffordshire Polytechnic, 1974*)

26. Why are the different competitive strategies necessary in
pricing new products? (*D.M.S., Polytechnic of Wales, 1976*)

27. In setting a price, factors other than cost can be extremely
important. Describe these factors and explain under what circumstances they would become important. (*D.M.S., Polytechnic
of Wales, 1976*)

28. (*a*) Why does a firm maximise its profit by producing up to
the point when marginal revenue is equal to marginal cost?

(*b*) Use the figures in the example below to determine the
output which is most profitable for the firm:

The oil crisis has created a renewed demand for coal. The
N.C.B. (National Coal Board), to meet the crisis, has intensified
its programme of open-cast mining and is now mining seams of
coal that were previously uneconomical but which are now
economical because of the rise in the price of coal.

The Government has issued instructions to the N.C.B. that
it must remain profitable and the mining of seams will be based
on this criteria.

Below is a table produced by N.C.B. economists showing the

amount of coal recovered against the amount of earth that has to be removed. As the thinner seams are worked more earth must be shifted per ton of coal.

The present costs incurred are 50p per ton for earth removal and 50p per ton for washing (i.e. washing the coal from the earth).

Given a price of £28 per ton, what output should the N.C.B. aim to produce?

Coal recovered	Earth removed
(1,000 tons)	*(1,000 tons)*
100	500
110	550
120	600
130	700
140	800
150	920
160	1,100
170	1,300
180	1,550
190	1,850
200	2,200

(D.M.S., North Staffordshire Polytechnic, 1974)

29. With reference to any study (or studies) with which you are familiar, discuss the usefulness of cost-benefit analysis for appraising public expenditure projects. *(B.A. (Business Studies), Part 3, Economics, Lanchester 1975)*

30. Consider the main problems involved in selecting a rate of discount for use in investment appraisal in the public sector. *(B.A. Hons. (Econ.), Part 3, Essay Paper, Lanchester 1973)*

31. Suggest reasons for the developing importance of attention to corporate strategy in large business firms, in the contemporary economic environment. *(B.A. Hons. (Econ.), Part 3, Economics of the Firm, Lanchester 1972)*

32. "Right at the start of the marketing process, the orientation is towards assets rather than customer needs. Strategy from strength is the emphasis" (Simmonds). Discuss. *(B.A. Hons. (Business Studies), Part 3, Economics of the Firm, Lanchester 1973)*

33. The implementation of strategy is probably the most difficult part of conducting a business. Discuss the difficulties which may arise in this process. *(B.A. Hons. (Econ.), Part 3, Business Administration and Policy, Lanchester 1974)*

34. Examine the relationship between strategy and structure, particularly in regard to the problems of implementing strategy. *(B.A. Hons. (Business Studies), Part 3, Economics of the Firm, Lanchester 1975)*

INDEX

INDEX

M&E Handbooks

Law

'A' Level Law/B Jones
Bankruptcy Law/P W D Redmond, I M McCallum
Basic Law/L B Curzon
Cases in Banking Law/P A Gheerbrant, D Palfreman
Cases in Company Law/M C Oliver
Cases in Consumer Law/G H Samuel
Cases in Contract Law/W T Major
Commercial and Industrial Law/A R Ruff
Company Law/M C Oliver
Constitutional and Administrative Law/I N Stevens
Consumer Law/M J Leder
Conveyancing Law/P H Kenny, C Bevan
Criminal Law/L B Curzon
English Legal History/L B Curzon
Equity and Trusts/L B Curzon
Family Law/P J Pace
General Principles of English Law/P W D Redmond, J Price, I N Stevens
Jurisprudence/L B Curzon
Labour Law/M Wright, C J Carr
Land Law/L B Curzon
Landlord and Tenant/J M Male
Law of Banking/D Palfreman
Law of Evidence/L B Curzon
Law of Succession/L B Curzon
Law of Torts/J G M Tyas
Law of Trusts/L B Curzon
Meetings: Their Law and Practice/L Hall, P Lawton, E Rigby
Mercantile Law/P W D Redmond, R G Lawson
Partnership Law/P W D Redmond
Private International Law/A W Scott
Public International Law/D H Ott
Roman Law/L B Curzon
Sale of Goods/W T Major
The Law of Contract/W T Major
Town and Country Planning Law/A M Williams

Business and Management

Advanced Economics/G L Thirkettle
Advertising/F Jefkins
An Outline of Monetary Theory/J L Hanson
Applied Economics/E Seddon, J D S Appleton
Applied Mathematics/H J Vincent
Basic Economics/G L Thirkettle
Business Administration/L Hall
Business and Financial Management/B K R Watts
Business Organisation/R R Pitfield
Business Mathematics/L W T Stafford
Business Systems/R G Anderson
Business Typewriting/S F Parks
Case Studies in System Design/R G Anderson
Computer Science/J K Atkin
Consumer Credit/R G Lawson
Data Processing and Management Information Systems/R G Anderson
Economics for 'O' Level/L B Curzon
Economics for Professional Studies/H Toch
Elements of Commerce/C O'Connor
Human Resources Management/H T Graham
Industrial Administration/J C Denyer, J Batty
International Marketing/L S Walsh
Labour Economics/J D S Appleton
Management, Planning and Control/R G Anderson
Management – Theory and Principles/T Proctor
Managerial Econonics/J R Davies, S Hughes
Marketing/G B Giles
Marketing Research/T Proctor, M A Stone
Mathematics for Economists/L W T Stafford
Microcomputing/R G Anderson
Modern Marketing/F Jefkins
Office Administration/J C Denyer, A L Mugridge
Operational Research/W M Harper, H C Lim
Organisation and Methods/R G Anderson
Production Management/H A Harding
Public Administration/M Barber, R Stacey
Public Relations/F Jefkins
Purchasing/C K Lysons
Sales and Sales Management/P Allen
Secretarial and Administrative Practice/L Hall
Statistics/W M Harper
Stores Management/R J Carter

Accounting and Finance

Auditing/L R Howard
Basic Accounting/J O Magee
Basic Book-keeping/J O Magee
Capital Gains Tax/V Di Palma
Company Accounts/J O Magee
Company Secretarial Practice/L Hall, G M Thom
Corporation Tax/B S Topple
Cost and Management Accounting – Vols 1 & 2/W M Harper
Elements of Banking/D P Whiting
Elements of Finance for Managers/B K R Watts
Elements of Insurance/D S Hansell
Finance of Foreign Trade/D P Whiting
Intermediate Accounts/L W J Owler
Partnership Accounts/J O Magee
Practice of Banking/E P Doyle, J E Kelly
Principles of Accounts/E F Castle, N P Owens
Taxation/H Toch

Humanities and Science

'A' Level Physics – Vols 1–3/M Chapple
Basic Botany/C Skellern, P Rogers
Biology Advanced Level/P T Marshall
British Government and Politics/F Randall
Chemistry for 'O' Level/G Usher
Economic Geography/H Robinson
English for Professional Examinations/J R L McIntyre
European History 1789–1914/C A Leeds
Geology/A W R Potter, H Robinson
Human Geography/H Robinson
Introduction to Ecology/J C Emberlin
Land Surveying/R J P Wilson
Modern Economic History/E Seddon
'O' Level Physics/M Chapple
Physical Geography/H Robinson
Political Studies/C A Leeds
Sociology 'O' Level/F Randall
Twentieth Century History 1900–45/C A Leeds
World History: 1900 to the Present Day/C A Leeds